DOCUMENTING THE VISUAL ARTS

Bringing together an international range of scholars, as well as filmmakers and curators, this book explores the rich variety in form and content of the contemporary art documentary.

Since their emergence in the late 1940s as a distinct genre, documentaries about the visual arts have made significant contributions to art education, public television, and documentary filmmaking, yet they have received little scholarly attention from either art history or film studies. *Documenting the Visual Arts* brings that attention to the fore. Whether considering documentaries about painting, sculpture, photography, performance art, site-specific installation, or fashion, the chapters of this book engage with the key question of intermediality: how film can reframe other visual arts through its specific audio-visual qualities, in order to generate new ways of understanding those arts. The essays illuminate furthermore how art documentaries raise some of the most critical issues of the contemporary global art world, specifically the discourse of the artist, the dynamics of documentation, and the visuality of the museum. Contributors discuss documentaries by filmmakers such as Frederick Wiseman, Lynn Hershman Leeson, Jia Zhangke, and Trisha Ziff, and about artists such as Michael Heizer, Ai Weiwei, Do Ho Suh, and Marina Abramović.

This collection of new international and interdisciplinary scholarship on visual art documentaries is ideal for students and scholars of visual arts and filmmaking, as well as art history, arts education, and media studies.

Roger Hallas is Associate Professor of English at Syracuse University. He is the author of *Reframing Bodies: AIDS, Bearing Witness, and the Queer Moving Image* (2009) and the co-editor of *The Image and the Witness: Trauma, Memory, and Visual Culture* (2007).

DOCUMENTING THE VISUAL ARTS

Edited by Roger Hallas

LONDON AND NEW YORK

First published 2020
by Routledge
2 Park Square, Milton Park, Abingdon, Oxon OX14 4RN

and by Routledge
52 Vanderbilt Avenue, New York, NY 10017

Routledge is an imprint of the Taylor & Francis Group, an informa business

© 2020 selection and editorial matter, Roger Hallas; individual chapters, the contributors

The right of Roger Hallas to be identified as the author of the editorial material, and of the authors for their individual chapters, has been asserted in accordance with sections 77 and 78 of the Copyright, Designs and Patents Act 1988.

All rights reserved. No part of this book may be reprinted or reproduced or utilised in any form or by any electronic, mechanical, or other means, now known or hereafter invented, including photocopying and recording, or in any information storage or retrieval system, without permission in writing from the publishers.

Trademark notice: Product or corporate names may be trademarks or registered trademarks, and are used only for identification and explanation without intent to infringe.

British Library Cataloguing-in-Publication Data
A catalogue record for this book is available from the British Library

Library of Congress Cataloging-in-Publication Data
Names: Hallas, Roger, 1970- editor.
Title: Documenting the visual arts / edited by Roger Hallas.
Description: London ; New York : Routledge, 2020. | Includes bibliographical references and index.
Identifiers: LCCN 2019033567 (print) | LCCN 2019033568 (ebook) | ISBN 9781138565999 (hardback) | ISBN 9781138565982 (paperback) | ISBN 9781315123301 (ebook)
Subjects: LCSH: Documentary films--History and criticism. | Art and motion pictures.
Classification: LCC PN1995.9.D6 D5824 2020 (print) | LCC PN1995.9.D6 (ebook) | DDC 070.1/8--dc23
LC record available at https://lccn.loc.gov/2019033567
LC ebook record available at https://lccn.loc.gov/2019033568

ISBN: 978-1-138-56599-9 (hbk)
ISBN: 978-1-138-56598-2 (pbk)
ISBN: 978-1-315-12330-1 (ebk)

Typeset in Bembo
by Swales & Willis, Exeter, Devon, UK

CONTENTS

List of figures vii
Acknowledgements ix
List of contributors x

Introduction 1
Roger Hallas

PART I
Historical foundations 21

1 Henri Storck's *Le Monde de Paul Delvaux* and Pygmalionist cinema 23
   Steven Jacobs

2 A sculptor's life on screen: John Read's film portraits
   of Henry Moore for BBC television 34
   Katerina Loukopoulou

PART II
Representing the artist 51

3 A portrait of the artist as automaton: creativity, labor, and
   technology in *Tim's Vermeer* 53
   Stephan Boman

4 Flesh and vision: Jia Zhangke's *Still Life* and *Dong* 68
   Amy Villarejo

5 Globalizing Ai Weiwei 82
   Luke Robinson

PART III
Questions of documentation 97

6 Film and the performance of Marina Abramović: documentary as documentation 99
   Chanda Laine Carey

7 Gained in translation: site-specificity in recent documentaries 113
   Vera Brunner-Sung

8 The wages of !W.A.R.: activist historiography and the feminist art movement 128
   Theresa L. Geller

PART IV
Museum gazing 143

9 When art exhibition met cinema exhibition: live documentary and the remediation of the museum experience 145
   Annabelle Honess Roe

10 Museum movies, documentary space, and the transmedial 160
    Asbjørn Grønstad

11 "Seeing too much is seeing nothing": the place of fashion within the documentary frame 174
    Matthew J. Fee

PART V
Art worlds and film worlds 189

12 Challenging the hierarchies of photographic history 191
    Trisha Ziff, interviewed by Roger Hallas

13 On the history (and future) of art documentaries and the film program at the National Gallery of Art 205
    Margaret Parsons, interviewed by Marsha Gordon

Index *221*

FIGURES

2.1	Advertisement for the 16mm print of *Henry Moore*, as published in *Art News Annual* 53, no. 7 (1955).	40
2.2	*Henry Moore: The Language of Sculpture* (John Read, 1974).	43
2.3	*Henry Moore: The Language of Sculpture* (John Read, 1974).	44
2.4	*Henry Moore: The Language of Sculpture* (John Read, 1974).	44
3.1	David Hockney tracing a live projection within a camera obscura. *David Hockney's Secret Knowledge* (Randall Wright, 2002).	56
3.2	Tim Jenison painting within his optical apparatus. *Tim's Vermeer* (Teller, 2013).	62
3.3	Jenison's perspective as he copies the image reflected in his shaving mirror. *Tim's Vermeer* (Teller, 2013).	64
3.4	Jenison using a computer to analyze perspective cues in Vermeer's *The Music Lesson*. *Tim's Vermeer* (Teller, 2013).	65
4.1	The director's signature. *Still Life* (Jia Zhangke, 2006).	70
4.2	Workers' flesh. *Still Life* (Jia Zhangke, 2006).	72
4.3	Liu Xiaodong painting Han Sanming. *Dong* (Jia Zhangke, 2006).	73
4.4	Detail of painting by Liu Xiaodong. *Dong* (Jia Zhangke, 2006).	77
5.1	*Ai Weiwei: Never Sorry* (Alison Klayman, 2012).	89
5.2	*Ai Weiwei: Never Sorry* (Alison Klayman, 2012).	89
5.3	*Ai Weiwei: Never Sorry* (Alison Klayman, 2012).	91
6.1	*Seven Easy Pieces* (Babette Mangolte, 2007).	105
6.2	*The Artist is Present* (Matthew Akers, 2012).	107
6.3	*The Space In Between: Marina Abramović in Brazil* (Marco del Fiol, 2016).	110
7.1	*Fallen Star: Finding Home* (Vera Brunner-Sung and Valerie Stadler, 2016). Courtesy of the Artist and Stuart Collection, University of California, San Diego. © Do Ho Suh.	119

7.2	*Fallen Star: Finding Home* (Vera Brunner-Sung and Valerie Stadler, 2016). Courtesy of the Artist and Stuart Collection, University of California, San Diego. © Do Ho Suh.	120
7.3	*Levitated Mass* (Doug Pray, 2013).	123
7.4	Interview subjects in multiple shots from *Levitated Mass*.	124
8.1	*!Women Art Revolution* (Lynn Hershman Leeson, 2010).	129
8.2	*!Women Art Revolution* (Lynn Hershman Leeson, 2010).	137
8.3	*!Women Art Revolution* (Lynn Hershman Leeson, 2010).	139
9.1	Presenter Tim Marlow discusses the exhibition's layout with curator Luke Syson. *Leonardo Live* (Phil Grabsky, 2011).	150
9.2	The British Museum's Twitter feed emphasizes the liveness of their forthcoming *Pompeii Live* broadcast on June 18, 2013.	155
10.1	*National Gallery* (Frederick Wiseman, 2014).	165
10.2	*The Great Museum* (Johannes Holzhausen, 2014).	168
10.3	*Museum Hours* (Jem Cohen, 2013).	171
10.4	*Museum Hours* (Jem Cohen, 2013).	171
11.1	*The First Monday in May* (Andrew Rossi, 2016).	181
11.2	*The First Monday in May* (Andrew Rossi, 2016).	182
11.3	*The First Monday in May* (Andrew Rossi, 2016).	182
11.4	*The First Monday in May* (Andrew Rossi, 2016).	185
12.1	*Chevolution* (Trisha Ziff, 2008).	194
12.2	*The Mexican Suitcase* (Trisha Ziff, 2011).	195
12.3	*The Man Who Saw Too Much* (Trisha Ziff, 2015).	199
12.4	*Witkin & Witkin* (Trisha Ziff, 2017).	202
13.1	Poster for the first *Films on Art* program at the National Gallery of Art, Washington, DC, 1979. Courtesy of the National Gallery of Art.	206
13.2	*De Artificiali Perspectiva or Anamorphosis* (The Brothers Quay and Roger Cardinal, 1991).	211
13.3	*Parabeton: Pier Luigi Nervi and Roman Concrete* (Heinz Emigholz, 2012). Courtesy of Grasshopper Film.	217

ACKNOWLEDGEMENTS

I would like to express my warmest gratitude to all the contributors for their rich ideas and rigorous scholarship that brought this collection together. Additionally, Steven Cohan, Matthew J. Fee, Marsha Gordon, Frances Guerin, Chris Hanson, Will Scheibel, Shawn Shimpach, and Patricia Zimmermann all gave sage advice along the way. I am very grateful for the research leave supported by the College of Arts and Sciences and the Humanities Center at Syracuse University, which enabled me to develop this project. I would also like to thank the College for providing subvention to support the publication of this book. I thank T.J. West for indexing, Andrew Melvin for copy-editing, and Natalie Thompson for managing the production of the book. Natalie Foster and Jennifer Vennall at Routledge have both been incredibly helpful, supportive, and patient throughout this process.

CONTRIBUTORS

Stephan Boman is Lecturer in the Department of Film and Media Studies at the University of California, Berkeley. He has written on issues at the intersection of film theory, visual culture, and documentary aesthetics in *ISLE: Interdisciplinary Studies in Literature and Environment* and *Discourse* (forthcoming). His dissertation, *Unstill Life: The Emergence and Evolution of Time-Lapse Photography*, explores the visual cultural sources and aesthetic implications of early, scientific time-lapse imagery.

Vera Brunner-Sung is a filmmaker and Assistant Professor in the Department of Theatre at The Ohio State University. Her work has screened at venues including the Ann Arbor Film Festival; CPH:DOX; International Film Festival Rotterdam; Leeum, Samsung Museum of Art; MoMA PS1; San Francisco International Film Festival; and Whitney Museum. Her writing on film has appeared in publications including *Cinema Scope*, *Millennium Film Journal*, and *Sight & Sound*.

Chanda Laine Carey is Assistant Professor of Creative Studies at the University of British Columbia, specializing in global contemporary art history, criticism, and theory. Her research focuses on art in global contexts, with emphasis on the lenses of cosmopolitanism and intersectionality to understand the diverse geographies of contemporary art. Her book project on Marina Abramović analyzes the development of her transcultural performance aesthetic as a reflection of her spiritual life and global travels.

Matthew J. Fee is Lecturer and Director of the Integral Honors Program at Le Moyne College, Syracuse. His primary areas of research and specialization are Irish cinema, Irish studies, and film genres. He has presented and published on Irish cinema, contemporary documentary, horror films, and post-9/11 cinema. Fee is currently completing a manuscript that explores how Irish cinema draws on the fantastic genre and its attendant spatial relations in order to define Irishness.

Theresa L. Geller will complete a three-year residency with the Beatrice Bain Research Group at the University of California, Berkeley in 2020–1. Before relocating to the Bay Area, she served as Associate Professor of Film Theory and History at Grinnell College. She is the author of *The X-Files* (2016) and several scholarly essays and articles on feminist theory, film, and television. Her co-edited volume, *Reframing Todd Haynes: Feminism's Indelible Mark*, is forthcoming.

Marsha Gordon is Professor of Film Studies at North Carolina State University. She is the author of *Film is Like a Battleground: Sam Fuller's War Movies* (2017) and *Hollywood Ambitions: Celebrity in the Movie Age* (2008), and co-editor of *Learning With the Lights Off: Educational Film in the United States* (2012) and *Screening Race in American Nontheatrical Film* (2019).

Asbjørn Grønstad is Professor of Visual Culture in the Department of Information Science and Media Studies, University of Bergen. He is founding director of the Nomadikon Center for Visual Culture and the author or editor of ten books, the most recent of which is *Invisibility in Visual and Material Culture* (co-edited with Øyvind Vågnes, 2019).

Roger Hallas is Associate Professor of English at Syracuse University. He is the author of *Reframing Bodies: AIDS, Bearing Witness, and the Queer Moving Image* (2009) and co-editor, with Frances Guerin, of *The Image and the Witness: Trauma, Memory, and Visual Culture* (2007). He is currently completing a book on the relationship between photography and documentary film.

Annabelle Honess Roe has published extensively on animation and documentary. Her 2013 book *Animated Documentary* was the recipient of the 2015 Society for Animation Studies McLaren–Lambart Award for best book. She is co-editor of *Vocal Projections: Voices in Documentary* (2018) and *The Animation Studies Reader* (2018). She is Program Director and Senior Lecturer in Film Studies at the University of Surrey.

Steven Jacobs is an art historian specialized in the interactions between film, the visual arts, and architecture. His publications include *The Wrong House: The Architecture of Alfred Hitchcock* (2007), *Framing Pictures: Film and the Visual Arts* (2011), *The Dark Galleries: A Museum Guide to Painted Portraits in Film Noir* (2013), *Screening Statues: Cinema and Sculpture* (2017), and *The City Symphony Phenomenon: Cinema, Art, and Urban Modernity Between the Wars* (2018). Together with Birgit Cleppe and Dimitrios Latsis, he is currently working on an edited volume on mid-twentieth-century art documentaries. He teaches at Ghent University and the University of Antwerp.

xii Contributors

Katerina Loukopoulou teaches Film History at the London College of Communication, University of the Arts London. After completing her PhD at Birkbeck College, Loukopoulou held the Henry Moore Foundation Post-doctoral Fellowship at UCL. Her research has featured in journals (*Film History*; *Visual Culture in Britain*) and edited collections (*Learning with the Lights Off* [2012] and *British Art Cinema* [2019]). Her current project, supported by the British Academy, investigates the relationship between pacifism and documentary cinema.

Margaret Parsons is Head of the Film Department at the National Gallery of Art in Washington, DC. She has organized media events for Corcoran Gallery of Art, the National Archives, Smithsonian National Museum of American History, Fenimore Art Museum, and other institutions. Her essays on film or preservation have appeared in *Curator: The Museum Journal*, *New York Folklore Quarterly*, *Revista Cultura*, and *The Moving Image*.

Luke Robinson is Senior Lecturer in Film Studies in the Department of Media and Film, University of Sussex. He is the author of *Independent Chinese Documentary: From the Studio to the Street* (2013), and the editor, with Chris Berry, of *Chinese Film Festivals: Sites of Translation* (2017).

Amy Villarejo is the Frederic J. Whiton Professor of Humanities in the Department of Performing and Media Arts at Cornell University. She is the author of *Lesbian Rule: Cultural Criticism and the Value of Desire* (2003), *Ethereal Queer: Television, Historicity, Desire* (2014) and *Film Studies: The Basics* (2nd ed., 2013); co-author of *Film Studies: A Global Introduction* (2015); and co-editor of *Keyframes: Popular Cinema and Cultural Studies* (2001).

Trisha Ziff is a documentary filmmaker and curator of photography based in Mexico City. She has curated exhibitions at the Victoria and Albert Museum, California Museum of Photography, International Center of Photography, and Centro de la Imagen in Mexico City. She has directed several award-winning documentary films on photography, including *Chevolution* (2008), *The Mexican Suitcase* (2011), *The Man Who Saw Too Much* (2015), and *Witkin & Witkin* (2017).

INTRODUCTION

Roger Hallas

To speak of art documentaries invokes two constitutive sets of relations – film/art and documentary/art – that have shaped discourse on cinema and documentary since the early twentieth century. The euphoric celebration of cinema as the "seventh art" by early film theorists, such as Ricciotto Canudo, rested on the understanding of this new art form as a synthesis of the classical arts of architecture, sculpture, painting, music, poetry, and dance;[1] modernist artists such as Ferdinand Léger, Marcel Duchamp, Man Ray, and László Moholy-Nagy all engaged in filmmaking as part of their avant-garde practice across media;[2] and the establishment of the Museum of Modern Art's Film Library in 1935, under the curatorial vision of Iris Barry, granted film unprecedented cultural legitimation by international modernism's preeminent institution.[3] Despite this centrality of cinema to the modernist avant-gardes of the 1920s and 1930s, as well as postwar movements, particularly pop art, it is only in the late twentieth century that major art institutions would fully embrace moving-image media within the sanctified white cube space of the gallery (rather than just the auxiliary space of their film auditoria).[4] In the post-medium condition of the contemporary global art world, moving-image installations have now become significant attractions for both curators and publics at the world's major art museums and biennales.[5] Recent contemporary art has also shown a strong conceptual interest in documentary, particularly in film-based work, some of which circulates fluidly between networks of film distribution and the art world.[6] Documentary scholar Michael Renov argues that this nexus between art and documentary is hardly new, but harkens back to the origins of documentary film in the late 1920s and early 1930s, when the avant-garde experimentation of Walter Ruttmann, Dziga Vertov, Jean Vigo, and others was a key component to the development of documentary as the "creative treatment of actuality" (John Grierson's seminal definition).[7] Although the Griersonian conception of documentary as a mass communicative tool of the modern public sphere marginalized the expressive or aesthetic function of documentary for much of the twentieth century, especially in the anglophone world, the resurgence of this expressive function over the past quarter century has placed it back at the center of documentary film innovation.[8]

As my previous endnotes indicate, this multifaceted nexus of film, documentary, and art has been substantively studied in a wide-ranging body of scholarship – but with the notable exception of art documentaries. While film scholars such as Angela Dalle Vacche, Susan Felleman, John A. Walker, and Steven Jacobs have published numerous books on art in narrative cinema, the English-language scholarship on art documentaries is limited to a relatively small number of journal articles and book chapters, and two books on British arts television.[9] What can explain such paucity? It is certainly not for a lack of primary objects of study, for art documentaries have been both abundant and formally diverse, as I will discuss below. Admittedly, documentary studies has only developed as a distinct field over the past twenty-five years, well after film studies' extensive theorization and historicization of narrative cinema and experimental film, thus causing many documentary genres still to await significant study. Yet, documentary studies has also demonstrated greater interest in documentaries that are seen to be directly addressing the social and the political. Even its engagement with ethnographic film (i.e., documenting culture) has predominantly focused on the ethics and politics of such representation. It is not as though the field has avoided engagement with art and aesthetics, for one of its most prolific areas of research growth recently has been the essay film, another sort of "art documentary," if you will, in which reflexive forms of aesthetic experimentation shape the manner of the essay film's social or political critique.[10] But documentaries about art may seem to have too attenuated a relationship to the world to warrant significant scholarly attention by documentary studies. In her interview in this book, Margaret Parsons also suggests that art history's own preoccupation with prioritizing proximity to its object of study, in this case the original artwork, can help explain why the discipline has paid such little attention to the art documentary.[11] Both documentary studies and art history thus position art documentaries as second-order representations, albeit in different ways.

Art documentaries exist in all shapes and sizes, ranging from educational short films and webisodes to theatrically-released feature films and "blue-chip" television series. Their diversity reflects the wide-ranging discursive and institutional contexts in which they have been produced and circulated – primarily educational institutions, art museums and galleries, public television, and the commercial film industry. This book explores the critical and conceptual issues shaping contemporary art documentaries within such contexts. The focus of the first two chapters on earlier art documentaries of the postwar period – Steven Jacobs's analysis of Henri Stork's *Le Monde de Paul Delvaux* (*The World of Paul Delvaux*, 1946) and Katerina Loukopoulou's study of John Read's six television portraits of Henry Moore (1951–1978) – provides the book's contemporary focus with an understanding of the genre's historical foundations and how it came to represent, respectively, the artwork and the artist. The main parts of *Documenting the Visual Arts* are then organized around three key concerns of the contemporary art documentary: the representation of the artist, the relationship between art documentation and documentary film, and the visual dynamics of the museum. The book concludes with two interviews with curators who have worked in different ways at the intersection of film and art worlds. Running throughout *Documenting the Visual Arts* as a conceptual preoccupation is the necessary question of intermediality; namely, of how film incorporates and reframes other art forms. This rich productive tension between the medium properties of film and those of other visual arts, which it represents in art documentaries, engenders a critical debate about the role of the filmmaker's aesthetic creativity in depicting that of another artist in another medium. It also raises the question of whether art documentaries have honored the integrity of specific artworks (and their medium) or have transformed the aesthetic material of those artworks into something different and autonomous. While much of the book concerns the age-old media of painting and sculpture, chapters also address the more recent art forms of performance art and site-specific installation, as well as fashion and photography, which have both generated enduring disputes about their status as art. Although cinema is itself a visual art – and similarly embroiled since its earliest years in the question of its aesthetic status – documentaries about film and filmmakers fall beyond the scope of this collection because they raise questions not of intermediality, but of a more direct medium self-reflexivity (and therefore deserve their own critical volume).[12] Before turning to the organizing concepts of this collection, I want to discuss some of the key historical developments in the art documentary.

Historicizing the art documentary

As Steven Jacobs notes, the treatment of art in early non-fiction cinema can be traced as far back as the later 1910s, with German travelogue films on architecture and monuments in European cities, and Sacha Guitry's *Ceux de chez nous* (*Those of Our Land*, 1915), which offered brief portraits of Claude Monet in his garden, Auguste Rodin in his studio, and other French artists.[13] This early appearance of art and artists remained, however, within the "view aesthetic" of early film *actualités*, which was grounded in the presentation of the world as "a view" for the spectator's visual pleasure.[14] In Hans Cürlis's *Kulturfilme* of the mid-1920s, we begin to see attempts to use film to document the process of artistic creation. His series of short films, *Schaffende Hände* (*Creative Hands*, 1923–1926), documented the aesthetic techniques of various German modernist artists, including Otto Dix, Käthe Kollwitz, and George Grosz, by positioning his camera behind the artists as they worked on canvas or paper, thus affording the viewer the opportunity to witness an artwork come into being. A decade later, in the US, this visual trope of "creative hands" would be put to a more explicit ideological purpose in *A Study of Negro Artists* (1935), one of several documentaries produced by the Harmon Foundation to promote its philanthropic support of African-American artists. In his analysis of the film, John Ott demonstrates how the film's intertitles and opening alternation between close-ups of hands performing manual labor and hands creating art de-professionalize black artists, framing their aesthetic practice as a secondary, "spare time" activity.[15]

Although German *Kulturfilme* dedicated to the visual arts proliferated in the 1930s, particularly during the Third Reich,[16] the art documentary would not come into its own as a specific subgenre until the postwar period with the "films on art" of Luciano Emmer, Henri Storck, and Alain Resnais, amongst others. Jacobs identifies this period as "the golden age of the art documentary,"[17] not just for the aesthetic innovation of its Italian, Belgian, and French filmmakers, but also for the institutional and commercial support it received (including the newly founded United Nations Educational, Scientific, and Cultural Organization and innovative film producers such as Anatole Dauman and Pierre Braunberger), as well as the critical discourse it stimulated amongst key film theorists, such as André Bazin, Siegfried Kracauer, and Rudolf Arnheim. Jacobs also connects the postwar art documentary to the mid-century popularization of fine art through book publication. While art reproduction had been central to the development of art history as a discipline in the nineteenth century (particularly glass slides), it was only in the mid-twentieth century that printing technology permitted the mass circulation of affordable art books, including André Malraux's *Le Musée imaginaire* (1947, published in English as *Museum Without Walls*, 1949). Malraux believed that the mass reproduction and montage of the art book would supersede the traditional art museum, creating the global circulation of a virtual archive of photographed artworks across cultures.[18] Filmmakers, critics, and institutions shared a similar universal humanistic vision for the art documentary. Yet, ideological conceptions of national traditions would also shape the development of the art documentary during the Cold War. For instance, the Division of International Motion Pictures at the US State Department commissioned a series of films in the late 1940s on American artists, such as Martha Graham, Georgia O'Keeffe, Edward Weston, and Frank Lloyd Wright. The films on Weston and O'Keeffe – *The Photographer* (Willard van Dyke, 1948) and *Land of Enchantment: Southwest U.S.A.* (Henwar Rodakiewicz, 1948) – were the only films to be completed and spent considerable screen time establishing the "American" character of the artists and their work by situating them in the natural landscapes of California and New Mexico respectively.

The postwar European art documentaries experimented considerably in their representation of European painting, but Emmer, Storck, and Resnais each differed in their methods and their ends. Emmer's documentaries about Italian Renaissance painting tended to isolate visual details to narrate the story depicted in the picture, rather than explore the narrative composition of the whole picture. His camera movement and editing temporalized spatial aspects of the picture and often created narrative suspense by delaying the revelation of the whole painting. He treated paintings as visual raw material for the construction of cinematic narrations of their subject matter. Although Storck was similarly invested in creating documentaries that worked autonomously from the art they depicted, he was committed to using the genre to examine art history, but not through the discipline's meticulous reproduction of individual artworks. In films such as *Le Monde de Paul Delvaux* and *Rubens* (1948), Storck combined a wide array of paintings from each artist to explore their aesthetic "worlds." Whereas the latter film deployed a range of special effects (split screens, multiple exposures, animation, iris shot, and a rotating camera) to analyze the visual dynamism of the baroque master, the former film combined

Delvaux's paintings, modernist music by André Souris, poetry by Paul Eluard, and an essayistic voiceover by René Micha into a deeply uncanny evocation of the Surrealist painter's universe. Jacobs's chapter in this book frames the Delvaux film as a *Gesamtkunstwerk* that brings together film, painting, music, and poetry to create an autonomous work that unsettles the distinction between "film on art" and "art film." Jacobs demonstrates how the film's treatment of the Pygmalion motif cherished by the Surrealists reflexively engages with the attempt to use film to "breathe life" into the stasis of painting. Resnais's films *Van Gogh* (1948) and *Gauguin* (1950) also drew from the *oeuvre* of each painter, but in the service of constructing their biographies as artists. He rearranged details from widely different paintings to create narrative sequences that emulate the conventions of continuity editing. Resnais noted, "What interested me in *Van Gogh* was the possibility to treat a painting as if it was a real space with real characters."[19] Resnais's close attention to Van Gogh's expressionist techniques construct the film's biographical narrative through the painter's subjectivity. Resnais's subsequent art documentaries would move away from artist biography as they became more political. His 1950 film *Guernica* uses Picasso's painting as the inspiration for a meditation on war and barbarism, drawing from other Picasso works far more than from his eponymous painting; *Les Statues meurent aussi* (*Statues Also Die*, 1953), Resnais's collaboration with Chris Marker and Ghislain Cloquet, integrates an analysis of how capitalism has transformed African art into a commodity fetish for the Western art market with a larger anti-colonial critique (which led to the film being censored by the French state).

In the 1950s and 1960s, the emergent institution of public television became an increasing funder and broadcaster of art documentaries, particularly in Western Europe (but to a far lesser extent in the US). In his history of British arts television, John Wyver proposes three fundamental modalities of television arts documentary – the lecture, the encounter, and the drama – which he identifies with three key figures within the BBC during its formative years: Kenneth Clark, John Read, and Ken Russell.[20]

The lecture mode draws from both the didactic function of talk in public service broadcasting and the art historical slide lecture developed in the German scholarly tradition by Heinrich Wölfflin. Wyver argues that it reaches its apotheosis in Kenneth Clark's prestige, high-budget series *Civilisation* (1969). Subtitled *A Personal View by Kenneth Clark*, the series adopts the intimate address of its charismatic presenter, who navigates his audience through centuries of Western civilization as he seamlessly travels across Europe from scene to scene, literalizing his intimate knowledge of the artifacts and buildings he discusses by consistently touching them tenderly as he speaks. Establishing the model of the authoritative male presenter, which would be embodied in the following decades by Robert Hughes, Simon Schama, Matthew Collings, Andrew Graham-Dixon, Waldemar Januszczak, and James Fox, Clark's series ensured that as Wyver notes, "opinions and interpretations, narratives and information are apparently derived only from the knowledge and sensitivity of the speaker" (145).[21] John Berger's 1972 series *Ways of Seeing* serves as a singular counter-model to the Clarkian televisual art lecture.[22] In the infamous opening scene of the series, Berger appears to take a knife to Botticelli's *Venus and Mars* (1483) in London's National Gallery and cut out a square from the canvas depicting Venus's head. As the camera pulls back, Berger's Brechtian move is revealed: he is in a film studio and the picture is a reproduction. This iconoclastic gesture both aims to shatter the auratic reverence of the artwork propagated by Clark and to introduce the ideas of Walter Benjamin's essay "The Work of Art in the Age of Mechanical Reproduction," which Berger explicitly acknowledges as the primary intellectual foundation of the series. Employing a range of Brechtian techniques to defamiliarize the conventional presentation of art on screen and encouraging its viewers to critically interrogate Berger's claims, the subsequent episodes examine patriarchy, patrimony, and the commodity fetish in European art history. Although Wyver argues that Berger's series (and accompanying book) had more influence in higher education (where it helped propagate Benjamin's artwork essay) than on the television lecture mode, the iconoclastic experimentalism and cultural materialist approach of *Ways of Seeing* would become an important influence on the alternative arts television that would emerge a decade later on Channel Four.

Wyver contends that if the lecture format prioritizes telling as its operative mode, the encounter format centers around the dynamics of showing: "The encounter requires only that the camera – and therefore the viewer – observes the artwork, the artist, or the process. This, the encounter suggests, is sufficient for knowledge to be imparted, values recognized, qualities experienced."[23] While most art documentaries include some level of telling (through voiceover or interview), the encounter emphasizes the empirical power of film to record and render the impression of visual presence. The earliest champion of this mode at the BBC was John Read, son of art historian Herbert Read and disciple of Grierson. Rejecting the format of live studio broadcast and its foundation in talk, Read insisted on using film for his profiles of contemporary British artists, which gave him the freedom to shoot in the artists' studios and homes, and to document the natural and social landscapes from which the artists drew their inspiration. Katerina Loukopoulou's chapter examines the six documentaries that Read made for the BBC about the sculptor Henry Moore from 1951–1978, tracing how Read's conception of a "film portrait" of the artist changed across the decades as Moore became ever more involved in the mediation of his own public identity (including his ongoing working relationship with Read). With their alternating attention to artist studio, exhibition space, and media interaction, Read's Moore films laid many of the foundations for the film portraits of the global art world's star artists, such as Ai Weiwei and Marina Abramović, whom Luke Robinson and Chanda Laine Carey examine in their chapters.

A fuller integration of showing and telling was achieved in the third, but less widely used, mode of art documentary that Wyver describes: the drama. Producing for the BBC's arts program *Monitor* (1958–1965), the young Ken Russell faced the perennial problem of documentary filmmakers working on historical material before the era of film: how to visualize the historical narrative without any archival film material? In a number of artistic biographies of major modern composers,

Russell elaborated an increasingly baroque use of dramatic reenactment, which drew on reflexivity, irony, and camp. Although Russell only made one drama-documentary about a visual artist (*Always on Sunday* [1965] on Henri Rousseau), his influence on films about painters was wide and lasting. His sophisticated and self-reflexive use of *mise-en-scène* would inspire his protégé Derek Jarman in making *Caravaggio* (1986) and John Maybury in his *Love Is the Devil: Study for a Portrait of Francis Bacon* (1998). While both of these studio-bound films are fictional art cinema rather than drama-documentaries, their evocation of the painters' visual style through experimental use of cinematography and *mise-en-scène* renders them more meditations on aesthetic vision than straightforward biographical narratives. Dramatic reenactments have now become a staple device that the lecture mode often employs as visual filler, such as in Schama's series *The Power of Art* (2007), but as Wyver notes, it is all too frequently "a farrago of costume drama clichés, all colour and movement and spurious mood" (157), rather than a genuinely aesthetic engagement with the possibilities of cinematic *mise-en-scène*.

In the 1980s, innovation flourished in the art documentary in several contexts for a number of reasons. A generation of artists, filmmakers, and broadcasters had emerged from art schools and universities having been exposed to critical theory ranging from materialist cultural studies to poststructuralism to feminist theory. Traditional artistic disciplines and media were also under pressure from the rise of new art practices and movements, such as performance art, land art, and conceptualism, that challenged the very materiality of the artwork itself and the conditions under which it is experienced. Cultural studies and postmodernism moreover pushed against the hierarchies of cultural value that stubbornly persisted in major art institutions. Within broadcast culture a major opportunity for independent film- and videomakers opened up with the establishment in 1982 of Britain's Channel Four, a commercial channel with a public service remit focused on program innovation and serving marginalized audiences. Often in conjunction with other institutions of public arts funding, such as the Arts Council of Great Britain and the British Film Institute, Channel Four commissioned a highly diverse and groundbreaking range of arts programming from independent producers in its first decade, frequently blurring the boundaries between art documentary and artist film/video.

Isaac Julien's *Looking for Langston* (1989) and Sandy Nairne's series *State of the Art* (1987) exemplify the kind of art documentaries made for the new channel. Produced by the Sankofa Film and Video Collective, which Julien co-founded in 1983, *Looking for Langston* constructs a highly poetic and performative mediation on the Black Atlantic resonance that poet Langston Hughes and the Harlem Renaissance held for Black British artists like Julien himself in the 1980s, particularly at the intersection of race and sexuality. The film's Benjaminian project, described by its script consultant Mark Nash as "the way it weaves the present into the past to look forward to the future,"[24] is partly accomplished through its reframing of footage from the Harmon Foundation documentaries about black visual artists and the complex appropriation of diverse photographers from the past and present (James Van Der Zee, George Platt Lynes, and Robert Mapplethorpe), creating an expansive visual mediation on historical identification, racial othering, and sexual desire. The film offers no clear-cut biographical, historical, or interpretative narrative about Hughes, nor the other artists of the Harlem Renaissance, but rather uses them to forge a space of cultural imagination for contemporary Black British artists. *Looking for Langston* thus offers a rich conception of the *arts* documentary, drawing together literary, visual, and musical arts. Although very different in scope and subject, Nairne's *State of the Art* shares in this embrace of holding multiple ideas in play and rejecting the demand for assertive exposition, interpretation, and evaluation of art. Drawing from the materialist approach of *Ways of Seeing* but without Berger's polemic tone, the six-part series explores the contemporary art world of the mid-1980s through a montage of artist interviews (including many more women artists and artists of color than in similar prior art series), critical quotations in dialogue with one another on voiceover, and slow contemplative footage of the artworks. Refusing biographical narrative or organization by art movement or medium, the series is structured around the predominant ideological issues of the increasingly globalized art world, such as the representation of history, commodity culture, creative labor, sexual politics, and cultural marginalization. In one of the more sympathetic responses amongst a largely negative critical reception, John Roberts indicated the limitations of its innovation: "On the one hand, it clearly offers an advance in the complexity and texture of argument over the profile and lecture, but given the tendency of anti-narrative strategies to weaken causality, it can reduce ideas to a heterogenous soup."[25]

Narrative returned as a major component of the art documentary during the boom in theatrically-released documentary feature films of the past several decades. Central to both the promotion and critical acclaim for the recent boom has been the mantra that non-fiction can provide as compelling characters and narratives as fiction – *Stranger Than Fiction*, the title of Thom Powers and Raphaela Neilhausen's long-running documentary program at the IFC Center in New York attests to this appeal. Institutional structures of production, distribution, exhibition, and reception in the film industry ensure the stability of the feature film's formal conventions. The complex mechanisms of co-production require documentary filmmakers to pass through various gatekeeping thresholds, including grant proposals, institute workshops, and pitches to commissioning editors and distributors. Art documentary features thus frequently rely on quest narratives (often with deadline structures) that are built around the artist's pursuit of a specific, challenging project, such as fashion designer Raf Simon's first show as creative director of Dior in *Dior and I* (Frédéric Tcheng, 2014), Cai Guo-Qiang's epic firework installation *Sky Ladder* in Kevin Macdonald's eponymous 2016 film, and Vik Muniz's collaborative art project with Brazilian trash recyclers in *Waste Land* (Lucy Walker, João Jardim, and Karen Harley, 2010). Distributors, exhibitors, and critics also all draw from a shared discourse around narrative cinema to frame documentaries for contexts dominated by fiction film. The genres of narrative cinema come to frame many art documentaries: slapstick comedy in Banksy's *Exit Through the Gift Shop* (2010), the road movie in JR and Agnès Varda's *Visages Villages (Faces Places*, 2017), the conspiracy thriller in Don Argott's *Art of the Steal* (2009), the coming-of-age tale in Nathaniel Kahn's *My Architect* (2003), and the romantic melodrama in Zachery Heinzerling's *Cutie and the Boxer* (2013). Trailers for art documentaries abound with the discourses of fictional intertextuality and genre: the trailer for *Waste Land*, for instance, quotes the *Huffington Post* with the line, "The *Slumdog Millionaire* of documentaries," while the trailer for Werner Herzog's 3-D spectacle *Cave of Forgotten Dreams* (2010) pitches it through the language and iconography of science fiction.[26]

Visual artists have also recognized the value to their public image in being the subjects of theatrically-released documentary features. Such films generally accrue greater cultural capital, garner more press coverage, travel further afield internationally, and potentially attract larger audiences than television programs, especially in the increasingly fragmented media ecology of digital television. Visual artists whose work is ephemeral, such as environmental artists, have built long-term relationships with specific filmmakers to document their work since visual documentation is critical to the wider exhibition of their work beyond its original temporary site. For instance, Christo and Jeanne-Claude maintained a working relationship for over thirty years with filmmakers David and Albert Maysles, which generated six films about specific installations. While the first, *Christo's Valley Curtain* (1974), was a 28-minute short film screened on television and at film festivals, the last, *The Gates* (2007), was an internationally acclaimed and widely-seen feature film distributed by Kino Lorber.[27] Similarly, fellow environmental artist Andy Goldsworthy collaborated with German filmmaker Thomas Riedelsheimer on a second documentary feature, *Leaning into the Wind* (2017), following the incredible success of *Rivers and Tides: Andy Goldsworthy Working with Time* (2001), which has gained somewhat of a cult following since its release. Canadian photographer Edward Burtynsky was so impressed with *Manufactured Landscapes* (2006), the film that Jennifer Baichwal (as director) and Nicholas de Pencier (as cinematographer and producer) made about his landscape photography, that his subsequent transmedia projects, *Watermark* (2013) and *Anthropocene* (2018), have been full collaborations with both of them.

Turning to our current moment, the impact of new digital technologies' varied affordances on the art documentary is still very much in process. Remediating the art documentary with the exhibition catalog, the CD-ROM, and later the webpage, facilitated the development of multimedia presentations that combined text, voice, photographic reproductions, and video. Social media streaming sites like YouTube and Vimeo have also renewed the life of the art documentary short: museums offer curatorial interviews, behind-the-scenes reports on preservation, and mini-artist biographies to supplement the visitor's experience before or after seeing the exhibition; and magazine-style arts television, like PBS's *Art in the Twenty-First Century* (*Art21*), has also been able to successfully transfer and expand its format on a web platform.[28]

Although virtual reality (VR) technologies have been widely used by digital artists since their invention, it is only very recently that art institutions have begun to explore their affordances for arts education. Rehearsing early art documentary's dual focus on either the artwork or the creative process, two primary applications of

VR to art documentary have emerged. In 2016, the Royal Museums of Fine Arts in Belgium collaborated with the Google Cultural Institute on a multimedia website, *Bruegel: Unseen Masterpieces*, which includes a 360-degree video on the painting *The Fall of the Rebel Angels* (1562) that allows the user to navigate around an animated rendering of the painting as a voiceover explains various details in the image.[29] In 2017, René Magritte's estate launched *Magritte VR*, which has toured film and arts festivals around the world. In a large viewing area in the shape of a bowler hat, up to fifty visitors can don VR headsets to "journey through the work" of the Surrealist master (created from imagery in forty of his paintings).[30] While each of these projects suggest digital remediations of Emmer's and Storck's postwar documentaries – by exploring the "aesthetic world" of a painting or an artist – they lack the earlier films' autonomy as cinematic artworks and allow their animated 3-D digital renderings of visual elements from the paintings to supplant the imagination of the viewer. The Tate Modern used VR to explore an artist's creative process and life in *Modigliani VR: The Ochre Studio*, which it commissioned for its blockbuster show on the artist in 2017.[31] Installed in a gallery room at the heart of the exhibition, *Modigliani VR* offered visitors a virtual tour of the artist's studio in Paris in 1919, shortly before he died. As the museum's website attests, Tate curators devoted enormous time and energy to reconstructing this studio (that had never been photographed) through meticulous research, which is conveyed through various voiceovers activated by the viewer looking around the virtual space.[32] Two of the paintings in the exhibition are displayed on easels in the studio, including Modigliani's last self-portrait. A paint palette sits on one side of the self-portrait and a mirror stands on the other, creating the rather uncanny sensation that the artist had momentarily stepped out the room. For all its visual stimulation, the experience offers little more than the snippets of contextual information that wall captions and audio guides can already, and more cheaply, provide. Only time will tell if VR can be marshaled in curatorial practice for more than its visual pleasure as a technological attraction.

Conceptualizing the art documentary

Intermedial representation in the art documentary always both exceeds and falls short in its reproduction of the original medium. This is arguably the root of art history's suspicion of the art documentary, but also the lure that draws filmmakers to make documentaries about other arts: to see a medium otherwise, in a different light, through a new lens, in an alternate frame, from a fresh angle. My phrasing here is not merely a clever play with metaphorical idiom, but actually points to the various qualities that film shares with some media but differs from others – its deployment of light, lenses, framing, and spatial mobility.

Film's intermedial relationship to painting was one of the first to be theorized in the context of the art documentary. In "Painting and Cinema," an essay that draws on the films of Emmer, Storck, and Resnais, Bazin contrasts what he calls the "centripetal" quality of the picture frame with the "centrifugal" quality of the film screen: a painting "polarizes space inwards" by masking and isolating a specific portion of reality, whereas film shows us "part of something prolonged indefinitely into the universe."[33] While both cinema and painting rely on the framing of the world, in painting it is fixed and permanent, while in cinema, the frame is radically contingent, always implying what is beyond it and anticipating a new frame, through an edit or a camera movement. Thus, Bazin contends that whenever a painting is filmed without ever showing its frame, it takes on the spatial properties of cinema and therefore becomes "part of that 'picturable' world that lies beyond it on all sides" (166). However, Philip Haas and David Hockney's film *A Day on the Grand Canal with the Emperor of China or: Surface Is Illusion But So Is Depth* (1988) reveals the Eurocentric assumption in Bazin's distinction. Hockney carefully analyzes a seventy-two-foot-long Chinese scroll painting, *The Kangxi Emperor's Southern Inspection Tour* (1689), by viewing it in the traditional way – on a flat surface unscrolling sections at a time – thus demonstrating the highly dynamic contingency of its frame and, by implication, its temporality and spatiality. As a reminder of the need to culturally contextualize our conceptions of medium specificity, Haas places a Canaletto painting (with classical Western perspective) on the wall behind Hockney.

The contingency of the frame is an aspect where film and photography also both meet and diverge. The camera viewfinder and the lens permit filmmaker and photographer to select how the profilmic space will be captured within a two-dimensional frame. Whereas the photographer searches for an intersecting spatial perspective and temporal moment to capture instantaneously in a still image, what Henri Cartier-Bresson famously called "the decisive moment,"[34] the filmmaker records and constructs a complex virtual mobility in time and space for the spectator through camera movement, editing, and special effects, what Erwin Panofsky called film's "dynamization of space" and "spatialization of time."[35] While the implication for filming photographs is one of emphasis on their fundamental arrest of the flow of time, even when a film shot moves across a photograph, the virtual mobility of cinema permits this two-dimensional medium a greater capacity to represent the three-dimensionality of the plastic and spatial arts, such as sculpture, installation art, and architecture, as well as applied arts, such as fashion and design. No sculpture, building, nor dress can be fully perceived from a single perspective; thus, film affords the chance for their visual contemplation in virtual time and space. But as architectural historian Barry Bergdoll notes, the agency of this dynamism lies with the filmmaker rather than the viewer:

> Space, the very essence of architecture, in the cinema is always represented or translated by a director or cameraman, rather than experienced directly. Knowledge, perception, and memory do not operate the same way in architectural space as they do in celluloid space.[36]

However naturalistic or affecting the cinematic depiction of an aesthetic object or architectural space may be, it always remains a particular visual interpretation of it, informationally richer than a photograph, but also considerably more constructed (by the filmmaker).

If the act of filming works of painting, sculpture, photography, and architecture has been preoccupied with translating them into the virtuality of cinematic time and space, then the act of filming artists has been more concerned with the preservation of the historical time and place of the profilmic, particularly with capturing the processes of artistic inspiration, creation, and reception. While the camera observes the artist perceiving the world, laboring in their studio, and interacting with those who are contemplating their completed work (usually friends, colleagues, dealers, collectors, or the filmmaker), the camera also often sutures the film viewer into those processes. In *The Photographer*, for instance, shots of Edward Weston gazing at the California landscape in search of photographic images are intercut with what appears to be Weston's point of view, thus tutoring us in a certain aesthetic mimicry; that is, in learning how to see the world as Weston does.[37] At one point, Van Dyke's film camera even looks through the lens of Weston's large-format photographic camera. *Une visite à Picasso* (*A Visit to Picasso*, Paul Haesaerts, 1949), *Jackson Pollack* (Hans Namuth, 1951), and *Le Mystère Picasso* (*The Mystery of Picasso*, Henri-Georges Clouzot, 1956) all include sequences in which the camera is placed behind or below a sheet of glass onto which the artist is painting, creating an unusual and uncanny alignment between the film screen and the surface of the painting.[38] However, these strategies for situating the film viewer viscerally within the aura of artistic creation were all paradoxically premised on the artist performing especially for the camera in a carefully configured set up – Pollack famously complained that the production of Namuth's film alienated him from his own artistic process.

Citing *Painters Painting* (1972), Emile De Antonio's film about American abstract expressionist and pop artists, as her primary example, Caroline A. Jones contends that art documentaries in the 1960s and 1970s increasingly moved away from figuring the artist as a highly mythologized and romanticized "inviolate individual," and towards a sharper, more self-conscious representation of artists' inscription within "the social web" of the art world in which they operate, "populated by assistants, dealers, and curators – a web woven of obligation and need."[39] Yet, the limitations of this widened focus become clearer if we compare *Painters Painting* to a contemporaneous short documentary, *Five* (Milton Meltzen and Alvin Yudkoff, 1971), which profiles five prominent African-American artists of the time (Barbara Chase Riboud, Charles White, Romare Bearden, Richard Hunt, and Betty Blayton).[40] Whereas De Antonio's film remains within the institutional context of the (white and overwhelmingly male) art world (as do the majority of contemporary art documentaries), *Five* situates each of its artists in relation to the social worlds of the cities in which they live and work, the cultural traditions of their community (rather than only to specific artists), and the imperatives of arts education and intergenerational cultural transmission.[41] This deeper social and cultural contextualization, as well as the group-focus on multiple artists in a single documentary, has characterized many of the documentaries produced about indigenous artists and artists of color – in contrast to the increasing attention to artist as star in many documentaries about contemporary artists.[42]

The three chapters in the second part of this book approach the representation of the artist in relation to several contexts: technology, social environment, and the global. Stephan Boman analyzes how *Tim's Vermeer* (Teller, 2013) updates and upends the representation of aesthetic creation in art documentaries through its documentation of software engineer Tim Jenison's quixotic attempt to recreate Johannes Vermeer's *The Music Lesson* (1662–1665) using a system of optical technologies that Vermeer may have used in the seventeenth century. In this exploration of technology's role in art, Boman demonstrates how the film uncouples automatism from its modernist conception as a mode of revelatory inspiration for artists and instead radically re-envisions artistic creation as the algorithmic – and thus banal – fulfillment of a pregiven, disembodied code. Turning to artists' relationships to the specific social environments they aim to represent in their work, Amy Villarejo discusses *Dong* (2006), Jia Zhangke's documentary portrait of Chinese painter Liu Xiaodong, in relation to its "companion" film, the more-widely-seen fictional narrative film *Still Life* (2006). Reading this narrative feature and documentary film, which are both set around the building of the Three Gorges Dam, against one another, Villarejo illuminates how the filmmaker (Jia) and painter (Liu) seek parallel formal solutions in their given media to representing the complex socio-political problems of contemporary China. Continuing the attention to contemporary Chinese artists, Luke Robinson examines how the focus of Alison Klayman's *Ai Weiwei: Never Sorry* (2012) on the performative aspects of Ai's practice emphasizes – and consolidates – his status as a global icon of the individual dissident artist, thus relegating the collaborative dimensions to the documentary aspect of his work within China. Rather than treat Klayman's representation of Ai as a globalized misconception of the "true" nature of Ai's practice, Robinson reads the film for moments that reveal Ai's self-aware negotiation of his own global iconification through being documented by foreign filmmakers, thus raising questions about the location of creative authority in the art documentary.

Part III turns to the question of documentation, which became a key issue for many artists in the late 1960s as their practice pushed ever more emphatically against existing conceptions of what could constitute an artwork. Despite their stark formal differences, performance art and land art both sought the de-objectification of art: in the former through the shift from material object to ephemeral event and in the latter through the scale and immobility of geographical inscription. Both thus functioned as anti-institutional practices resisting commodification; yet their de-objectification also prompted the desire for their documentation. The ephemeral singularity of performance art limited their potential audience in time and place, as did the wild, isolated locations of much land art, such as Michael Heizer's *Double Negative* (1969) in the Nevada desert and Robert Smithson's *Spiral Jetty* (1970) on Great Salt Lake, Utah. As performance artist Stuart Brisley argues for photographic documentation: "It releases the performance from the tyranny of being held in the time of its revelation. It extends duration and opens the performance to another life albeit one that is different."[43] Documentation would likewise produce an archival record of the artwork in order to secure its place within art history. While recognizing the need for documentation, performance artists have often felt a strong ambivalence towards it, for if the ontology of performance art rests in its liveness – its presence, immediacy, and singularity – then mediating it would erode the conditions of its being.[44] But, as Philip Auslander points out, "the live is actually an effect of mediatization, not the other way around."[45] As a supplement (in the Derridean sense), the documentation of a performance serves as a post-facto guarantor of its singularity as an event.

During the initial heyday of performance art, photographic documentation was favored by most artists over filmic or videographic documentation. On the one hand, photographs were mere traces of the original work and could never substitute for, in the sense of offering an impression of experiencing, the performance itself, as film or video could, with their capacity for movement and duration. In their suspension of time, photographs also paradoxically keep in play the potentiality of liveness. On the other hand, a photograph can serve as a visual reaction to the performance, an impression of the spectator's perception of the performance. Photographer and filmmaker Babette Mangolte, who has documented many performance artists in both media, explains their distinction:

> Shooting photographs requires improvisation, daring, and immediacy. Those qualities are the opposite of what you need for filmmaking where long term planning and a conceptual grasp of what you want to do are all important. Unlike photography, filmmaking is not primarily a reaction to an event.[46]

Aware of the pitfalls in allowing such reactions to become an expression of her own aesthetic framing of the experience, Mangolte recognizes the need to balance intuition and technique, or, in Barbara Clausen's words, "to grasp the atmosphere between the performer and the audience."[47] Neither a reproduction nor an interpretation of the artwork, documentation maintains an interstitial supplementary status, hovering between being interior and anterior to it. This ambiguity was heightened by the increasing prevalence of artworks in the post-medium age that are wholly constituted by forms of documentation, such as Hans Haacke's provocative works about art patronage and provenance in the 1970s. The processes of documentation had become a mode of art creation in their own right.

All three chapters in Part III engage with this question of how to understand the relationship between artwork and documentation within the context of the art documentary. Moreover, as artists develop increasingly collaborative relationships with the filmmakers documenting their practice, the distinction between art documentation and art documentary becomes a critical question. In her analysis of documentary films about performance artist Marina Abramović, ranging from *The Great Wall of China: Lovers at the Brink* (Murray Grigor, 1989) to *The Space in Between: Marina Abramović and Brazil* (Marco del Fiol, 2016), Chanda Laine Carey argues that they blur the lines between mass media and performance art documentation. The fragmentation and reconstitution of documentation of Abramović's performances that circulates fluidly between gallery spaces and mass-media screens cause a reconceptualization, according to Carey, of both curatorial practice and documentary filmmaking. Shifting to the documentation of site-specific artists, such as Heizer, Christo and Jeanne-Claude, and Do Ho Suh, Vera

Brunner-Sung draws on Miwon Kwon's analytical paradigms of site-specificity to illuminate how documentary filmmakers, including herself, have adopted different filmic techniques to most effectively document phenomenological, social/institutional, and discursive modes of site-specific art. Although many filmmakers become full-on collaborators with artists as they work to extend the parameters of the artwork, Brunner-Sung also recognizes ways in which a filmmaker, such as Doug Pray in his eponymous film about Heizer's installation *Levitated Mass* (2012), can radically marginalize artistic intent (in this case of the phenomenological sort), in favor of an investigation of how the work's construction impacted a wide range of people outside of the art world. Expanding the discussion of documentation to its function within feminist and art historiography, Theresa L. Geller's chapter examines how Lynn Hershman Leeson's documentary film and transmedia project *!Women Art Revolution* (a.k.a. *!W.A.R.*, 2010) forges a genealogical counter-history of the feminist art movement from the forty years of documentary material that Hershman Leeson has shot in and about the movement. Geller demonstrates how *!W.A.R.* both documents and participates in feminist art activism through the deployment of consciousness-raising strategies, the reclamation of marginalized artists and practices, and the refusal to abide by the disciplinary distinctions between aesthetic and political practice.

Part IV investigates the documentary representation of art museums, which has flourished in recent years, including three acclaimed feature films on major European institutions released in a single year: *National Gallery* (Frederick Wiseman, 2014), *The Great Museum* (Johannes Holzhausen, 2014), and *The New Rijksmuseum* (Oeke Hoogendijk, 2014). An institution of modernity, the museum shares several key characteristics with cinema.[48] As Tony Bennett elaborates in his discussion of the "exhibitionary complex" of nineteenth-century modernity, the museum is a technology of display that disciplines its visitors not only in viewing its objects through particular ideological frames and narratives, but also in a social identification with their fellow museum visitors as a public.[49] As much film historiography since the late 1980s has argued, cinema has performed similar functions in generating publics from collective acts of film viewing. Furthermore, just as cinema renders the world as picture, museums transform all objects that enter them into objects of visual interest, and thus aesthetic contemplation, what Svetlana Alpers calls the "museum effect," which she defines as "the tendency to isolate something from its world, to offer it up for attentive looking and thus transform it into art like our own."[50] But, as Stephen Greenblatt reminds us, the "exalted attention" of "wonder" towards the object in a museum is often in tension with a counter-balancing curatorial model of "resonance" that evokes to the viewer "the complex, dynamic cultural forces from which [the displayed object] has emerged."[51] One could argue that this productive tension between resonance and wonder is common to many art documentaries as they seek to both intensify our visual perception of artworks and deepen our understanding of their cultural contexts.

Art museums have in fact deployed cinema as a tool for disciplining their visitors since the early 1920s. In her research on the early-twentieth-century "museum films" made by the Metropolitan Museum of Art in New York, Haidee Wasson illuminates how these short educational films about the museum's collection were originally produced to train the visitor's visual attention in the museum rather than to disseminate the collection beyond the walls of the museum.[52] Amidst growing concern about the problem of "museum fatigue," these films, which were screened in the museum's auditorium, were designed to simplify the experience of the museum:

> the attractions of cinema at the Met lay less in the capacity of projected celluloid to surprise or seduce or shock, and more in its capacity to diminish the size, direct the eye, order the clutter, and tame the experience of a vast museum and its art. (181)

While museum technologies for disciplining visitor behavior have shifted out of their film auditoria and into other media, such as the audio tour, the museum film has survived in the form of "treasures of"-style DVD souvenirs and more recently in the successful brand of *Exhibition on Screen* documentaries that showcase blockbuster art exhibitions at major institutions.

Annabelle Honess Roe's chapter investigates a short-lived phenomenon in the UK that attempted to combine the exhibition documentary subgenre with the live-broadcast format of "event cinema." Analyzing broadcasts from the Tate Modern, the National Gallery, and the British Museum into UK movie theaters, Honess Roe reveals how the incongruities between the visualities of live television, theatrical film exhibition, and the art museum caused this emergent subgenre to founder under the weight of its own contradictory aims. By contrast, Asbjørn Grønstad's chapter explores the generative interaction of cinematic and museum gazes in Wiseman's *National Gallery*, Holzhausen's *The Great Museum*, and Jem Cohen's fictional narrative film *Museum Hours* (2012), which he argues produce a transmedial gaze. For Grønstad, such a transmedial gaze permits not only a renewed perception of artworks in the gallery space but also a richer understanding of the image ecology in which the museum and its art are embedded. Focusing on *The First Monday in May* (2016), Andrew Rossi's documentary about the Met's 2015 fashion exhibition *China: Through the Looking Glass*, Matthew J. Fee's chapter discusses how the film's dual attention to the curation of the exhibition and the preparations for its opening benefit gala illuminates the ongoing debate about fashion's place within the art museum. By comparing Rossi's documentary with *The September Issue* (R. J. Cutler, 2009) and *Scatter My Ashes at Bergdorf's* (Matthew Miele, 2013), which respectively examine the fashion magazine and the department store window, Fee further situates the museum effect on fashion in relation to consumerist technologies of display that also render it as an object of purely visual contemplation.

Documenting the Visual Arts concludes with two interviews that consider the relationship between film worlds and art worlds. In my interview with photography curator and documentary filmmaker Trisha Ziff, she discusses the differing dynamics of exhibition curation, book editing, and documentary filmmaking that have shaped her career-long engagement with photographic history. In whichever medium she is working (and her projects often involve all three), Ziff endeavors to use it in the service of contesting dominant conceptions of photographic history, especially those that prioritize the discourse of master artists and the aesthetic hierarchies that produce them. Marsha Gordon interviews Margaret Parsons, Head of the Film Department at the National Gallery of Art in Washington, DC, who discusses the history of the museum's film program since she began in 1981. As a curator working at the interstices of film and art worlds, Parsons elucidates the impact of funding, distribution, festivals, institutions, and economics on art documentaries, as well as art historical institutions' own experimental engagements with documentary film production, such as *Art on Film*, a collaboration between the Getty and the Met in the late 1980s. Both Ziff and Parsons remind us that to understand the contemporary art documentary, we must attend as much to the institutional dynamics of the film and art worlds as to the aesthetic challenges of film's intermedial representation of other visual arts.

Although this book shines critical illumination onto a genre largely overlooked thus far by documentary studies and art history, it is, like most edited collections, neither comprehensive in scope nor without any regrettable lacunae. I thus hope that its accomplishments – and its limitations – will encourage more scholarship on the continually burgeoning body of art documentaries.

Notes

1 See Richard Abel, *French Film Theory and Criticism: A History/Anthology, 1907–1939*, vol. 1 (Princeton: Princeton University Press, 1993), 5–34; and D. N. Rodowick, *Elegy for Theory* (Cambridge, MA: Harvard University Press, 2014), 72–89.
2 See Malcolm Turvey, *The Filming of Modern Life: European Avant Garde Films of the 1920s* (Cambridge, MA: MIT Press, 2013). On the initial impact of cinema on avant-garde movements, see Jennifer Wild, *The Parisian Avant-Garde in the Age of Cinema, 1900–1923* (Berkeley: University of California Press, 2015). On the emergent networks and institutions that facilitated European avant-garde film in the interwar period, see Malte Hagener, *Moving Forward, Looking Back: The European Avant-garde and the Invention of Film Culture, 1919–1939* (Amsterdam: University of Amsterdam Press, 2007).
3 See Haidee Wasson, *Museum Movies: The Museum of Modern Art and the Birth of Art Cinema* (Berkeley: University of California Press, 2005).
4 On the nexus between art and the moving image after 1945, see Kelly Brougher, *Art and Film since 1945: Hall of Mirrors* (Los Angeles: Museum of Contemporary Art, 1996); and Tanya Leighton, ed., *Art and the Moving Image: A Critical Reader* (London: Tate Publishing, 2008). On the history and theory of moving image installation, see Andrew V. Uroskie, *Between the Black Box and the White Cube: Expanded Cinema and Postwar Art* (Chicago: University of Chicago Press, 2014); Kate Mondlich, *Screens: Viewing Media Installation Art* (Minneapolis: University of Minnesota Press, 2010); and Catherine Elwes, *Installation and the Moving Image* (London and New York: Wallflower Press, 2015).
5 Okwui Enwezor's inclusion of a substantial amount of film-based work in *documenta 11* in 2002 marked a critical moment for the global art world's embrace of contemporary moving-image art. Another key exhibition was Kelly Brougher's 2008 two-part exhibition at the Hirschhorn Museum in Washington, DC, *The Cinema Effect: Illusion, Reality, and the Moving Image*.
6 See Claudia Spinelli, ed., *Reprocessing Reality: New Perspectives on Art and Documentary* (Zurich: JRP Ringier, 2005); T. J. Demos, *The Migrant Image: The Art and Politics of*

Documentary during Global Crisis (Durham: Duke University Press, 2013); and Julian Stallybrass, ed., *Documentary* (London: Whitechapel Gallery, 2013).
7 Michael Renov, "Art, Documentary as Art," in *The Documentary Film Book*, ed. Brian Winston (London and Basingstoke: British Film Institute and Palgrave Macmillan, 2013), 348.
8 A key critical recognition of this shift came from Bill Nichols in the early 1990s when he defined a new mode of documentary film, the "performative," which prioritizes evocation over indexical referentiality in the service of exploring the affective dimensions of social subjectivity. Bill Nichols, "Performing Documentary," in *Blurred Boundaries: Questions of Meaning in Contemporary Culture* (Bloomington: Indiana University Press, 1994), 92–106.
9 See Angela Dalle Vacche, *Cinema and Painting: How Art is Used in Film* (Austin: University of Texas Press, 1996); Dalle Vacche, ed. *Film, Art, New Media: Museum without Walls?* (Basingstoke: Palgrave Macmillan, 2016); Susan Felleman, *Art in the Cinematic Imagination* (Austin: University of Texas Press, 2006); Felleman, *Real Objects in Unreal Situations: Modern Art in Fiction Films* (Bristol: Intellect, 2014); John A. Walker, *Art and Artists on Screen* (Manchester: Manchester University Press, 1993), Steven Jacobs, *Framing Pictures: Film and the Visual Arts* (Edinburgh: Edinburgh University Press, 2011); Jacobs, Susan Felleman, Vito Adriaensens, and Lisa Colpaert, *Screening Statues: Sculpture and Cinema* (Edinburgh: Edinburgh University Press, 2017). Jacobs has consistently devoted attention to art documentaries in his books and is currently co-editing a volume on art documentaries of the 1940s and 1950s. British arts television has garnered two book-length histories: Walker's *Arts TV: A History of Arts Television in Britain* (London: John Libbey and the Arts Council of Great Britain, 1993) and John Wyver's *Vision On: Film, Television, and the Arts in Britain* (London: Wallflower, 2007). French scholarship on the history of art documentaries has been more prolific: Yves Chevrefils Desbiolles, ed. *Le Film sur l'art et ses frontières* (Aix-en-Provence: Publications de l'Université de Provence, 1998); Fanny Etienne, *Films d'art/films sur l'art* (Paris: Harmattan, 2002); and Valentine Robert, Laurent Le Forestier, and François Albera, eds., *Le Film sur l'art: entre histoire de l'art et documentaire de creation* (Rennes: Presses Universitaires de Rennes, 2015).
10 See Timothy Corrigan, *The Essay Film: From Montaigne, after Marker* (Oxford: Oxford University Press, 2011); Laura Rascaroli, *How the Essay Film Thinks* (Oxford: Oxford University Press, 2017); Nora M. Alter and Corrigan, eds., *Essays on the Essay Film* (New York: Columbia University Press, 2017); and Alter, *The Essay Film after Fact and Fiction* (New York: Columbia University Press, 2018).
11 Art historian Caroline A. Jones has also noted her discipline's dismissal of the art documentary: "Yet despite [the] promise of plenitude and seductiveness – science, magic, and glimpses of hidden truths – films in particular have been virtually ignored by art historians. If they appear at all in the art-historical literature, they are used primarily as verbal sources (mined for quotes) or viewed as stylistic subjects (analyzed formally). … Few films have been examined for the flesh they might add to the bones of historical chronology, or the information on practice that they might provide." *Machine in the Studio: Constructing the Postwar American Artist* (Chicago: University of Chicago Press, 1996), 63.
12 While reflexive documentaries about their own making, such as Dziga Vertov's *Man with a Movie Camera* (1929) or Jafar Panahi's *This Is Not a Film* (2011), have attracted significant scholarly attention, documentaries about the history of film, filmmakers, and individual films have generated surprisingly scant critical study, with a few exceptions, such as Jean Luc Godard's *Histoire(s) du cinema* (1988–1998) and the subgenre of "making of" documentaries on DVDs.
13 Jacobs, *Framing Pictures*, 1. My discussion here of early art documentaries draws substantively from Jacobs's excellent account in the first chapter of his book.

14 See Tom Gunning, "Before Documentary: Early Non-fiction Films and the 'View' Aesthetic," in *Uncharted Territory: Essays on Early Nonfiction Film*, ed. Daan Hertogs and Nico de Klerk (Amsterdam: Stichting Nederlands Filmmuseum, 1997), 9–25.
15 John Ott, "Labored Stereotypes: Palmer Hayden's *The Janitor Who Paints*," *American Art* 22, no. 1 (2008): 102–115.
16 See Robert Ziegler, *Kunst und Architektur im Kulturfilm, 1919–1945* (Konstanz: UVK Verlagsgesellschaft, 2003).
17 Jacobs, *Framing Pictures*, 4.
18 For a comprehensive history of Malraux's project, see Walter Grasskamp, *The Book on the Floor: André Malraux and the Imaginary Museum* (Los Angeles: Getty Publications, 2016).
19 Cited in Jacobs, *Framing Pictures*, 25.
20 Wyver, *Vision On*, 137.
21 Wyver, *Vision On*, 145. The exception to British television's obsession with male art historical authority appears to be the late Wendy Beckett, better known to television audiences as Sister Wendy, and more recently cultural historian Janina Ramirez. Even *Civilisations* (2018), the BBC's recent multicultural revision of Clark's series, retained the authoritative presenter format, albeit with a more diverse tripartite cast of Schama, classicist Mary Beard, and historian David Olusoga.
22 For a critical account of the heated intellectual debate about Berger's series and its relationship to Clark's *Civilisation*, see Jonathan Conlin, "'An Irresponsible Flow of Images': Berger, Clark and the Art of Television, 1958–1988," in *On John Berger: Telling Stories*, ed. Ralf Hertel and David Malcolm (Leiden: Brill Rodopi, 2015), 269–291.
23 Wyver, *Vision On*, 151.
24 Mark Nash, "Langston in Retrospect," in booklet accompanying *Looking for Langston*, DVD. Directed by Isaac Julien. London: British Film Institute, 2005.
25 John Roberts, "Postmodernism, Television and the Visual Arts: A Critical Consideration of *State of the Art*," in *Picture This: Media Representations of Visual Arts and Artists*, ed. Philip Hayward (London: John Libbey, 1998), 61.
26 Herzog had repeatedly referred to the film in interviews during his press junket as "a science fiction fantasy." See Rob Munday, "Cave of Forgotten Dreams," *Director Notes*, accessed March 26, 2011, https://directorsnotes.com/2011/03/26/cave-of-forgotten-dreams/.
27 In the 2000s, Christo and Jeanne-Claude also developed a working relationship with German filmmakers Wolfram and Jörg-Daniel Hissen, who made a number of short documentaries for European television.
28 Beginning its first broadcast season on PBS in 2001, *Art21* launched its internet presence in 2008 with its web-only series, *Exclusive* (later rebranded as *Extended Play*). "History," *Art21*, accessed June 12, 2019, https://art21.org/about/history/.
29 Royal Museums of Fine Arts in Belgium, "Bruegel: A Fall with the Rebel Angels (Virtual Reality)," YouTube, March 14, 2016, www.youtube.com/watch?v=bXR9EEmb-JU.
30 "Magritte VR," BDH, accessed June 12, 2019, www.bdh.net/immersive/magritte-vr.
31 See Preloaded, "Modigliani VR – Full Demo," Vimeo, accessed June 12, 2019, https://vimeo.com/257108192/22d0d1c94f.
32 "Behind the Scenes: Modigliani VR: The Ochre Studio," Tate Modern, accessed June 12, 2019, www.tate.org.uk/whats-on/tate-modern/exhibition/modigliani/modigliani-vr-ochre-atelier.
33 André Bazin, *What is Cinema?* vol. 1, trans. Hugh Gray (Berkeley: University of California Press, 1967), 166.
34 Cartier-Bresson's seminal 1952 monograph was published as *The Decisive Moment* (New York: Simon and Schuster) in English and *Images à la sauvette* (Paris: Verve) in French (which roughly translates as "images on the run"). In the English edition, Cartier-Bresson

writes, "To me, photography is the simultaneous recognition, in a fraction of a second, of the significance of an event as well as of a precise organization of forms which give that event its proper expression" (42).
35 Erwin Panofsky, "Style and Medium in the Motion Pictures," in *Film: An Anthology*, ed. Daniel Talbot (Berkeley: University of California Press, 1966), 18.
36 Barry Bergdoll, "Altered States of Vision: Film, Video, and the Teaching of Architectural History," in *Architecture on Screen*, ed. Nadine Covert (New York: Metropolitan Museum of Art, 1994), xvii.
37 This form of aesthetic mimicry has remained a popular technique for documentaries about photographers, utilized in films such as *War Photographer* (Christian Frei, 2000) and *Magnum Photos: The Changing of a Myth* (Reiner Holzemer, 2000).
38 Particularly in *Jackson Pollack*, this novel technique presents painting as the trace of the artist's bodily movement. Caroline Jones discusses how Namuth's film, along with Paul Falkenberg's related photographs, played a highly significant role in Pollack's reception in the 1950s, arguably consolidating the idea of his "action painting" in a more immediate way than the paintings themselves. See *Machine in the Studio*, 72–80.
39 Jones, 108.
40 *Five* was sponsored by Seagram Distillers and later circulated internationally by the US Information Agency.
41 Whereas Herbert Matter's short documentary about sculptor Alexander Calder, *Work of Calder* (1950), used the character of a child as the epitome of wonderous contemplation of the heroic artist and his creative process, *Five* repeatedly invokes children as figures of intergenerational cultural continuity of the past, present, and future.
42 See for example, Australian Aboriginal (Wiradjuri/Kamilaroi) filmmaker Michael Riley's *Boomalli: Five Koorie Artists* (1988), about Bronwyn Bancroft, Fiona Foley, Tracey Moffatt, Raymond Meeks, and Jeffrey Samuels; and Canadian Indigenous (Métis/Cree) filmmaker Loretta Todd's *Hands of History* (1994), about four Indigenous female artists in Canada: Doreen Jensen, Rena Point Bolton, Jane Ash Poitras, and Joane Cardinal-Schubert.
43 Stuart Brisley, "The Photographer and the Performer," in *Live Art on Camera: Performance and Photography*, ed. Alice Maude-Roxby (Southampton: John Hansard Gallery, 2007), 83.
44 See Peggy Phelan, "The Ontology of Performance: Representation without Reproduction," in *Unmarked: The Politics of Performance* (London: Routledge, 1993), 146.
45 Philip Auslander, *Liveness: Performance in a Mediatized Culture*, 2nd ed. (London: Routledge, 1999), 55.
46 Babette Mangolte, "My History (The Intractable)," in *Live Art on Camera*, 137.
47 Barbara Clausen, "Performing Histories: Why the Point Is Not to Make a Point … " *Afterall* 23 (Spring 2010): 39.
48 Alison Griffiths has arguably offered the most sustained historical investigation of this nexus in her two books, *Wonderous Difference: Cinema, Anthropology, and Turn-of-the-Century Visual Culture* (New York: Columbia University Press, 2001) and *Shivers Down Your Spine: Cinema, Museums, and the Immersive View* (New York: Columbia University Press, 2013).
49 See Tony Bennett, "The Exhibitionary Complex," *New Formations* 4 (Spring 1988): 73–102.
50 Svetlana Alpers, "The Museum as a Way of Seeing," in *Exhibiting Cultures: The Poetics and Politics of Museum Display*, eds. Ivan Karp and Steven D. Lavine (Washington, DC: Smithsonian Institution Press, 1991): 27.
51 Stephen Greenblatt, "Resonance and Wonder," in *Exhibiting Cultures*, 42.
52 Haidee Wasson, "Big, Fast Museums/Small, Slow Movies: Film, Scale, and the Art Museum," in *Useful Cinema*, eds. Charles R. Acland and Haidee Wasson (Durham: Duke University Press, 2011), 178–204.

PART I
Historical foundations

1

HENRI STORCK'S *LE MONDE DE PAUL DELVAUX* AND PYGMALIONIST CINEMA

Steven Jacobs

Delvaux and cinema

The 1940s and 1950s can be considered the "Golden Age" of the art documentary. In those decades, literally hundreds of art documentary shorts were produced, many of them being made by leading filmmakers such as Henri Alékan, Henri-Georges Clouzot, Carl Theodor Dreyer, Robert Flaherty, Jean Grémillon, Alain Resnais, and Willard S. Van Dyke, among others. In addition, prominent critics and film theorists such as André Bazin, Siegfried Kracauer, and Rudolf Arnheim paid attention to the art documentary in their writings while the phenomenon was also extensively discussed in leading film and art journals. Furthermore, in the decades immediately following the Second World War, the production and distribution of art documentaries were backed by international cultural organizations such as UNESCO, FIAF (Fédération internationale des archives du film), IAFF (International Art Film Federation), CIDALC (Comité internationale pour la diffusion des arts et des lettres par le cinéma), and IIFA (International Institute of Films on Art). Last but not least, in 1948 leading filmmakers, producers, and museum officials founded FIFA (Fédération internationale du film sur l'art), which would play an important role in the dissemination and critical contextualization of these films. In the 1940s and 1950s, conventions were established that are still in use in art documentaries today, but many seminal works from that period remain striking because of their audacious experiments. This was particularly the case in Italy, France, and Belgium, where filmmakers such as Luciano Emmer, Alain Resnais, and Paul Haesaerts presented their "documentaries" not as mere registrations or reproductions but as experimental shorts that were new filmic artworks in their own right. These films became visual laboratories to investigate the tensions between movement and stasis, the two- and three-dimensional, and the real and the artificial; a film on art was thus self-consciously presented as an art film. Many of the art documentaries of the era are highly personal, poetic, reflexive, and experimental films that still offer a thrilling cinematic experience, in contrast with many of the didactic and instructive art documentaries produced during the following decades.[1]

One of the key figures in the development of the postwar lyrical art documentary is Belgian filmmaker Henri Storck (1907–1999), who had close personal contacts with painters such as James Ensor, Léon Spilliaert, Constant Permeke, and Félix Labisse, who were all living in the seaside town of Ostend, where Storck grew up.[2] Storck started making films on art in the mid-1930s, but his most important contributions to the genre date from the late 1940s, when he was also personally involved in FIFA. In particular, *Le Monde de Paul Delvaux* (*The World of Paul Delvaux*, 1946) and *Rubens* (1948) would become landmark art documentaries that were abundantly screened and discussed in the immediate postwar era. *Rubens* was made in collaboration with the art historian Paul Haesaerts, who later also made art documentaries such as the widely acclaimed *Visite à Picasso* (*Visit to Picasso*, 1950). Rather than dealing with the life or the historical context of the famous baroque artist, *Rubens* first and foremost presents an analysis of the style and compositions of the painter with the help of camera movements, split screens, dissolves, and animation techniques. In so doing, Storck and Haesaerts employed the revealing power of cinema as an instrument of formalist art criticism, showing that it could liberate itself from dependence on a dominating voice-over narration.

Equally significant and influential as *Rubens* is the 11-minute black-and-white short *Le Monde de Paul Delvaux*, which Storck made two years earlier in collaboration with poet, essayist, and art critic René Micha, who wrote the screenplay. As its title suggests, the film deals with Belgian Surrealist artist Paul Delvaux, who had become famous for his paintings of uncanny nudes in nocturnal cityscapes. Throughout the 1930s, Delvaux had developed his set of personal themes and syntax, centering on the classical female nude, which is for him less an ideal to be pursued than an object of reverie.[3] In Delvaux's world, these nudes are juxtaposed to men dressed in the fashion of the day, wandering in desolate streets and squares, which are rendered in emphatic Quattrocento perspective. In the 1940s, Delvaux's paintings increasingly combined elements of classical architecture with tokens of urban modernity, such as tram lines or gas lights, as well as marble statues and skeletons. When Storck made his film in the mid-1940s, Delvaux was at the height of his international popularity with a retrospective exhibition at the Palais des Beaux-Arts in Brussels in December 1944, only a few months after the liberation.[4] Stimulated by the popularization of Surrealism in the United States, Delvaux's fame had crossed the Atlantic in the very same months – Lee Miller photographed the artist with some of his paintings at the Palais des Beaux-Arts for *Vogue* magazine.

Hollywood also recognized the aptness of Delvaux's art for the film camera. Together with Max Ernst and Salvador Dali, among others, Delvaux participated in the notorious art competition for a painting representing *The Temptation of Saint Anthony* to appear in Albert Lewin's production of *The Private Affairs of Bel Ami* (1947). Eventually a jury decided to include Ernst's painting although the film itself clearly shares, as Susan Felleman notes, some pictorial characteristics with Delvaux's paintings.[5] Fifteen years later, the interconnections between Delvaux, Ernst, and film would also mark the production of Resnais's *L'Année dernière à Marienbad* (*Last Year at Marienbad*, 1961). Although Resnais initially thought of Ernst for the production of the statue featured prominently in the film, the classical sculpture reminiscent of a Poussin painting was eventually made by prop artists.[6] Yet, with its eerie tableau-like imagery, *Marienbad* reminds us in its entirety of Delvaux, while the statuesque actress of the theater play in the opening sequence seems to have directly stepped out of a Delvaux painting. Several scholars have noticed these affinities with Delvaux's paintings, and British film critic Raymond Durgnat even linked *Marienbad* to Henri Storck's visualization of the Surrealist painter. In his review of the film, Durgnat states that *Marienbad* recalls Storck's *Le Monde de Paul Delvaux* "with its Surrealist canvasses of sad-eyes nudes and aimless men straying against ruins and crumbling statues."[7] Resnais undoubtedly knew about Storck's Delvaux film as he recognized the importance of "the Belgian School" when making art documentaries himself in the late 1940s and early 1950s.[8]

Staging perspectives on the nude

It was *Marienbad*'s oneirism, as well as its morbid fascination for lifeless bodies, that reminded Durgnat of Storck's *Le Monde de Paul Delvaux*. Produced by the so-called "Séminaire des Arts," under the direction of Luc Haesaerts at the Palais des Beaux-Arts, the film was shot on 35mm during the retrospective at the Palais and released in 1946 with a soundtrack that combined music by André Souris and a Paul Éluard poem recited by the Surrealist poet himself.[9] Written in 1938, when Delvaux contributed to the *Exposition internationale du Surréalisme* at the Galerie des Beaux-Arts in Paris, Éluard's *Exil (à Paul Delvaux)* was based on two 1937 paintings by Delvaux, *L'Appel de la nuit* (*The Call of the Night*) and *L'Aurore* (*Aurora*), and refers to "grandes femmes immobiles" or "grand immobile women" who are "tranquilles et plus belles d'être semblables" or "tranquil and too beautiful to be alike."[10]

Stork divides Éluard's poem into small fragments and integrates them into the Stravinsky-inspired score by Souris, a musician close to the Surrealist movement, who wrote that "the determining function of the film was the tempo, a function which is essentially musical. Delvaux's painting is implicitly slow, and Storck has established the unity of the film on the slowness of his travelling shots."[11] Bringing together film, painting, music, and poetry, *Le Monde de Paul Delvaux* presented itself as a modern *Gesamtkunstwerk* in the age of mechanical reproduction. Art critic and film historian Paul Davay described it as

> an almost perfect meeting and fusion of different artistic disciplines subject to a new means of expression – the cinema. Under Storck's direction, the painter Delvaux, the script-writer René Micha, the musician André Souris, and the poet Paul Éluard found a common ground.[12]

For Storck, Delvaux's paintings were a perfect subject for a film as they are characterized by structures that resemble forms of staging. In a 1970 conversation with the painter, Storck compared Delvaux's paintings with

> the preoccupations of a theater scenographer. One can say that his paintings are constructed like a theater. [...] and this is why these paintings work perfectly in cinema, why they go well on the screen. In addition to a composition and its plastic elements, there is a mise-en-scène.[13]

In Delvaux's paintings, public squares, temple forecourts, and paved loggias create the scene for a mute drama.[14] It is precisely in these stage-like settings that Delvaux's nude bodies eroticize their environment. Enhanced by colonnades and other architectural features, the exaggerated or receding perspectives guide our gaze into the depth of the painting. This magnetic effect of Delvaux's perspectives is closely connected to the theme of expectation since his paintings evoke a moment that endures for eternity, "pregnant with ill-defined but nonetheless profound desire."[15] In addition, with his nudes captured within receding perspective, Delvaux does not only present the woman as an object of male phantasies and desires, he also implicates the viewer in acts of voyeurism – a theme also evoked by the abundant presence of mirrors, frames, spectacles, and lamps in Delvaux's *oeuvre*. This voyeuristic effect is emphasized by Delvaux's practice of showing the same woman (or similar-looking women) multiple times, as if they surrender themselves to the gaze of the spectator. Storck's moving camera accentuates this submission. Storck, for instance, often shows only a part of a painting, particularly when he opens a new sequence. As a result, the compositional organization within the frame differs from that of the original painting. The off-center position of the camera creates a certain tension, heightening the uncanny character of Delvaux's perspectives. For André Bazin, this confrontation between the fixed and centripetal frame of the painting with the mobile and centrifugal frame of the film camera was precisely one of the most fascinating aspects of the art documentaries of the late 1940s.[16] According to Bazin, the fixed frame of painting encloses a world that exists entirely by and for itself; it draws the viewer's attention in a centripetal way to a static composition. The frame of the film camera, by contrast, is mobile and implies a centrifugal space extending beyond the frame into the smallest and most remote corners of everyday life. When we show a part of a painting on a film screen, the space of the painting loses its orientation; it is presented as something borderless and hence something that extends beyond the frame.

Storck precisely introduces this centrifugal space of film into the centripetal space of painting. By switching between paintings and by letting the camera glide over surfaces, the limits of which remain invisible, he breaks through the spatial restraints of painting. As the film's title indicates, rather than focusing on a few specific paintings, *Le Monde de Paul Delvaux* deals with the entire oeuvre of the Surrealist painter or with his "world" consisting of desolate streets with classical buildings, trains, and tram lines, where naked women seem to pass along men dressed in black suits with bowler hats. The film creates an organically integrated melancholic and oneiric universe constructed out of fragments drawn from twenty Delvaux paintings (all made between 1939 and 1944), which were brought together at the Palais des Beaux-Arts retrospective.[17] Furthermore, Storck and Delvaux did away with the frames of the pictures and, in some cases, lined them up one next to the other so that Storck's camera could pass without interruption from one to the other.[18] By switching from one painting to the other, the film emphasizes the persistence of recurrent iconographic motifs and the element of repetition in Delvaux's paintings. In so doing, Storck demonstrates the ways art documentaries are able to create an entire world by means of different artworks. Many art documentaries bring artworks together, comparing them by switching from one painting to another. In *Van Gogh* (1948), for instance, another landmark film of the late 1940s, Alain Resnais draws our attention to all kinds of plastic details in Vincent Van Gogh paintings, but he also constructs a plot, which violates the original works of art. His camera, for instance, approaches a door of a building in a painting and suddenly enters its interior by means of another painting. Paintings are linked in a way a director would use real locations. A forward track to the window in the painting of *The Yellow House* (1888) is, for instance, followed by a backward tracking shot, which starts from a window and gradually reveals the entire interior of *Bedroom in Arles* (1888). This cinematic logic can also be found in Storck's film on Delvaux, whose art is characterized by imposing perspectives rather than by the modernist flatness of Van Gogh's paintings. Storck presents various Delvaux paintings as parts of a coherent world. Entire sequences of his film are like a tour through a Delvaux-like cityscape. His camera movements and the editing create spatial relations between different paintings.

Throughout the entire film, Storck's mobile camera gently scans Delvaux's canvasses, scrutinizing as well as cherishing them. On the one hand, with these camera movements as well as his close-ups, Storck focuses on the tactile aspects of the paintings. As American film historian and critic Arthur Knight noted in a 1952 survey of innovative art documentaries, "Storck creates an awareness of texture, of technique, of how the paint is laid on."[19] On the other hand, Storck succeeds in evoking the immaterial and dream-like world of Delvaux's paintings, the camera capturing their eerie spaces and lunar gloss. Storck's black-and-white film corresponds to Delvaux's uncannily nocturnal light, which transforms his women into mysteriously lunar beings. According to Storck, "one can never say if it is daylight or nocturnal light. It is like a great nocturnal light seen during the day."[20] Furthermore, Storck notes that, in Delvaux's paintings,

> shadows on the ground are sharp and vigorous, often contradictory, adding to the strangeness of the ensemble. It is the light of ore, of which Breton spoke, a miraculous invention of Delvaux, a necessary invention to light the domains of the night, to light the fires that illuminate the corners of the scene, the burning lights and lanterns, the brilliant windows, the mirrors, the jewels.[21]

The use of black-and-white perfectly tallies with Delvaux's austere use (or sometimes virtual absence) of color, which emphasizes his graphic style as well as his fascination with lines, visualized by the presence of telegraph wires, train tracks, and architectural or skeletal forms. This graphic linearity echoes Delvaux's linear perspective, which is frequently enhanced by colonnades or other architectural features. Storck emphasizes these characteristics in the opening sequence of the film, using forward tracking shots that underline Delvaux's receding perspective. Moreover, Storck's black-and-white film evokes the studio lighting of academic painting, which promotes the visibility of objects but at the same time fixes figures and things. The surreal or hallucinatory quality of Delvaux's paintings is partly the result of the evocation of a timeless realm. This is of course also the result of Delvaux's "classicism." During his journey to Italy in the late 1930s, Delvaux studied the painters of the Quattrocento, who confirmed him in his aesthetic taste for linear perspective, architecture, and women of ideal proportions.[22]

The Surrealist documentary and Pygmalionism

With *Le Monde de Paul Delvaux*, Storck made an important contribution to the development and dissemination of Surrealism in the 1940s. The Surrealist aspect of this film, however, is not only the result of film's subject matter. To a certain extent, *Le Monde de Paul Delvaux* can also be considered itself a Surrealist film. Already in the late 1920s, Storck himself had close connections to Surrealist artists such as Félix Labisse. The French painter scripted two of Storck's early films, *Pour vos beaux yeux* (*For Your Beautiful Eyes*, 1929) and *La Mort de Vénus* (*The Death of Venus*, 1930), which include narratives, themes, motifs, and imagery that are marked by Surrealism, such as the eroticism of the sea or a strange story of a young man who buys a glass eye and sends it by mail. Much later, in 1962, Storck would make two films dealing with Labisse's paintings, *Le Bonheur d'être aimé* (*The Happiness to Be Loved*) and *Les Malheurs de la guerre* (*The Troubles of War*). Other early Storck films such as *Images d'Ostende* (*Images of Ostend*, 1929), *Idylle à la Plage* (*Idyll at the Beach*, 1931), and *Sur les bords de la caméra* (*At the Borders of the Camera*, 1932) are likewise characterized by Surrealist preoccupations, such as a preference for striking contrasts and disjunctions, a fascination for the eye and the gaze, and a predilection for the combination of sensual beauty and decay.

Storck contributed as well to the development of the Surrealist documentary. Both Ado Kyrou and Michael Richardson in their books on Surrealist cinema explicitly mention Storck as a documentary filmmaker influenced by Surrealism.[23] Although Surrealism is often associated with an anti-realist aesthetic grounded in dreams and the marvelous, there was always a certain documentary element to Surrealism present in all its manifestations.[24] In fact, the Surrealists favored the documentary image, in both photography and film, because it could anchor or reveal the surreal in the real. Surrealism precisely demonstrated the ambiguity, opacity, or non-transparency of the documentary image by juxtaposing photographs with each other or with captions, thus generating new meanings or revealing latent ones. Illustrated journals close to the Surrealist movement, such as *Documents* or *Variétés*, demonstrated in text, image, and lay-out that meanings could shift and that representations never resulted in unified realistic worlds.[25]

As a medium that inherently combines images, film offered these options too. Many avant-garde artists were attracted to film precisely because of its capacity to juggle with the indexical representations of the documentary image and to create radical juxtapositions through cinematic montage. Right from its inception in the 1920s, documentary filmmaking was characterized by the use of "modernist elements of fragmentation, defamiliarization (*ostranenie*, *Verfremdungseffekte*), collage, abstraction, relativity, anti-illusionism and a general rejection of the transparency of realist representation."[26] In his found-footage films of the early 1930s, such as *Sur les bords de la camera* and *Histoire du soldat inconnu* (1932), Storck played on this dimension precisely, transforming the original meanings of the film fragments and creating formal, rhythmic, narrative, or symbolic connections between images taken from different sources and contexts. *Le Monde de Paul Delvaux* is evidently a documentary on painting; it relies on the documentary indexicality of the film camera; however, its subject is not the historical world or "reality" but "le monde de Paul Delvaux," an artificial, oneiric world created by a painter. Yet, the film is at the same time a Surrealist documentary itself. Using painted imagery as found footage reminiscent of the Surrealist *objet trouvé*, Storck combines highly idiosyncratic poetic forms with documentary practices, thus exploring the borders between documentary and fiction, reality and fantasy, as well as painting and cinema. Focusing on the dream-like and uncanny characters of Delvaux, Storck deploys the medium of film to transform stasis into movement, death into life, and paint into flesh. Although Storck's gentle camera movements seem to emphasize the fixity of Delvaux's cityscapes and his figures, he also brings Delvaux's nudes to life, presenting them as sleepwalking phantoms or as beings somewhere halfway between living and dead.

With a camera caressing the nudes of Delvaux, Storck's film evokes the cool eroticism and *agalmatophilia* – humans falling in love with statues – cherished by the Surrealists. In so doing, Storck presents himself as a modern Pygmalion, who had become a Surrealist icon.[27] Not coincidentally, Storck's *Le Monde de Paul Delvaux* includes the painter's own interpretation of the myth of Pygmalion, which deals with the desire on the part of the artist to breathe life into his own creation. In the decade leading up to Storck's film, particularly between 1937 and 1943, Delvaux painted numerous works dealing with the Pygmalion theme. In the painting featured in the film, Delvaux inverted the myth by showing a nude woman caressing a sculpted male body. Instead of Pygmalion adoring his stone Galatea, Delvaux shows a naked woman embracing a *kouros*. In Delvaux's version, it is the painter who is metamorphized into a marble statue with amputated legs. Both Delvaux and Storck not only refer to the classical myth of Pygmalion, they unmistakably evoke a Surrealist "Pygmalionism" or a form of sexual responsiveness directed toward a statue.[28] This Pygmalion effect, as Victor Stoichita calls it, relies on an uncanny combination of stone and flesh, matter and spirit, or death and life.

Desire is dependent on its confrontation with lifeless matter. Not coincidentally, Storck includes footage of Delvaux's 1944 painting *Sleeping Venus*, a theme that also confronts lifeless bodies with desire.[29] At the time Storck made his film, male presences had become increasingly rare in Delvaux's paintings, while marble statues and skeletons had gained greater importance. A traditional symbol of death, the skeleton also tallied with the Surrealist notion of convulsive beauty, a beauty that is both alluring and repellent, as the sleeping or sleepwalking nudes in Delvaux's paintings seem to be dreaming of Death or of seduction by Death.

Storck and Delvaux's fascination for the Pygmalion myth tallies with many artworks and films of the 1940s. The fascination of the living statue can be found in contemporaneous art films that were greatly affected by Surrealism, such as Jean Cocteau's *La Belle et la bête* (*The Beauty and the Beast*, 1946) or Hans Richter's *Dreams That Money Can Buy* (1947), as well as in the Surrealist-inspired films of the American postwar avant-garde, such as *Ritual in Transfigured Time* (Maya Deren, 1946), *The Petrified Dog* (Sidney Peterson, 1948), *Image in the Snow* (Willard Maas, 1952), or *Eaux d'artifice* (Kenneth Anger, 1953). In addition, living statues abound in Hollywood productions of the period. Films such as *One Touch of Venus* (William Seiter, 1948) and *The Barefoot Contessa* (Joseph Mankiewicz, 1954), both starring a highly "statuesque" Ava Gardner, feature statues that become objects of desire, thus hinting at problems of corporeality, carnality, embodiment, and morbid sexuality.[30] Likewise, numerous 1940s Gothic melodramas, such as *Rebecca* (Alfred Hitchcock, 1940), *Laura* (Otto Preminger, 1944), *Gaslight* (George Cukor, 1944), *The Ghost and Mrs. Muir* (Joseph Mankiewicz, 1947), and *Pandora and the Flying Dutchman* (Albert Lewin, 1950), contain key scenes with haunting portraits.[31] The latter film even demonstrates that, following the *Bel Ami* art competition, Delvaux remained an important source of inspiration for Lewin. With its juxtaposition of modern and classical elements, his *Pandora and the Flying Dutchman* shares many similarities with the paintings of De Chirico and Delvaux. Often celebrated by the Surrealists themselves, these noir thrillers are marked by the illusion that a portrait or a statue is coming to life, haunting the film's characters. This illusion is created with the help of montage effects, sounds, light, and camera movements, which are comparable with the ways in which Storck animates the still image in the paintings of Delvaux, which have a kind of noiresque quality with their dreamy characters wandering through nocturnal cityscapes. Moreover, Delvaux's paintings feature nudes who, according to David Scott, possess some of the photogenic qualities of Hollywood goddesses of the 1930s and 1940s.[32]

Just as the portraits in noir thrillers and gothic melodramas are often presented as enigmatic or uncanny due to their stillness and immobility in the flow of the film, Delvaux's petrified nudes are rendered even more statuesque by Storck's gliding camera. In contrast with many other art documentaries that use camera movements and editing to mobilize or animate static pictures, Storck's moving camera rather emphasizes the fixity of Delvaux's nudes – an issue that is inherent to the general theme of Delvaux's paintings, which often deal with the juxtaposition between nude and skeleton, eroticism and death, flesh and marble, the living and the inanimate. Presenting his nudes as petrified figures or fossilized icons, Delvaux emphasizes their lifeless nature. His paintings are marked by an architectural gravitas and an emphatically anti-dynamic (and, in that sense, highly uncinematic) style. Paradoxically denying the dynamic nature of cinema, Storck emphasizes the very stillness of Delvaux's paintings through his use of cinematography.

Sequel

Winning a gold medal at the Venice Film Festival in 1948, *Le Monde de Paul Delvaux* attracted international acclaim from critics. According to H.W. Janson, Storck's film has demonstrated

> how effectively the moving camera can guide the beholder's eye so as to focus his attention and heighten his perceptions. There is a strange excitement about viewing paintings thus spread out upon the movie screen. A new dimension, we feel, has been added to our experience, and we find ourselves in a state of visual alertness that makes the forms speak to us with particular eloquence and intensity.[33]

Delvaux, Storck, and Micha collaborated again on later occasions. In 1968, Delvaux designed the sets for Lucien Deroisy and René Mischa's film adaptation of Alain Robbe-Grillet's novel *Les Gommes*. Two years later, and almost a quarter century after *Le Monde de Paul Delvaux*, Storck and Micha returned to the work of the Surrealist painter in *Paul Delvaux ou les femmes défendues* (*Paul Delvaux or the Forbidden Women*, 1970). In a prologue, we see Delvaux at work in his studio while his voice-over shares his fondness for drawing and the things that inspire him. Meanwhile, the camera explores the space of his studio and shows us how these things (miniature trains, lamps, and skeletons) are to be found in the artist's everyday environment. At times, we are confronted with surreal juxtapositions, such as a miniature train next to a death mask. We also see the artist comparing preparatory sketches with a painting and looking at his work in a mirror. The main part of the film consists of a succession of close-ups of paintings with the focus on the skeletons, women, and trains that typify Delvaux's oeuvre. The calm mobile camera is accompanied by a voice-over by Micha, a poem by Henry Bauchau and a drifting score by Philippe Arthuys. The use of color enables the filmmaker to show the texture of the paintings but paradoxically also contributes to the film's cold visual temperature and distant atmosphere. The general tone, however, is quite different from the 1946 film. Today, the 1970 sequel looks much more conventional than the highly personal and lyrical original film, which predates the breakthrough of television in most European countries and its impact on the standardization of the art documentary. While *Paul Delvaux ou les femmes défendues* attempts to relate Delvaux's paintings to reality (the artist, his studio, his sources of inspiration), *Le Monde de Paul Delvaux* fully remains inside the fictional world created by Éluard's poem and Delvaux's paintings.

Notes

1 On the postwar art documentary, see Steven Jacobs, *Framing Pictures: Film and the Visual Arts* (Edinburgh: Edinburgh University Press, 2011), 1–37.
2 On Storck, see the "Storck Issue" of *Revue belge du cinéma* (August 1979); *Hommage aan Henri Storck: Films 1928–1985, Oeuvrecatalogus* (Brussels: Fonds Henri Storck, 1997); Vincent Geens, "Le temps des utopies: L'ambition cinématographique d'Henri Storck, de 1907 à 1940," *Bijdragen tot de Eigentijdse Geschiedenis* 7 (2000): 189–237; Laura Vichi, *Henri Storck: de l'avant-garde au documentaire social* (Crisnée: Yellow Now, 2002); and Johan Swinnen and Luc Deneulin, eds., *Henri Storck memoreren* (Brussels: VUB Press, 2007).
3 David Scott, *Paul Delvaux: Surrealizing the Nude* (London: Reaktion Books, 1992), 65.
4 The Paul Delvaux exhibition at the Palais des Beaux-Arts Brussels took place from December 16, 1944, to January 15, 1945.
5 Susan Fellemann, *Botticelli in Hollywood: The Films of Albert Lewin* (New York, NY: Twayne Publishers, 1997), 68. Delvaux was also one of the artists that Lewin collected. The *Bel Ami* art competition was won by Max Ernst. All entries (including the one by Delvaux) travelled throughout the US.
6 Jacques Saulnier, quoted in *L'Arc* 31 (1967): 55. Resnais had made a documentary on Max Ernst working in his studio in 1947.
7 Raymond Durgnat, "*Marienbad*: Reviewed by Raymond Durgnat," *Films and Filming* (March 1962): 31. See also Steven Jacobs, Susan Felleman, Vito Adriaensens, and Lisa Colpaert, *Screening Statues: Sculptures and Cinema* (Edinburgh: Edinburgh University Press, 2017), 118–36.
8 See Marcel Oms, *Alain Resnais* (Paris: Éditions Rivages, 1988), 12. In 1946–1947, Resnais made a series of film portraits of artists such as Henri Goetz, Hans Hartung, César Doméla, Lucien Coutaud, Christine Boumeester, Félix Labisse, Oscar Dominguez, and Max Ernst. His early art documentaries include *Van Gogh* (1948), *Guernica* (1950), *Gauguin* (1950), and *Les Statues meurent aussi* (with Chris Marker, 1953). See also Jacobs, *Framing Pictures*, 1–37.
9 Other (uncredited) collaborators included Albert Putteman, who assisted Storck as a cinematographer. Storck was also in charge of the editing while Marthe Jaubert took care of the sound editing.
10 Jean-Charles Gateau, *Paul Éluard et la peinture surréaliste, 1910–1939* (Paris: Droz, 1982). Éluard and Breton also included a reproduction of Delvaux's *L'Appel de la nuit* in their *Dictionnaire abrégé du surréalisme* (Paris: Galerie des Beaux-Arts, 1938). "Exil (à Paul Delvaux)" is published in Paul Éluard, *Oeuvres complètes I* (Paris: Gallimard, 1968), 1004. An English translation of the poem by Roland Penrose and E.L.T. Mesens was published alongside the original in the June 1940 issue (no. 18–20) of the *London Bulletin* (page 14), https://monoskop.org/images/0/0e/London_Bulletin_18-20_1940.pdf. Accessed August 13, 2019.
11 André Souris, "Music and Filmed Paintings," in *Films on Art* (Paris: UNESCO; Brussels: Éditions de la connaissance, 1949), 28.
12 Paul Davay, "Compelled to See," in *Films on Art*, 9–18.
13 "Entretien avec Paul Delvaux (10 Juin 1970)," typescript of a conversation between Paul Delvaux, Paul De Bock, Dr. De Mol, Henri Storck, and Virginia Leirens (25 pages), 9–10. Henri Storck Foundation. Author's translation.
14 Shortly after Storck's film, Delvaux was commissioned in 1947 to design the decor for Jean Genet's ballet project *'Adame Miroir*, which premiered on May 31, 1948, at the Théâtre Marigny in Paris. See Gene A. Plunka, *The Rites of Passage of Jean Genet: The Art*

and Aesthetics of Risk Taking (Rutherford, NJ: Fairleigh Dickinson University Press, 1992), 115–16.
15 Scott, *Paul Delvaux*, 90.
16 André Bazin, "Painting and Cinema," in *What is Cinema?* Vol. 1, trans. Hugh Gray (Berkeley, CA: University of California Press, 1967), 164–72.
17 The film features 20 Delvaux paintings: *Nocturne* (1939), *L'Appel* (1944), *La Femme verte* (1943), *Le Temple* (1944), *La Prisonnière* (1942), *La Vénus endormie* (1944), *Nymphes des eaux* (1938), *Le Village des Sirènes* (1942), *Les Phases de la lune I* (1939), *Les Phases de la lune III* (1942), *Pygmalion* (1939), *L'Entrée de la ville* (1940), *Le Jardin nocturne* (1942), *L'Aube sur la ville* (1940), *La Rencontre* (1942), *Le Chemin de la ville* (1939), *La Visite* (1939), *L'Éveil de la forêt* (1939), *La Ville inquiète* (1941), and *Les Courtisanes* (1943).
18 Davay, "Compelled to See," 16–17.
19 Arthur Knight, "A Short History of Art Films," in *Films on Art 1952*, ed. William McKissack Chapman (New York, NY: The American Federation of Arts, 1953), 13.
20 "Entretien avec Paul Delvaux (10 Juin 1970)," 15.
21 Henri Storck, Undated typescript of a speech (9 pages), 2. Henri Storck Foundation.
22 Scott, *Paul Delvaux*, 43.
23 Ado Kyrou, *Le Surréalisme au cinéma* (Paris: Le Terrain vague, 1963), 47, 139–40, 159, and 197; Michael Richardson, *Surrealism and Cinema* (Oxford: Berg, 2006), 77–92.
24 Ian Walker, *City Gorged with Dreams: Surrealism and Photography in Interwar Paris* (Manchester: Manchester University Press, 2002); David Bate, *Photography & Surrealism: Sexuality, Colonialism, and Social Dissent* (London: I.B. Tauris, 2011).
25 James Clifford, "On Ethnographic Surrealism," in *The Predicament of Culture: Twentieth-Century Ethnography, Literature, and Art* (Cambridge, MA: Harvard University Press, 1988), 146; Steven Jacobs, "*Variétés* and the Surrealist Aesthetics of Urban Picture Spreads," in *Paper Cities: Urban Portraits in Photographic Books*, eds. Susana Martins and Anne Reverseau (Leuven: Leuven University Press, 2016), 21–40.
26 Bill Nichols, "Documentary Film and the Modernist Avant-Garde," *Critical Inquiry* 27, no. 4 (Summer 2001): 593.
27 Robert Desnos, "Pygmalion et le Sphinx," *Documents* 1 (January 1930): 32–39; Simon Baker, *Surrealism, History, and Revolution* (Bern: Peter Lang, 2008), 188–99.
28 On Pygmalionism in the visual arts, see Victor Stoichita, *The Pygmalion Effect: From Ovid to Hitchcock* (Chicago, IL: University of Chicago Press, 2008). Stoichita argues that it was only with the invention of moving pictures that the modern age found a fitting embodiment of the Pygmalion story's influence.
29 Several scholars have focused on Delvaux's expression of desire. See, for instance, Jean Clair, "Un Rêve autobiographique," in *Delvaux: Catalogue de l'oeuvre peint*, eds. Michel Butor, Jean Clair, and Suzanne Houbart-Wilkin (Lausanne: La Bibliothèque des arts, 1975); and Marcel Paquet, *Delvaux et l'essence de la peinture* (Paris, 1982).
30 Susan Felleman, *Art in the Cinematic Imagination* (Austin, TX: University of Texas Press, 2006), 56–73.
31 Steven Jacobs and Lisa Colpaert, *The Dark Galleries: A Museum Guide to Painted in Film Noir, Gothic Melodramas, and Ghost Stories of the 1940s and 1950s* (Ghent: AraMer, 2014).
32 Scott, *Paul Delvaux*, 75.
33 H.W. Janson, "College Use of Films on Art," in *Films on Art 1952*, 40.

2

A SCULPTOR'S LIFE ON SCREEN

John Read's film portraits of Henry Moore for BBC television

Katerina Loukopoulou

The construction of Henry Moore's public identity has received renewed interest in the early twenty-first century.[1] But little attention has been paid to the ways in which his iconic status was shaped by the emergence of television in the UK from the 1950s onwards. This historiographical neglect could be related to art-historical bias against popular media, such as television, by the institutions that establish art canons. To give an example, for some time Moore's likeness has been very well represented in the collections of London's National Portrait Gallery. He has featured in no less than eighty-five portraits, consisting predominantly of photographs but also of drawings, caricatures, an etching, and a bronze head. But our understanding of his public image is incomplete without a consideration of Moore on film and television, since it is through these media that Moore became an iconic figure of twentieth-century art. Moreover, the digitization of the BBC productions on Moore in 2010 altered this media ecology. Hitherto-neglected film and television sources have started to feature more prominently in art history at large and in Henry Moore studies in particular, the latter exemplified in the painstaking documentation of the "myriad mediations" of the sculptor by film and television historian John Wyver.[2]

This chapter builds on Wyver's work by focusing on a particularly important set of mediations: six portrait films, which were all scripted, produced, and directed by John Read from 1951 to 1978. Read was the director who most frequently and consistently portrayed Moore on film. This long-term relationship between sculptor and director owed its origins to Read's upbringing as the eldest son of the art critic Herbert Read, one of Moore's most consistent advocates and life-long friends. John Read was thereby granted privileged access not only to the sculptor himself, but also to the critical apparatus through which Herbert Read and other critics constructed Moore's public identity.

The films' titles offer clues to their emphasis, alternating from the biographical to the art historical to the celebratory: *Henry Moore* (1951), *A Sculptor's Landscape* (1958),

Henry Moore: One Yorkshireman Looks at His World (1967), *Henry Moore: The Language of Sculpture* (1974), *Henry Moore at Home: A Private View of a Personal Collection* (1974), and *Henry Moore at Eighty* (1978).[3] The latter four films were made during Moore's "great communicator period" (1960–86), during which he gave countless interviews that shaped the public discourse on his life and influences.[4] Their distinctiveness as a group of films can be attributed to what Read often described as a "collaboration."[5] However, Read's films on Moore have not been studied before as a corpus.[6] This chapter explores the crucial contributions these six films made to Moore's public identity. By analyzing them as "portrait films," I argue that they stand out from the early conventions of television arts programming and from their other historical origins in "films on art." In the 1950s, nonfiction films about art and artists, like Read's, were described interchangeably as "art films" and "films on art." This genre came to international prominence after the Second World War when its production and circulation were entangled in UNESCO's postwar vision of cultural democracy.[7] The genre's codes and conventions ranged in style, incorporating experimental, pictorial, and documentary modes. The production of Read's first film on Moore in 1951 was a catalyst for BBC television to endorse the genre, since he was the most celebrated British sculptor and had won the international prize for sculpture at the Venice Biennale in 1948. By 1978, with the film *Henry Moore at Eighty*, the genre had become a staple of public service broadcasting, by then most commonly known as "art documentaries." Moore's screen presence had developed alongside television's growth into the predominant audiovisual medium of communication in the UK. From transmitting to a few thousand viewers in the South of England in the late 1940s, the BBC would go on to broadcast to thirty million viewers across the country by the late 1970s.

Read's films do not only chart the sculptor's evolving public image in postwar Britain, they also index Read's own development as a filmmaker. After 1951, Read became a prolific BBC producer and director of art films that were steered toward what he understood, following John Grierson, as the "documentary" mode.[8] Read's approach would increasingly prioritize the artist's point of view, and by 1967 his films would often be described as "film portraits." At the time of his retirement from the BBC in 1983, he was widely regarded as a "portrait maker."[9] With the exception of the painter L.S. Lowry (about whom Read made two films, in 1957 and 1977), Moore was the only artist with whom the director collaborated consistently over the span of his career.

Film portraiture

The very notion of a "film portrait" hardly existed when Read directed his first film on Moore. It was then conceived and promoted as an "art film" or "film on art." In *Theory of Film*, Siegfried Kracauer prioritized this genre amongst postwar trends in the development of the documentary film, and singled out Read's films amongst the most promising ones.[10] But from the late 1960s onwards, art documentaries dedicated to a single personality became more often described as "film portraits." According to Paul Arthur, the term gained currency thanks to the growth of experimental film portraits in the 1960s, such as those by Andy Warhol and Gregory Markopoulos, and the "subjective turn" in documentary film practices.[11] It is indicative that upon Read's retirement in 1983, the BBC ran a seven-part series of his documentaries, *Portraits and Reflections*, which appraised him as a "portrait maker."[12]

Of the approximately one hundred television programmes that Read produced (mainly art documentaries), his six films on Henry Moore, made over three decades, record the changes in the sculptor's physical appearance and public role, thereby creating a detailed portrait of his life on screen. Of course, Read's films on Moore can be interpreted and appreciated in many other ways: as unique insights into filming the fine arts and sculpture, especially in relation to the uses of the mobile camera to frame the embodied perception of sculpture; for their innovative early use of film in British television in the 1950s, when it was a predominantly a live medium; for shaping the language of the art documentary genre; and for consolidating arts programmes as a staple genre of British television.[13] But the focus of this chapter is on "moments" of portraiture; that is to say, how filmic language constructed and examined Moore's artistic identity and selfhood.

The digitization of these films for the BBC's online archive platform once again made them available to the various audiences they had previously garnered. These films were not only broadcast to thousands and subsequently millions of television viewers, but up to the mid-1980s, most of them (especially the early ones) were also available for rental to arts schools and other institutions in the educational sector as 16mm nontheatrical viewing copies, both in the UK and abroad. But when video (VHS) replaced 16mm film in the early 1980s, Read's films were not transferred to video and thus gradually fell out of circulation. It is important to consider distribution and exhibition, because one of the main "functions" of portraits, according to art historian Shearer West, is that they are "normally created with the understanding that they will be in the public domain … and serve a multiplicity of aesthetic, political, and social functions."[14] In a similar way, documentary films have historically been exhibited in more wide-ranging public spaces than fiction films, entangled with contingencies of political and social functionality as well as aesthetics.

Despite the circulation of Read's films as 16mm copies (after they were first broadcast), they were initially conceived for the medium of television, which has favored close-up shots of faces for most of its history. As Marcia Pointon explains in her study *Portrayal*, "our need to engage visually through facial encounters, whether with ourselves or with others, remains central in all societies. Yet the face and its replication in works of art is contingent historically and perceptually."[15] The historical framing of the face on television through close-up shots is of special interest because of the close resemblance to real human dimensions, resulting in what television historians have described as the aesthetics of "intimacy" and "immediacy," especially during the first three decades of the medium's history.[16] The very titles of Read's films demonstrate the oscillation between "likeness" and "type" that is inherent in all visual forms of portraiture. Moore's identity is externalized as a "type" in the case of the three films that place him within a larger context (landscape, language, the world): *A Sculptor's Landscape*, *One Yorkshireman Looks at His World*, *The Language of Sculpture*. However, in the other three films (*Henry Moore*, *Henry Moore at Home*, *Henry Moore at Eighty*), the audiovisual discourse focuses more intimately on Moore as an individual, on the process of his becoming Moore, the iconic artist figure, but within more personal ("at home") and temporal contexts ("at eighty").

What distinguishes a film portrait from a regular art documentary focused on an individual artist? To a certain extent, they share similarities, but what makes a documentary come closer to the art of portraiture is what art historian Richard Brilliant has described as a "heightened degree of self-composure that responds to the formality of the portrait-making situation."[17] In the case of film portraits, the four key performative elements of the subject (facial, gestural, corporeal, vocal) that are inherent in all documentaries become more pronounced.[18] The encounter between the artist and the camera becomes an act of (self-)presentation in a time-based medium, which retains the aspects described by Brilliant, but transposed to a constructed film world. For example, the recurrent motif of close-ups of the artist at work enhances the documentation of the creative process to the level of cinematic spectacle, which adheres to the "occasionality" of portraiture.[19]

Nonfiction performance has a long history that can be traced back to the early days of cinema when the practice of soliciting performances from all sorts of social and cultural settings was quite common and provided early nonfiction films with new subject matter and attractions.[20] One of the first uses of the term "cine-portrait" is associated with a specific mode of filmmaking used in the Soviet Union in the 1920s, to describe the cinematic spectacle of "workers at work."[21] After the Second World War, the artist at work became an attraction for documentary filmmakers. Throughout the 1940s and 1950s, many modernist artists alongside Moore engaged with films on art, most famously Jackson Pollock and Pablo Picasso.[22] Film has uniquely preserved the creative vitality of all three artists, but only in Moore's case has it spanned his artistic career.

The making of the filmic sculptor

On the occasion of the Festival of Britain in 1951, the BBC approached Moore with the idea of a programme dedicated to him. The initial plan was to invite Moore to be interviewed live at the television studio to discuss his sculpture commissioned for the festival near the time of its opening.[23] Mary Adams, the influential Head of Television Talks, assigned the programme to her new recruit, John Read, who had joined the BBC in 1949. Read fully understood that he owed the opportunity to produce a program on Moore to his father's close association with the sculptor.[24] His creative impulse to challenge the BBC's standard practices of live programming by making a "television film" on Moore was derived from his admiration for the films of the British Documentary Movement in the 1930s.[25]

Soon after his graduation from Oxford, Read approached John Grierson with an article-cum-manifesto about the future of postwar documentary. Thanks to Grierson's intervention, *Sight and Sound* published the article, which advocated for new types of documentaries in which "the educational is implicit in the artistic."[26] Accordingly, aesthetic display rather than outright didacticism would prevail in his films. With these aspirations, Read was an exception in 1940s BBC television, where the majority of producers came mainly from radio or print journalism. Read was attracted by television's potential, but not its liveness; instead, he considered television as a "marvellous method of film distribution" and an ideal medium for expanding the range of a documentary's subject matter.[27] Live transmission (with live and linear editing) was the norm for television at the time, whereas film (shot and edited prior to transmission) was rarely used.[28] As evidenced in their initial correspondence, both Read and Moore favored film rather than live transmission.[29] Read was eager to produce a program that would realize his aspirations for documentary film and Moore was more interested in being filmed at work in his studio rather than interviewed live in the artificial setting of a television studio. This was not the first time that the sculptor had featured in a documentary film. Moore had already been filmed for Jill Craigie's *Out of Chaos* (1944), a propaganda short about war artists, in which he had re-enacted the creative process for his *Shelter Drawings* (1940–2) of Londoners sleeping in the Underground during wartime bombing. He had also appeared in the promotional film *Henry Moore* (J.J. Sweeney, 1946), produced as a record of his first museum exhibition in 1946 at the Museum of Modern Art (MoMA) in New York.

Read and cameraman Alan Lawson filmed Moore on location intermittently for six months while the sculptor was working on his festival commission, which resulted in his first bronze sculpture, *Reclining Figure: Festival* (1951). Moore's strong engagement with the filming process intrigued Read, who wrote a memo to the BBC's publicity officer during the shoot to emphasize that "the film should be unique among art films because of the unusual co-operation and advice which the artist has given."[30] At the time, few films on living artists at work existed. The most notable was *Visite à Picasso* (*Visit to Picasso*, Paul Haesaerts, 1950), in which Picasso performs for the camera by painting on glass. At the same time that Read was working on the Moore film in the UK, photographer Hans Namuth and documentarian Paul Falkenberg in the US were making *Jackson Pollock*, a short film on the artist's process of action painting, which premiered at MoMA in June 1951.[31] This was a critical moment in the history of art documentaries, when these three highly influential and pioneering films were being made almost simultaneously. Their shared emphasis on documenting the manual process of artistic creation would become a constitutive convention of the art documentary in the subsequent decades.

The films about Picasso and Pollock evidently involved collaboration between the artists and the filmmakers in order to capture the creation of artworks. But Read's film differs in terms of developing and intertwining two narratives: the evolving creative process and the biographical account. For example, two minutes into the film, Moore is introduced through a montage of close-ups of his hands and his tools. The staccato montage that gradually reveals Moore at work in his studio reinforces the depiction of the sculptor as the force that mediates between nature and culture, echoing Moore's 1930s doctrine of "truth to materials."[32] As the film progresses, these fragmented views gradually form a more cohesive narrative of Moore's "becoming" a modernist sculptor, creating a timeline of influences and working practices, which will be repeated and refined in subsequent biographical narratives.[33] Moore's aesthetic education is narrated with an audiovisual parade of his encounters with modern and ancient art at London's museums, with a key sequence devoted to modern painting (Cézanne, Seurat, Picasso) at the National Gallery. The sculptor is then introduced again, this time in his living room, where we see him first in a framed photograph. The camera then slowly pans to the left to reveal the "real" Moore sitting next to a television set. This reflexive progression from framed paintings to a framed photograph of Moore and then to the artist positioned next to a television shapes the film's rhetoric of equivalence: the artist and his influences have been "framed" in the mass media age, becoming cultural artefacts. The film thus reinforced a highly stylized mediation of Moore through photographs and the moving image, contributing to the sculptor's growing status as a highly recognizable iconic artist in the postwar British public sphere and the international art world.

In comparison to Moore's other media appearances at the time, Read's film introduces a new aspect of Moore in the rendering of the previously private act of the creative process as a public one. The second half of the film documents how Moore made *Reclining Figure: Festival* through the process of modelling rather than carving, which had defined his working practice until then. The sculpture's genesis is visualized from the moment of ideation, through the construction of the plaster, up to the final bronze casting in the foundry. Apart from the last stage, Moore is constantly shown at work, as if to dispel the myth that modelling distances the sculptor from the material. The historical significance of Read's meticulous documenting of the creative process can be compared to the Namuth and Falkenberg film about Pollock. Art historian Caroline Jones has argued that the impact of the film was more crucial than Pollock's own paintings in terms of introducing audiences and other artists to the process of action painting, which very few people had witnessed before then.[34] Similarly, Read's film on Moore anatomized and celebrated the creative process of the sculptor who had persistently defended and disseminated modernism in British sculpture. By doing so, the film also asserted the authority of the modernist sculptor's identity as a public personality, as mediated through the new medium of television.

Henry Moore was televised on April 30, 1951, to coincide with the opening of Moore's Tate Gallery exhibition (his first museum show in the UK) and two days before the opening of the Festival of Britain. This multifaceted occasion was the culmination of an uphill struggle for Moore after three decades of consolidating his place within the art world. At the same time, this film marked the beginning of a new era of his engagement with the public service medium of television in the UK and internationally through the extensive circulation of the film at film

40 Katerina Loukopoulou

festivals and film societies. After its initial transmission, *Henry Moore* circulated for decades as a 16mm print, not only in Britain, but also in Europe and the US. An advertisement for the film's distribution in the US promotes Moore as a leading figure in modernist sculpture (Figure 2.1).

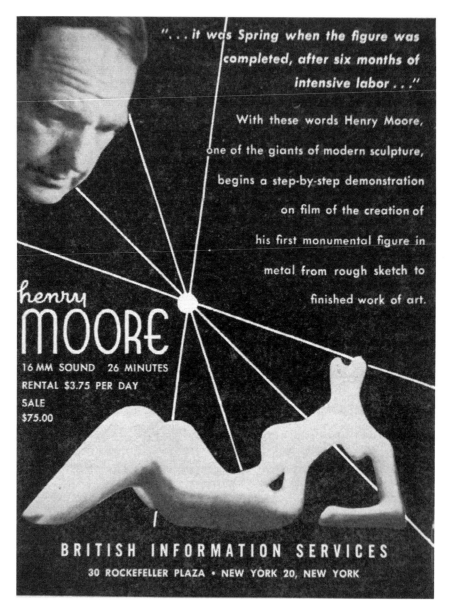

FIGURE 2.1 Advertisement for the 16mm print of *Henry Moore*, as published in *Art News Annual* 53, no. 7 (1955)

The advertisement's dynamic design places Moore's disembodied god-like head at the top left corner, overseeing his sculpture, which is positioned at the diametrically opposite end of the poster. As depicted here, Moore had literally become a giant with his proportionally overblown head hovering over his creation. The lines linking the sculptor's head with his sculpture resemble rays of light, projecting outwards, as if predicting and anticipating the future apotheosis of Moore.

Expanding Moore's point of view

With his second and third films on Moore, *A Sculptor's Landscape* and *One Yorkshireman Looks at His World*, Read aligned each film's audiovisual rhetoric with the sculptor's evolving visions by placing the artist and his sculpture against a wider range of settings. By the time Read made his second film on Moore in 1958, he had also established himself as an auteur of art documentaries on contemporary British artists with such films as *Artists Must Live* (1953), *Graham Sutherland* (1953), *John Piper* (1954), *Stanley Spencer* (1956), and *L.S. Lowry* (1957). With the film on Lowry, Read had pioneered the use of the tape recorder to allow more time for the artist to speak continuously without the interruption of the 35mm reel changeover, which ultimately offered the filmmaker more freedom in the editing of the sound. This technique allowed Read to foreground the artists' voices and perspective even more, a feature that attracted praise from film critics.[35] Writing for the journal of the Society for Education through Art in 1957, Read asserted: "I do not myself believe that the art film is a legitimate instrument of criticism … I prefer building up commentary and explanation from the artist's own opinions and statements."[36] Although an artist's views may be construed as a form of criticism, the implication of Read's point was to challenge the ostensible objectivity attributed to documentary as a film mode.

In *A Sculptor's Landscape*, Moore engaged even more closely with the planning and the actual filming. Soon after its first broadcast on June 29, 1958, Read published an insightful account of the filming process:

> [Moore] often looked through the camera himself in order to discuss the shots with us. The collaboration rarely became a difficulty and it created freedom of action rather than inhibited it. When the shots were assembled he saw these with me and pointed out the ones that to him seemed the most successful.[37]

Rather than suggest aspects of self-portraiture, such collaborative dynamics are indeed fundamental to all forms of portraiture, in which the agency of creating representation is negotiated between the portrait maker and the sitter.

Moore was increasingly interested in landscape at this stage of his career. Following a series of open-air exhibitions in London parks in the late 1940s and 1950s, the relationship between sculpture and landscape had become a new terrain of exploration for modern sculptors. A series of key sequences emphasize Moore's evolving relationship with place, space, and nature as forces of creativity. Moore, his sculpture, and his new studios are emphatically framed against the landscape, surrounded by tall trees and the expansive horizon, while long takes explore his collection of stones, bones, and shells displayed in his studio. *A Sculptor's Landscape* thus visualized the shift from the 1930s conception of the modernist artist's studio as a "fortress" and a "lab" toward an idealization of the sculptor set against landscapes.[38] The prevalence of nature was aligned with the Neo-Romantic celebration of landscapes that became popular in postwar British cinema, such as in the films of Michael Powell and Emeric Pressburger, as well as across media and the arts.[39]

The evolving relationship between the sculptor and his surroundings was also picked up in the subsequent film, *One Yorkshireman Looks at His World*. While the first part establishes Moore's evolving "life on screen," the second part explores Moore's new "worlds" and "environments." Structured as the final part of a trilogy, Read re-edited extracts from his 1951 and 1958 films with new material shot in 1967, explaining that, "This year we have completed the sequence and brought together into a single film the entire story of the man and his work."[40] To render the "entire story" audiovisually, Read also repurposed extracts from other films and television programmes about Moore (such as *Out of Chaos* and a 1960 interview of Moore for the BBC *Face to Face* series), underpinning the intended "biographical film" mode.[41] The film's narrative gradually moves to the present and to the expanding spaces of the sculptor's workplace. The Moore of 1967 is first shown as a small figure in the distance approaching his newly built studio hangar. Fluid 16mm camerawork documents Moore supervising his assistants while they are dissecting the enormous plaster of *Double Oval* (1966), ready for transportation to a German foundry, where it will be cast in bronze. The film's final sequence transports the viewer from the factory-like operations of Moore's studios in Hertfordshire to the even-larger-scale enterprises of the Carrara quarries in Italy, from where Michelangelo sourced his marble. Here, the camera follows Moore, first shown to be drawing on a piece of stone at the highest peak of the mountains and then carving at a stone-yard. The ending functions to portray the apotheosis of Moore, elevated as a modern equal of Michelangelo. At the same time, it echoes one of the film's earlier sequences, where Moore narrates how he first encountered Michelangelo as a schoolboy. Both sequences frame a narrative and a discourse that became even more prominent in later interviews in which Moore aligned himself with "the great masters" rather than with his contemporaries.[42]

Read's construction of a filmic serialization of Moore's life reveals the self-conscious effort of his films to become entangled in the historiography of the sculptor's life. The contemporaneous publication of new biographies, such as Herbert Read's *Henry Moore: A Study of His Life and Work* (1965) and Donald Hall's *The Life and Work of a Great Sculptor: Henry Moore* (1966), must have enhanced this sense of historicity. *One Yorkshireman* complemented the biographical texts, but not as an inferior illustration. Read achieved this by adhering to the Griersonian ethos of "the creative treatment of actuality" that would foreground the aesthetic coherence of a film's narrative.[43] In the case of Read's films about Moore, this "creative treatment" developed into the then novel documentary mode of film portraiture. This kind of biographical documentation of a living artist, which combined multiple archival sources with brand new footage, was not only unprecedented but also proved influential on subsequent BBC documentary production.

Portraiture, canonicity, and iconicity

Moore emerges as a fully iconic figure in Read's second trilogy, which includes *Henry Moore: The Language of Sculpture*, *Henry Moore at Home: A Private View of a Personal Collection*, and *Henry Moore at Eighty*. The first two films were shot together and then edited as separate television programmes to be broadcast in 1974. The interviews with Moore take place in his studio and his living room with the sculptor's own discourse now shaping each film's narrative. Long takes linger on Moore analyzing his own sculpture in great depth and often relating it through gesture to his collection of modern art and ethnographic artefacts. Moore here acts as a presenter, as a guide to his own work and its contexts, reminiscent of art historian Kenneth Clark's powerful performance in the landmark BBC series *Civilisation* (1969), which millions of viewers had watched in Britain and the US.

The Language of Sculpture acknowledges that by 1974 Moore had become a fully-fledged canonical artist. Moore is introduced with a series of close-up shots within the ancient walls of Forte de Belvedere in Florence, followed by long shots of him walking as he is being filmed by another crew (Figures 2.2–2.4). These reflexive

FIGURE 2.2 *Henry Moore: The Language of Sculpture*
(John Read, 1974)

44 Katerina Loukopoulou

FIGURE 2.3 *Henry Moore: The Language of Sculpture*
(John Read, 1974)

FIGURE 2.4 *Henry Moore: The Language of Sculpture*
(John Read, 1974)

cinéma-vérité shots of Moore caught between cameras indicate his level of media iconicity, which had never before been associated with a modern sculptor. In both 1974 films, the majority of Moore's screen time becomes interview time, in which he speaks directly to the camera. Moreover, editing does not disrupt the flow and development of his comments. As Read put it,

> it soon became clear that the finished film would fall naturally into two separate parts—the first about the Florentine exhibition concerned with the meaning of sculpture; and the second in which Moore's reserve about talking of himself and his work was somewhat broken down, treating more intimately of the artist as a person.[44]

Moore's growing confidence in front of the camera allowed these later films to move closer to the illusion of close-up intimacy that the television screen enhances. At the same time, Moore's own sense of performativity had been refined, especially in relation to his ease in gesturing toward objects and his own work.

The Language of Sculpture was scheduled in a primetime evening slot on BBC2 on New Year's Day, while its companion piece, *Henry Moore at Home*, followed a week later in the same time-slot. Moore's life and canonicity had by now become a television series, bound to attract large audiences and positive press coverage across the political spectrum, from the conservative *Daily Mail* to the socialist *Morning Star*. Criticism vis-à-vis this level of iconicity was not uncommon, although paradoxically it only confirmed Moore's status. In the *Evening Standard* reviews of the 1974 programmes, art critic Richard Cork criticized the overall "trumpeting Hollywood-style" canonization and adulation of Moore. But apropos of the man, he conceded that "Moore was mercifully unpretentious" and praised the sculptor's "ability to talk about his work with plain, unaffected, northern good sense and then suddenly launch into an elevated train of thought."[45] Reminiscent of sculptor Anthony Caro's 1960 critique of Moore's stardom, Cork also seeks to distinguish between the "Hollywood-style" and the "real" Moore.[46]

In Read's final film, *Henry Moore at Eighty*, the artist continues to control the dramatic action. The close-up shots of Moore speaking directly to the camera alternate with over-the-shoulder, point-of-view shots of him demonstrating drawings from his whole career, from the *Shelter Drawings* to self-portraits of his own hands from the mid-1970s. The choice of the latter confers a new level of reflexivity in relation to the film's engagement with Moore's own representation of himself. The film foregrounds Moore as a multimedia artist, as he is first shown carving, then drawing, staging, and photographing his sculpture, and finally etching. It is the seemingly spontaneous execution of a drawing, though, that stands out in the film. While a series of drawings parade for the camera through Moore's hands and point of view, he poses in front of Dürer's drawing *Conrad Verkell* (1508), whose lines and shapes he analyses by copying them, assuming the role of a teacher eagerly communicating the secret language of a drawing's schemata to his audience.

That Moore performs with such ease while the camera is rolling over his shoulder suggests how used to being filmed he had become. This scene also reveals the alignment of his screen performances with his artistic production. What Moore started in this scene as an apparently spontaneous exploration of a Dürer drawing was later fully materialized into his 1979 etching *Interpretation from Dürer's Portrait of Conrad Verkell with Landscape*. By this stage in Moore's career, his artistic life seems to unfold on screen. With a growing sense of the sculptor's place in art history and posterity, Read envisioned this last film as a testament to the "sculptor's mind" for the future generations of artists, critics, and scholars.[47]

Henry Moore at Eighty was broadcast on July 30, Moore's birthday. He was the only living British artist whose birthday was celebrated by both UK television channels on the same day during their evening schedules: the BBC with Read's film, scheduled at the primetime slot of 8 p.m., and ITV with the more grandiosely entitled program *The Majesty of Henry Moore*, at the less competitive slot of 11:45 p.m. *Henry Moore at Eighty* extended the myths of "intimacy" and "personal" communication that had characterized the rhetoric of *Henry Moore at Home*. The film thus combined the ostensibly contradictory figures of Moore the everyman and Moore the exceptional iconic artist.

Conclusion

In 1979, Read published a short biographical account with the title *Henry Moore: Portrait of an Artist*.[48] The bulk of the text derives from his scripts and from Moore's statements in the films. The book therefore reads more like a film script and an open conversation with the artist. Read's choice of the term "portrait" points to a transition in his Moore documentaries, from the experimental mixed-mode of the 1950s art films to the emphasis on biography in the later films. The shift in later years toward intimate views of the artist is indicative of Moore's own movement toward increasing self-referentiality in his work.

Read produced a final tribute to Moore by compiling a film obituary in 1986. Broadcast one week after Moore's death as part of the BBC arts program *Arena*, Read addressed the camera directly like a newscaster to narrate his memories of Moore through his own films. In this compilation film, Read's "real" Moore and the "screen-sized" Moore fused to form a "sculptor's life on film." Extracts from all six films punctuated Read's narration, delivered in a moving tone and intensified by the very presence of the filmic Moore, whose liveliness remained registered on a medium that defies death and stasis. Read's *Arena* tribute turned his six films into chapters of an audiovisual lecture about Moore's life as had been captured and become familiar to audiences through television. The metaphorical narrative of Moore as the artist who "sculpted the twentieth century" would have been far less known had it not been for the public service medium of BBC television and Read, who documented Moore's evolving identity for future generations. Read's films of Moore across the decades of British television shaped the film portrait both as a mode of documentary filmmaking and as a staple of the art world. Their influence can still be felt in the current proliferation of art documentaries across screens, platforms, and exhibition spaces, as it has become conventional for museums and galleries to project art documentaries about artists alongside their work in the gallery space. In 2010, Read's first film on Moore once again set a trend during the *Henry Moore* retrospective at Tate Britain when it was screened alongside the sculpture, whose making it documented. And the film has also become a permanent exhibit since Tate Britain's rehanging of its collection in 2013. The institutions that had long excluded arts documentaries and film portraits have now endorsed them.

Read's films on Moore constitute a significant contribution to the history of the visual arts documentary genre. The longevity of this particular collaboration between filmmaker and artist charts not only Moore's rise to become the iconic British artist of the late twentieth century, but also the evolution of the arts documentary over the same period as it increasingly, and self-reflexively, attends to the mediation of the contemporary artist's identity within the public sphere. To view Read's documentaries as film portraits permits us to gauge the shifting negotiation of representational agency between filmmaker and subject as Moore built trust with Read, grew more comfortable with the camera's presence, and developed his public identity not only as an iconic artist but also as a "great communicator" of aesthetic value and meaning.

Notes

1 *Henry Moore: Sculptural Process and Public Identity*, Tate Research Publication, 2015, accessed July 20, 2018, www.tate.org.uk/art/research-publications/henry-moore/public-identity-r1175678.
2 John Wyver, "Myriad Mediations: Henry Moore and his Works on Screen 1937–83," in *Henry Moore: Sculptural Process and Public Identity* (Tate Research Publication, 2015), accessed August 10, 2017, www.tate.org.uk/art/research-publications/henry-moore/john-wyver-myriad-mediations-henry-moore-and-his-works-on-screen-1937-83-r1151304.
3 All six films are available to view online, alongside other BBC radio and television programmes on Moore. "Henry Moore at the BBC," BBC, accessed May 10, 2019, www.bbc.co.uk/archive/henrymoore.
4 Alan Wilkinson, "Introduction," in *Henry Moore: Writings and Conversations* (Berkeley: University of California Press, 2002), 28–9.
5 In interviews and writings, Read emphasized the "collaborative" nature of his documentaries. See, for example, John Read interview, BECTU History Project, tape no. 146, June 25, 1990. BECTU interviews can be accessed via the British Film Institute Library in London.
6 Histories of arts television only briefly consider Read's first two films on Moore: John A. Walker, *Arts TV: A History of Arts Television in Britain* (London: John Libbey, 1993); John Wyver, *Vision On: Film, Television and the Arts in Britain* (London: Wallflower Press, 2007).
7 J. Urlik, "Films Bring Art to the People," *UNESCO Courier* II, no. 12 (1950): 6–7.
8 John Read, "The Film on Art as Documentary," *Film Culture* 3, no. 3 (1957): 6–7.
9 John Read, "Henry Moore," *Radio Times*, November 9, 1967, 535; Peter Lennon, "Portrait Maker," *The Listener*, January 15–21, 1983, 27.

10 Siegfried Kracauer, *Theory of Film: The Redemption of Physical Reality* (Oxford: Oxford University Press, 1960), 193–201.
11 Paul Arthur, "No Longer Absolute: Portraiture in American Avant-Garde and Documentary Films of the Sixties," in *Rites of Realism: Essays on Corporeal Cinema*, ed. Ivone Margulies (Durham: Duke University Press, 2003), 93–118.
12 Lennon, "Portrait Maker," 27.
13 John Wyver has made a case for the recognition of Read's place in the canon of television creators. See John Wyver, "Representing Art or Reproducing Culture? Tradition and Innovation in British Television's Coverage of the Arts from the 1950s–1980s," in *Picture This: Media Representations of Visual Art and Artists*, ed. Philip Hayward (London: John Libbey, 1988), 27–46.
14 Shearer West, *Portraiture* (Oxford: Oxford University Press, 2004), 43.
15 Marcia Pointon, *Portrayal and the Search for Identity* (London: Reaktion, 2012), 8.
16 John Ellis, *Visible Fictions: Cinema, Television, Video* (London: Routledge, 1982); Roy Armes, *On Video* (London: Routledge, 1988).
17 Richard Brilliant, *Portraiture* (London: Reaktion, 1991), 10.
18 Elizabeth Marquis, "Conceptualizing Documentary Performance," *Studies in Documentary Film* 7, no. 1 (2013): 45–60.
19 Brilliant, *Portraiture*, 7; West, *Portraiture*, 50.
20 Vinicius Navarro, "Nonfictional Performance from Portrait Films to the Internet," *Cinema Journal* 5, no. 3 (2012): 136–41.
21 Graham Roberts, *Forward Soviet! History of Soviet Non-fiction Film* (London: I.B. Tauris, 1999), 21.
22 *Jackson Pollock* (Hans Namuth and Paul Falkenberg, 1951); *Visite à Picasso* (*Visit to Picasso*, Paul Haesaerts, 1950); *Picasso* (Luciano Emmer, 1954); *Le Mystère Picasso* (*The Mystery of Picasso*, Henri-Georges Clouzot, 1956).
23 For a discussion of the film's cultural contexts, see Katerina Loukopoulou, "The Mobile Framing of Henry Moore's Sculpture in Post-War Britain," *Visual Culture in Britain* 13, no. 1 (2012): 63–81.
24 Read interview, BECTU History Project.
25 John Read, "I Don't Know Why You Bother." *Art and Artists*, August 1983, 6.
26 John Read, "Is There a Documentary Art?" *Sight and Sound* 17, no. 68 (1948–1949): 158.
27 Lennon, "Portrait Maker," 27.
28 The main reasons for live transmission were industrial, as the BBC had to avoid a clash of interests with the film industry. See Armes, *On Video*.
29 BBC Written Archives Centre, T6/168/1 TV Films *Henry Moore*, File 1A, March 1950–May 1951, (hereafter BBC WAC T6/168/1).
30 Memo from John Read to Television Publicity Officer, January 15, 1951, BBC WAC T6/168/1.
31 For a contextual history of this film's production, see Katerina Loukopoulou, "Museum at Large: Aesthetic Education through Film," in *Learning with the Lights Off: Educational Film in the United States*, ed. Devin Orgeron, Marsha Orgeron and Dan Streible (New York: Oxford University Press, 2011), 356–376.
32 For early statements on "truth to material," see Moore's contribution to the 1934 group publication *Unit One: The Modern Movement in English Architecture, Painting and Sculpture*, edited by Herbert Read, reproduced in Wilkinson, ed. *Henry Moore: Writings and Conversations*, 191.
33 Hannah Higham, ed. *Becoming Henry Moore* (Perry Green: The Henry Moore Foundation, 2017).

34 Caroline A. Jones, *Machine in the Studio: Constructing the Postwar American Artist* (Chicago: Chicago University Press, 1996), 72.
35 Patrick Hayman, "Art Films by John Read," *Sight and Sound* 26, no. 4 (1957): 217. On the novelty of introducing tape-recording in art documentaries, see John Read, "Artist into Film," *The Studio,* 155, no. 780 (1958): 91.
36 John Read, "The Art Film and Television," *Athene* 7, no. 4 (1956): 18.
37 John Read, "Filming A Sculptor's Landscape," *Painter and Sculptor* (Summer 1958): 4.
38 Anne Wagner, *Mother Stone: The Vitality of Modern British Sculpture* (New Haven and London: Yale University Press 2005), 143–4.
39 David Mellor, ed., *A Paradise Lost: The Neo-Romantic Imagination in Britain, 1935–1955* (London: Lund Humphries, 1987).
40 Read, "Henry Moore," 535.
41 Max Wykes-Joyce, "Interview with John Read – Film Director," *Arts Review*, February 23, 1974, 81.
42 Wyver, "Myriad Mediations."
43 Read, "Is There a Documentary Art?"
44 Wykes-Joyce, "Interview with John Read," 81.
45 Richard Cork, "Last Night"s TV," *Evening Standard,* January 2, 1974; Richard Cork, "Television Review," *Evening Standard*, January 9, 1974.
46 Anthony Caro, "The Master Sculptor," *The Observer*, November 27, 1960.
47 John Read quoted in the *Yorkshire Post*, July 29, 1978.
48 John Read, *Portrait of an Artist: Henry Moore* (London: Whizzard Press, 1979), 9.

Acknowledgements

This essay draws on research that I conducted thanks to the Henry Moore Foundation (HMF) Postdoctoral Fellowship, hosted by the History of Art Department, University College London (2010–12). I thank the HMF archivists for advice and support with my research of primary sources; John Wyver for valuable comments on earlier drafts; and Roger Hallas for his constructive feedback that helped me to steer this essay to its current shape.

PART II
Representing the artist

3
A PORTRAIT OF THE ARTIST AS AUTOMATON

Creativity, labor, and technology in *Tim's Vermeer*

Stephan Boman

Tim's Vermeer (Teller, 2013) is a portrait of Tim Jenison, a retired software designer with abundant free time, ample means, a knack for mechanics, and a weird obsession. Where plenty of retirees try their hand at watercolors, landscapes, or still life, Jenison is determined to use his technical savvy to paint his own version of Johannes Vermeer's *The Music Lesson* (1665). At once grandiose and trivial, Jenison's project makes an apt subject for a documentary: can a mere amateur recreate a masterpiece just by exploiting optical equipment? But the film also invests this experiment with great philosophical and historical significance. If successful, it would supposedly unsettle standard accounts of how artists used technology, suggesting that old masters were not just influenced or inspired by optical images, but that they in fact painted over the image projected by a camera obscura. If optics were the key to Vermeer's method, then perhaps he was not a divinely gifted contriver of realistic views; perhaps, instead, he was a scientifically proficient tinkerer, like Jenison.

Throughout *Tim's Vermeer*, there is an intriguing counterpoint between the seriousness of the so-called "optical hypothesis," and the jovial, winking tone of the film and its titular subject. Narrated and directed by the popular magician duo Penn and Teller, the film skillfully manages our curiosity, pivoting artfully between the mysterious naturalism of Vermeer's paintings and the elegance of Jenison's optical apparatus. Our curiosity is likewise piqued by the absurd scale of Jenison's endeavor and the spectacle of his commitment to it, spanning years of planning and preparation, and months of laborious painting. Even granting the importance of the hypothesis, Jenison's efforts seem out of proportion to their value as evidence: once he has recreated one corner of Vermeer's painting, what more is proved by filling in the rest of it? In the end, the film uses this exorbitant expenditure of leisure time to pose several discomfiting questions. Could Vermeer *really* have painted his masterpieces just by tracing an optical projection? Can Jenison *really* paint a counterfeit "Vermeer" with no outside assistance? And if so, what does this mean for our appreciation of art and artists from centuries past?

While these are legitimate questions, I would suggest that in this case they are a bit of *misdirection*. The real challenge of Vermeer's paintings, after all, is not to decide if their hypothesized reliance on optics disqualifies them as art, but to see how these instruments might have served his artistic ambitions. Sidestepping this fuzzier question, the film focuses on our uncertainties and anxieties regarding art, especially our ambivalence about the nature and meaning of automatism. Where art is concerned, automatism and mechanical reproduction have largely been defined and debated in relation to photography: whether a mechanically produced image can convey artistic intent or provoke aesthetic response. *Tim's Vermeer* is instructive for how it reframes the notion of automatism in ways that call upon photography's historical endpoints, staging a potentially illuminating encounter between the optically-informed paintings of Vermeer and Tim Jenison's algorithmically-motivated process. While the film urges us to marvel at the resemblance of Jenison's "Vermeer" to *The Music Lesson*, at the affinity between Jenison and Vermeer, and at how technological progress explains the evolution of visual art, I will urge a different conclusion. Even if we imagine Vermeer using Jenison's device, these two applications of the same mechanism nevertheless manifest different underlying logics, and minister to different values and worldviews: which is to say, they embody different *automatisms*. To show how *Tim's Vermeer* enables this insight, I will briefly consider how it compares to classic documentaries about artistic process, and how the notion of automatism has been theorized in recent years, before finally analyzing the nature of the automatism dramatized by Jenison's optical machine.

Tim's Vermeer and the artist at work

As the chapters in this volume make clear, films "documenting the visual arts" take many forms and address an array of epistemological desires, interrogating art's cultural significance, its popular reception, and its modes of circulation. While *Tim's Vermeer* draws more directly from reality TV and mockumentary than from earlier canons of documentary, it resonates with an important subgenre of the art documentary: a cycle of "portrait films" covering notable artists and observing their working processes. The main features of this subgenre are given in two early prototypes: Hans Namuth's *Jackson Pollock* (1951) and Henri-Georges Clouzot's *The Mystery of Picasso* (*Le Mystère Picasso*, 1956). In both cases, the filmmakers focus on the artist's active, creative labor as an occasion for two adjacent media, film and painting, to interrogate one another. Namuth trains his camera on Pollock's full-bodied thrusts as the latter sidles around his floor-bound canvas flinging globs of paint. The filmmaker asserts the movie camera's capacity to catch Abstract Expressionism in the act, constituting "action painting" as a suite of sinuous, performative gestures. The dynamism of motion pictures transfers our interest from the finished object to its genesis, its active formation over time. In an especially provocative move, Namuth places his camera beneath a sheet of glass upon which Pollock drips point, suggesting a graphic interface between cinematic gaze and artistic gesture. Clouzot, in his Picasso film, further elaborates this impulse toward intermedial dialogue, inducing Picasso to paint a glass pane as the camera observes from its opposite side. Both films invite the viewer to imagine herself "looking through" a real canvas as it is painted in real time – an experience that inspired André Bazin to call *The Mystery of Picasso* a "Bergsonian film."[1]

These glass intermediaries literalize a fantasy of artistic transparency, so that *seeing through* the canvas bespeaks a novel form of intimacy with the works and their makers. More abstractly, they suggest a contact zone between the media of film and painting as such, a frame in which the painter directly confronts the camera's viewfinder, acknowledging how both modernist painting and cinema animate the relation between liveness and permanence, action and form. This fascination with artistic process, while not always as self-conscious and experimental as in these two works, remains conspicuous in a range of later art documentaries, like *Painters Painting* (Emile de Antonio, 1973), *Golub* (Jerry Blumenthal and Gordon Quinn, 1988), and *Gerhard Richter Painting* (Corinna Belz, 2011), to name just a few. These films attest to our enduring desire to witness the becoming of art, to understand the personalities and methods that endow it with life, to see, more generally, how vibrant forms evolve out of inert material.

This investment in the enigma of creative process is given a provocative turn in the BBC arts documentary, *David Hockney: Secret Knowledge* (Randall Wright, 2002), a television program that in many ways sets the stage for the intervention of *Tim's Vermeer*. Narrated almost entirely by Hockney himself, the documentary complements the artist's best-selling book of the same title, promoting the thesis that Western painters, beginning around 1420, made extensive use of optics to achieve a range of realistic effects.[2] The program narrates the germ and development of this pet theory, beginning with Hockney's hunch, during an exhibition of portraits by Ingres, that these drawings from the 1820s must have been made with the assistance of the camera lucida. Hockney then searched for comparable effects – seemingly traced lines, objects painted out-of-focus, impossibly perfect perspective in still-life subjects, intensely detailed patterns on clothes and textiles – which could be accounted for by the use of optical aids. In recounting this radical discovery and the accumulation of clues – clues enticingly hidden in plain sight, winking out of the paintings themselves – the documentary embraces the air of conspiracy and mystery. Here, the "artist at work" is a painter-cum-detective straining to recover methods that, despite once being in wide circulation, were meticulously concealed before being lost to time. Like other TV detectives, Hockney restages the "scene of the crime," setting up a camera obscura of his own and trying his expert hand at tracing its seductive, inverted image.

As Hockney paints within the camera, he is keen to compare optical painting and cinema, alluding to a "straight line" running from the Renaissance to the television signal. He likens the camera obscura's projection of a live, moving, color image to a cinematic image, a motion picture witnessed centuries before the invention of the cinematograph. He refers to his work space – with its stagey reproductions of views from several Renaissance cities – as "my own kind of Hollywood set." He describes how Caravaggio integrated separate optical renderings into complex compositions, comparing this process to an editor splicing close-ups into a film. As he works in his camera, adding judicious marks here and there over the projection and "directing" his models, Hockney sports a T-shirt proclaiming one of the mottos from his book: "Optics Don't Make Marks." This is a reminder that, where optics or cinematography are concerned, it still takes an artist to put these scientific instruments to use. The trouble, though, is that it is unclear whether Hockney's attempts to paint via camera obscura will bear fruit. The spectacle of his efforts is compelling in its own way, but we never see convincing results, paintings that resemble the realist masterpieces he analyzes. Undeterred in his theory, Hockney acknowledges this frustration: "I knew the problems, and I'm still dealing them."

As a kind of sequel to *Secret Knowledge*, *Tim's Vermeer* takes up Hockney's desire to know "how they did it," and suggests an unexpected solution to the artist's abortive experiments. Jenison is presented as a technical savant, a man whose fluency with machinery goes back to adolescence, when he dismantled and rebuilt an old player piano, and who later earned a fortune as a video software engineer. With his penchant for tinkering and his enthusiasm for Hockney's theory, Jenison reimagines optical painting as an engineering puzzle. Where Hockney seeks to accommodate optics within traditional artistic methods, Jenison simply reduces human talent and skill from the image-making equation entirely. The film narrates the process by which Jenison hits upon technical improvements to the camera obscura as a device for mindlessly copying images, then follows him as he demonstrates the viability of this method, makes elaborate preparations for his "Vermeer" experiment (which includes

FIGURE 3.1 David Hockney tracing a live projection within a camera obscura.
David Hockney's Secret Knowledge
(Randall Wright, 2002)

a full-scale replica of the room and decors depicted in *The Music Lesson*), and, finally, fulfills his role as painting automaton – his slow, plodding progress captured by an unmanned video camera poised over the canvas. Though we are, as Jenison jokes, literally "watching paint dry," this last portion of the film is in some ways captivating, a reminder of art documentaries' predilection for images coming to life.

Art, illusionism, and automatism

Tim's Vermeer gives us what *Secret Knowledge* only hints at: an object that demonstrates the viability of optical methods, a full production of a painting that seems to look a great deal like Vermeer's *Music Lesson*. But this object, and the way in which the film documents its production, raise a series of questions. How convincing *is* Jenison's painting – how closely *does* it resemble Vermeer's original?[3] Assuming the resemblance between Jenison's painting and Vermeer's is as uncanny as the film insists, how compelling is this as evidence that Vermeer actually employed Jenison's method, or one like it? How compelling, for that matter, is the optical hypothesis as such? What exactly is explained by the discovery that painters hundreds of years ago used optical aids? In short, why and how does the optical hypothesis and the operation of Jenison's machine *matter* to us?

Tim's Vermeer presents itself as a potentially scandalous experiment, acknowledging some of the real-world controversy that surrounded Hockney's book, but declining to flesh out the objections raised by art historians.[4] Though visually and formally prosaic, the film channels the personae of Penn and Teller in instructive ways – especially their irreverent humor, their concern with revealing how illusions work, and their willingness to undermine their own credibility. Just as Jenison assesses Vermeer through the lens of his technical expertise, so the filmmakers approach Jenison's project and the optical hypothesis from the vantage of practiced illusionists: they are all determined to figure out *how the trick is done*. The filmmakers recognize something important about the emotional significance of this sort of inquiry, converting our aesthetic ambivalence about the stunt into a more concrete uncertainty: whether we should believe what we are seeing in the film.

Several critics and viewers remark on feeling ill at ease with the film, not just because they are uncomfortable with its underlying thesis, but because they suspect its central stunt – Jenison's laborious but convincing replica – might actually be some sort of hoax.[5] Such hoaxing is by no means unheard of in recent documentary, given the fluid boundaries between pseudodocumentaries, mockumentaries, and hoax documentaries.[6] In this case, perhaps Penn and Teller's toying with documentary reliability can count as a form of cultural commentary, a perception that American movie audiences are uncomfortable talking about art, that we are uneasy with high-cultural distinctions, that we are leery of being duped. There is something apt in how *Tim's Vermeer* activates the uncanny pleasures of a good magic act while poking holes in the notion of artistic "genius." Are we relieved or disturbed by the conjecture that old masterpieces are elaborate deceptions, mechanical copies posing as manual creations? Are we amused or scandalized when, instead of the image of a great artist at work, we behold Tim Jenison, hunched and bored as he slaves over an optically configured paint-by-numbers kit? The film focuses these lines of anxious curiosity into the blunt question that Philip Steadman, one of Jenison's academic accomplices, poses: "Was Vermeer a machine?" Where, in these paintings, does the optical device's functioning end and Vermeer's human contribution begin? These sorts of questions and anxieties are at the heart of the notion of *automatism*.

The concept of "automatism" is complex and historically layered, often bespeaking a swirl of categorical uncertainties. The word's roots lie in nineteenth-century psychology, describing either the mindless and routine itineraries of the body or, conversely, the programmable systems of the mind.[7] Its etymology draws as well on the uncanny clockwork automaton dolls whose life-imitating performances were popular in Enlightenment Europe – elaborate, brilliantly configured machines that included defecating ducks, talking children, and a chess-playing "Turk."[8] The term similarly informs twentieth-century emblems of industrial automation and computerization.[9] In the arts, the psychoanalytic account of automatism was embraced as a creative principle by André Breton and other Surrealists, a way to harness the resources of the unconscious mind.[10] More recently, the term has been appropriated for media theory, especially to describe the image-making paradigm inaugurated by the invention of photography and, perhaps, dissolved by the emergence of digital media.[11]

Automatism's theoretical richness lies in how the term evokes the interplay of media technologies, industrial systems of production, and a field of related feelings and cultural categories. As Scott Selisker shows, the cultural significance of automatism is as a term which confuses ontological categories, and against which we try to define the nature of our humanity.[12] The distinctly human virtues of freedom, creativity, and individual agency are ones we try to conceptualize by negating their antitheses: constraint, reproduction, and unconscious or externally determined behavior. Automatism points to an absenting or reduction of conscious control, the significance of which is negotiated in a patchwork of objects, texts, narratives, and discourses. Its "aesthetic effects" are similarly generated by "moments of ontological uncertainty" that confuse "categories for personhood and objecthood"(8). To take just one poignant example, consider the inspiration and complex influence of E.T.A. Hoffmann's 1816 story, "The Sandman," which tells of a young man who is first deceived by a lifelike mechanical girl, Olympia, then haunted by his uncertainty about who else might be an automaton. The figure of Olympia recalls the real-life humanoid machines devised in the eighteenth century, curiosities that beguiled onlookers and toyed with their ability to tell vital behaviors from mechanical ones. For the young man in Hoffmann's tale, this categorical confusion of person and thing, agent and automaton, triggers a general psychic breakdown, leading later critics to read the story as an illustration of the aesthetic/affective category of the uncanny.[13] This interplay of unsettled feelings, uncanny aesthetics, and conceptual confusion extends from Hoffmann through other fictions of zombies, robots, and somnambulists – but it also pertains to the aesthetic and ontological attraction of photography as a form of self-generating image.

Categorical ambiguity was central to the nineteenth-century reception of photography, especially within polemics that either contested or defended the new technology's viability as an artistic medium. These arguments were generally disputed on aesthetic grounds, committing naysayers to the truism that the artist's *hand* must be central to the meaning of art, or that a work of art must be an *original* creation, whereas the photograph was only ever a copy of something first conceived in nature.[14] But these arguments were never very far from broader cultural debates, especially insofar as photography was taken as a species of industrialization and the "machine age" – an accomplice to the unchecked spread of railroads, pit mines, and factories.[15] Later, modernist-era critics digested the aesthetic and cultural implications of photographic automatism into alternative artistic paradigms: the decline of the art object's unique, unapproachable, and inimitable "aura," as Walter Benjamin saw it; the plastic arts' resolution of their "mummy complex," in André Bazin's account.

Stanley Cavell's re-tooling of automatism in the 1970s begins by modifying this insight of Bazin's. Photography did something automatically that had previously been done manually, but the underlying *wish* that it satisfied was not the painter's wish to make realistic images, but the pervasive, philosophical wish "to escape subjectivity and metaphysical isolation."[16] Photography's cultural significance involves forms of physical and psychic *relief*: it enables the production of realistic pictures with minimal effort, and, Cavell submits, it naturalizes our relation to the phenomenal world by giving us "views" of it that are not predigested by an intervening personality. This last, mythic accomplishment is due to the fact of automatism itself:

> Photography overcame subjectivity in a way undreamed of by painting, a way that could not satisfy painting, one which does not so much defeat the act of painting as escape it altogether: by *automatism*, by removing the human agent from the task of reproduction. (23)

To "get to the right depth of this fact of automatism" (21), Cavell draws attention to how the term operates within theories of artistic media – how debates over "medium specificity" attempt to fix the nature and "possibilities" of the artist's tools and materials, but how works of art also utilize formal resources in ways that are, in some sense, automatic. In describing film and photography, then, we can speak of two different sorts of automatisms, the first literal or concrete, the second figurative or metaphorical. Film is first of all a complex of photographic exposures, the automatic spooling of celluloid through a camera, and the projection of these recorded images on a screen: Cavell refers to this physical basis as a "succession of automatic world projections" (72). But film's automatisms also include Hollywood's genres, cycles, plots, stars, and types, which are the true *media* of the movies, in that it is through these traditional, iterative forms that filmmakers come to discover the "possibilities" of motion pictures (60). In short, we cannot truly know what film's physical basis *is* or what its capacities are just by studying its underlying mechanisms. Rather, we gain knowledge about a given medium's "specificity" only through the production and critical reception of successful works within that medium. If, for example, photography tends to give "ontological equality" to human beings and inanimate objects, this fact only becomes legible to us through eloquent instances of genre, style, and type – through, for instance, the comic characters established by Chaplin, Keaton, and Lloyd, and how those characters are able to conjure humor from their interactions with stubborn objects and rebellious devices. "What gives significance to features of [film's] physical basis" – to, in this instance, the mechanical automatisms of photography – "are artistic discoveries of form and genre and type and technique, which I have been calling automatisms" (105).

Referring to cycles and genres and star personas as "automatisms" is bound to raise confusion. Cavell's point in sowing this sort of confusion, I take it, is to show how working within a vital tradition is *like* working with a physical medium – how in both cases our plans and designs must be negotiated through materials and forms that do certain things on their own, *automatically*, without our having to tell them to. Photography's automatism is central to the art of film, in this theoretical scheme, both as a "material basis" and as a paradigm for artistic intervention. Several critics have accordingly asked how deeply that paradigm might be disturbed by the dominance of digital processes in our contemporary mediascape. Mary Ann Doane reasons that the concept of a medium is one that involves a seeming contradiction, a form of agency that *depends* on a negative constraint: "the potential of a medium would thus lie in the notion of material resistances or even of matter/materiality itself as, somewhat paradoxically, an *enabling impediment*."[17] The risk, she finds, in the emergence of digital technologies is that so much emphasis is put on the encumbered transmission of the digital animator's vision, to the point that the notion of a *medium* – with its unpredictably instructive resistances – disappears entirely. While digital imagery's lack of a physical basis, its abstract ontology as 1's and 0's, need not invalidate it as a medium, what Doane's insight seems to point to is a paradigm shift: the end of photography as an instrument and model for artistic innovation. True, digital films still mobilize the forms and conventions they inherit from cinema's celluloid history, making use of these artistic automatisms. But something has changed when we no longer know how to imagine the relationship between these aesthetic statements and the physical stuff out of which they are formed.

Rosalind Krauss, writing about artists working in the aftermath of conceptualism, refers to this current situation as "the post-medium condition." Much like the artists that Cavell saw as having constantly to rediscover or redefine their chosen medium, Krauss notes that contemporary artists face an institutional environment in which plastic media, as such, are often deemed exhausted. Some, she argues, respond creatively to the culture of rapid and enforced obsolescence by embracing obsolete technologies. Two central figures in Krauss's argument are James Coleman and William Kentridge, both of whom employ outmoded materials like slide projectors, charcoal, and sequential photography to create unusual motion picture installations. She finds that, in embracing obsolete devices and materials, these artists pointedly decline the dominant equation of creativity with intellectual property;

instead, they stake their creative acts in the investigation of these physical materials and technologies, in the behaviors and modes of thought these technologies seem to foster.[18] Against the tide of information economies, immaterial media platforms, and the paradigm of Conceptual Art, part of what these artists are trying to reclaim is the very *notion* of "a medium." They seize on the automatisms of the technologies they use – the intermittent progress of still photographs through the slide projector's carousel, the timed exposures in a stop-motion-animation set-up – and work out ways to interact with these automatisms. These interactions are themselves repetitive and iterative, not unlike a classical artist's activation of an inherited formal tradition, and much of their creative potency lies in "mining" the possibilities of given technologies and semi-conscious routines.

Krauss illustrates this circuit of technology and manual technique through a discussion of William Kentridge's idiosyncratic version of stop-motion animation.[19] Kentridge's self-imposed technique involves trekking back and forth between a painting canvas and a film camera – adding a few new marks and adjustments to his drawing on one end, then returning to his camera to take a single exposure of the drawing, then repeating the cycle. The camera shutter, the trek, and the mindset of his painting all suggest automatic, half-conscious qualities – routine behaviors whose repetitive nature relaxes the need to plan one's marks in advance. The virtue of this rule-bound circuit is that it yields unanticipated discoveries for his animation, as when his incremental marks cause the plunger on a French coffee press to morph into a mine-shaft. Kentridge calls this method for catching serendipitous insights *fortuna*. For Krauss, it epitomizes the process of inventing something new by interacting, routinely and dialogically, with a palpable medium.

Tim's automatisms and Vermeer's

With Coleman and Kentridge in mind, I would like to return to Jenison's painting apparatus and its presentation in *Tim's Vermeer*, and to reconsider what the film and the apparatus actually imply about art, technology, and the notion of automatism. If the apparatus can be seen as an automated ensemble, what manual task does it take over? What deeper psychic or mythic needs does it address? What does the success or failure of Jenison's project tell us about Vermeer and his art? What, finally, does it tell us about the relationship between art and technology in our own time?

We are to understand that Jenison's painting method makes no demands on the user's talent or skill. His apparatus is an elaborate optical machine based on a traditional camera obscura: a lens projects and focuses an image of the illuminated room, this image is then reflected and sharpened by a concave mirror placed on the rear wall of the camera chamber, and this mirror image is then reflected once more in a small shaving mirror suspended over the painting surface at a 45° angle. The machine's human user is still obliged to apply paint, matching it point by point to whatever appears in the shaving mirror. But this labor is as mindless as it is tedious, and its result depends in no way on the personality, vision, or aptitudes of the painter. Rather, the look of the finished product depends only on the calibration

FIGURE 3.2 Tim Jenison painting within his optical apparatus. *Tim's Vermeer* (Teller, 2013)

of the device and the external scene it pictures – much like a photograph. The method, Jenison boasts, "isn't subjective, it's *objective*. You're a piece of photographic film at that point." *It*, the method, does the work; and it does so by turning you, the painter, into a machine – an additional cog in the camera obscura's mechanics.

While *Tim's Vermeer* invites us to see Jenison as rediscovering a lost method, a forgotten midway point between freehand painting and chemical photography, Jenison's technical means and theoretical ends seem to negate core features of photographic aesthetics. It is striking, for instance, how Jenison's method precludes the intrusion of *accident*. The photograph's automatism has often been associated with the inclusion in the image of details that are in some sense *not* intended by the photographer – an undesired flinch in the subject of a portrait, a fly that alights on a shoulder unnoticed. Photography's emergence as a medium of art involved critical and artistic acknowledgments of these unmeant, undetermined, yet often affecting intrusions of accident – new aesthetic categories, like Barthes's *punctum*; new stylistic protocols, like Bazin's celebration of long takes and deep spatial compositions; new lines of ethical and political investment in the image.[20] The photographic image's flouting of conscious control spoke to a conception of nature as aesthetically fertile, a source of invention and inspiration. Within this paradigm the artist, whether painter or photographer or filmmaker, could model her methods on the camera's faithfulness to life.

In hollowing out the relevance of human skill, Jenison's machine eliminates the possibility of accident and, more importantly, the possibility of investing unintended details with human significance. His precisely configured optical set-up compels him to follow an ironclad directive: any detail he can see in the reflection he must reproduce in paint. Once the apparatus has been assembled, the result of Jenison's brushstrokes is wholly determined by the mirrors and the method. Because the scene he depicts – his spatially exact reconstruction of the room in *The Music Lesson* – is perfectly arrested, the time it takes Jenison to complete his painting is lengthy, but insubstantial. Accidents and missteps do occur in the course of the film: a storm disrupts a lighting fixture; Jenison realizes that his outdoor heaters are probably unsafe for indoor use; he discovers and corrects a flaw in his painting, the result of having briefly upset one of his mirrors. But these episodes come across as brief and contrived, breaking the monotony of Jenison's work, but in no way imperiling its momentum. His progress is as inevitable as it is slow. This mode of painting admits no accidents, no discoveries, no personal inflections, so that neither time nor Tim can make any difference in the final result.[21]

Compare Jenison's painting process to Krauss's description of William Kentridge. Both men follow prescribed rules as they interact with an imaging set-up. But where Kentridge experiences his technically orchestrated routine as a device for producing inventions, Jenison's device is designed only to prove a point. The project is conceived as an unusually elaborate "proof of concept," to demonstrate that a talent-negating mechanical device like Jenison's can produce a painting that resembles Vermeer's. In its mission and in its figuring of creative process, Jenison's machine is also designed to demystify artistic creation by, as several critics note, reducing it to a species of technological invention.[22] The function of this optical apparatus is to show that artistic labor is replaceable by a mechanical device, and that art, more broadly, can be comprehended by science, obviating the need for humanistic interpretation, theory, or criticism.

In its functioning, its conception, and its implied ethic, the logic of Jenison's machine is pointedly not that of photography: it is that of digital imaging.[23] This is true, first of all, of how Jenison and the film characterize creative process. The manual labor of painting has been de-skilled and standardized in a way that voids it as a medium of art: the brushstrokes map inputs to outputs, light to pigment, in a rigorously determined way. The process is automated, not in the world-imprinting spirit of photographic exposure and development, but in the sense of an algorithm, reflecting Jenison's experience with video-editing software.[24] Following that impulse, then, the outlet for creativity, as modeled by digital work flows, is in the laying down of the code itself – not in the drudgery of painting, but in the design of the optical machine itself. Indeed, much of the film's attraction is in its presentation of the practical difficulties with painting from a camera projection, and then showing Jenison assess and resolve those difficulties. The chamber of the camera is dim and the projected image fuzzy, so he introduces the concave mirror to brighten and sharpen the image. Matching paint to the camera projection is impossible, but he is able to circumvent this obstacle when he realizes that he can employ an angled shaving mirror rather than attempt to trace the projection directly. He describes this breakthrough as a "eureka" moment, a lightbulb switching on his mind as he marinates in a bathtub. It is the surest example of a creative inspiration anywhere in the film. Tellingly, it occurs offscreen, during Jenison's unfilmed bath. The insight is treated as a purely mental phenomenon, so that it would have been impossible to film anyway.

I am suggesting that this treatment of creative labor as mental and abstract, as opposed to manual and embodied, fits the cultural ethos of Silicon Valley, but that we should not presume to extend it to Vermeer's Delft. Though Jenison ultimately works with period-accurate oils and pigments, brush and canvas, his experience of creative activity is still modeled by his experience working with digital codes, graphical interfaces, and video arrays. *Tim's Vermeer* seems to acknowledge this through two recurring visual motifs that complement the digital framework of Jenison's experiment. The first of these visual motifs consists in how the film attempts to demonstrate the mechanics of Jenison's method. Having positioned his shaving mirror so that it catches the image from the camera, Jenison explains his painting procedure: by bobbing his head up and down, he can continually compare his painting to the image in the mirror, adding and mixing small regions of paint until they "match" the corresponding area of the reflection, at which point the edge of the mirror seems to "disappear." To illustrate what Jenison is describing, the camera shifts its perspective up and down to compare the canvas and the mirror reflection. Later, the film elaborates this comparative gaze into a recurring gesture, *scanning* from left to right over the mirror to show how exactly it matches the painting below. While the film includes many shots of Jenison's hunched, bored, laboring body as he picks away at his canvas, the magic of the method is more striking in these "scanning" gestures. The camera makes successive passes over the shaving mirror, each time showing ever nearer equivalence between reflection and painting. It is as if the mirror itself were the agent, or implement, effecting the painting – an effect not unlike Photoshop's texture-mapping cursor.

The other visual motif that evokes the sensibility of digital imaging is the use of time-lapse to show the progress of Jenison's painting, condensing months of work

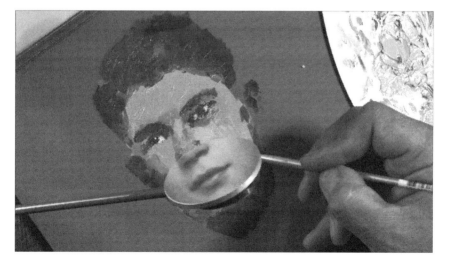

FIGURE 3.3 Jenison's perspective as he copies the image reflected in his shaving mirror. *Tim's Vermeer* (Teller, 2013)

FIGURE 3.4 Jenison using a computer to analyze perspective cues in Vermeer's *The Music Lesson*. *Tim's Vermeer* (Teller, 2013)

into a few seconds of screen time. The most striking example of this comes near the end of the film, rendering the evolution of Jenison's painting from start to finish. The background is laid down first, then windows and furniture, tiles and fabrics, girl and teacher all successively emerging into the field of the canvas. This telescoping of time removes the figure of the human painter from the picture, so that the painting seems to direct its own development, as if we were witnessing some advanced form of autopoiesis. While the occlusion of labor is a mainstay of cinematic illusions, in this case it is particularly evocative of the creative logic animating Jenison's project. Jenison is blunt in describing his affinity for Vermeer. He invokes his background as "a video guy" to explain why is drawn to these paintings that, to him, look like video displays. He describes the paintings in terms of color grading, "definition," and "resolution," as if paint and pixels were already ontologically equivalent. The impression we get is not so much of a period-accurate recreation than of a digital savant who has "hacked" Northern Renaissance painting. This tendency, in both Jenison and in the film, is vexing for how it declines to meet Vermeer halfway.

The film is almost certainly right that Vermeer made rigorous use of some sort of optical contraption, but it refuses to imagine what inspired this use, what optical technology might have meant to a painter like Vermeer, how it might have addressed his depictive desires, articulated his worldview, or mediated the claims of craft and technology, art and science, in his own time. These questions are, of course, the domain of art historians; that the film sidesteps them is disappointing, but perhaps not surprising, given its ultimate thesis.[25] "Is Tim an artist or an inventor?" Penn asks near the film's conclusion. "Perhaps the problem is that we have that distinction." Perhaps Penn is right that the boundaries we draw between art and science are worth questioning, but the film's program, as critics have noted, is not to broker a new peace between C.P. Snow's "two cultures," but to subsume one of them within the other. Art, in the film's optic, can be reduced to a minor species of technological invention; image-making since the Renaissance, a story of technical improvements culminating in the triumph of virtual reality and computer simulations. Hewing to this story, though, means ignoring what is potentially strange in Vermeer's paintings, and refusing to revise one's perspective in their light. So when Jonathan Jones remarks that Jenison's "Vermeer" looks very much like a digital rendering – a sort of labor-intensive print-out, a copy of a poster – this is because its DNA, its underlying codes and commitments, are digital. It indexes and expresses, not the photographic ideal of fidelity to the light-borne world, of faith in the world as a source of vital forms, but the recession of this ideal in the wake of digital convergence.

Notes

1 André Bazin, "A Bergsonian Film: *The Picasso Mystery*," in *Bazin at Work: Major Essays and Reviews from the Forties and Fifties*, ed. Bert Cardullo (New York, NY: Routledge, 1997), 211–220.
2 David Hockney, *Secret Knowledge: Rediscovering the Lost Techniques of the Old Masters* (London: Thames and Hudson, 2001).
3 As Jonathan Jones suggests, there is some "crude sleight of hand" here, as we are technically never shown Vermeer's original painting, only reproductions of it. Jonathan Jones, "DIY Vermeer Documentary Utterly Misses the Point," *The Guardian,* January 28, 2014. www.theguardian.com/artanddesign/jonathanjonesblog/2014/jan/28/tims-vermeer-fails.
4 Much of that controversy was concentrated into a series of articles on Hockney's conjecture, academic responses to it, and a symposium organized at New York University to encourage debate among Hockney (and his fellow travelers Philip Steadman and Charles Falco) and his critics. See Sarah Boxer, "Paintings Too Perfect? The Great Optics Debate," *New York Times*, December 4, 2001. www.nytimes.com/2001/12/04/arts/paintings-too-perfect-the-great-optics-debate.html.
5 Joshua Gans, "10 Reasons to Doubt Tim's Vermeer," *Medium*, June 15, 2014. https://medium.com/@joshgans/10-reasons-to-doubt-tims-vermeer-c183bb3ce7a2.
6 Examples would include *Exit through the Giftshop* (Banksy, 2010) and *I'm Still Here* (Casey Affleck, 2010).
7 Henri Ellenberger, *Discovery of the Unconscious* (New York, NY: Basic Books, 1979).
8 Gaby Wood, *Living Dolls: A Magical History of the Quest for Mechanical Life* (London: Faber and Faber, 2002).
9 Fred Turner, "Romantic Automatism: Art, Technology, and Collaborative Labor in Cold War America," *Journal of Visual Culture* 5, no. 1 (2008): 5–26.
10 André Breton, "First Surrealist Manifesto" (Paris: Éditions du Sagittaire, 1924); Susan Laxton, "*Flou*: Rayographs and the Dada Automatic," *October* 127 (2009): 25–48.
11 David Norman Rodowick, *The Virtual Life of Film* (Cambridge, MA: Harvard University Press, 2007).
12 Scott Selisker, *Human Programming: Brainwashing, Automatons, and American Unfreedom* (Minneapolis, MN: University of Minnesota Press, 2016).
13 Sigmund Freud, "The Uncanny," trans. Alix Strachey, in *Sigmund Freud: Collected Papers, vol. 4*, ed. Ernest Jones (New York, NY: Basic Books, 1959), 368–407.
14 Lady Elizabeth Eastlake, "Photography" (1857), in *Classic Essays on Photography*, ed. Alan Trachtenberg (New Haven, CT: Yale University Press, 1980), 39–68.

15 See John Ruskin's early embrace and later rejection of photography, as discussed in Michael Harvey, "Ruskin and Photography," *Oxford Art Journal* 17, no. 2 (1984): 25–33.
16 Stanley Cavell, *The World Viewed: Reflections on the Ontology of Film*, enl. ed. (Cambridge, MA: Harvard University Press, 1979), 21.
17 Mary Ann Doane, "Indexicality and the Concept of Medium Specificity," *Differences* 18, no. 1 (2007): 130; original emphasis.
18 Rosalind Krauss, "Reinventing the Medium," *Critical Inquiry* 25, no. 2 (1999): 289–305; and "'… And Then Turn Away?' An Essay on James Coleman," *October* 81 (1997): 5–33.
19 Rosalind Krauss, "'The Rock': William Kentridge's Drawings for Projection," *October* 92 (2000): 3–35.
20 Roland Barthes, *Camera Lucida*, trans. Richard Howard (New York, NY: Hill and Wang, 1981); on cinephilia and contingency, see Paul Willemen, *Looks and Fictions: Essays in Cultural Studies and Film Theory* (Bloomington, IN: Indiana University Press, 1994).
21 In this respect, *Tim's Vermeer* is strikingly *un*-Bergsonian.
22 As Manohla Dargis puts it, "despite being couched in the nominally objective language of science, [the film] has the feel of a 21st-century rationalist's attempt to vanquish a 17th-century mystery." "Dutch Masterwork, Under Reconstruction," *New York Times*, January 30, 2014. www.nytimes.com/2014/01/31/movies/tims-vermeer-chronicles-an-attempt-to-make-one.html.
23 As described by Doane.
24 In this respect, Jenison's few flirtations with error could count as *glitches*, rather than accidents.
25 These questions are explored compellingly in Lawrence Gowing's classic monograph, *Vermeer* (Berkeley, CA: University of California Press, 1952).

4

FLESH AND VISION

Jia Zhangke's *Still Life* and *Dong*

Amy Villarejo

Jia Zhangke, perhaps the most internationally known of the People's Republic of China's (PRC's) "Sixth Generation" filmmakers, submitted not one but two films to the 2006 Venice International Film Festival: the narrative feature film *Still Life* and the shorter documentary film *Dong*. Despite their formal differences, these are both intimate projects: *Still Life* follows two familial characters, one of them played by Jia's cousin Han Sanming and one played by his wife and longtime collaborator Zhao Tao. In a different mode of intimacy, *Dong* is putatively an "artist's documentary," a study of Jia's friend, the painter Liu Xiaodong, who teaches at the Central Academy of Fine Arts (CAFA) in Beijing. Intended as companion pieces, the two films are both set in and study the vicious transformation of the Three Gorges Dam area around the Yangtze River in Hubei Province. Now the site of the world's largest power station, the dam serves as official evidence of China's success (demonstrated by a number of monumental infrastructure projects that are variously the biggest, longest, tallest, largest, fastest, and so on). In the region, however, the dam has caused the displacement of more than a million residents, the destruction of archaeological sites, flooding, landslides, and the risk of severe ecological devastation.

In both of his films, however, Jia seeks to capture neither monumentality nor destruction alone. His lenses are trained instead on the interaction of the body and the land, a convergence of what I will here be calling *flesh* and *vision*, in which a string of encounters – between workers and the built environment, between dwellers and their homes and region, between the filmmaker and his actor/characters, between an artist and those same workers/actors/characters, and between the painter Liu Xiaodong and the filmmaker Jia Zhangke – beckon and demand reflection. It is as though these two films serve as an invitation to find *forms*, in the mediums of paint and film respectively, adequate to the violence *and* redemption Jia and his subjects witness along the riverbank (and then, as I will explain, in Bangkok, where the second part of *Dong* unfolds). Simply put, I mean by "flesh" those workers' bodies that both Jia and Dong encounter and struggle to represent through the "vision" of the two art forms, brought together in the companion films. In emulation of this invitation, the form of this chapter is itself a layering that evokes conjoined artmaking, showing prismatically some aspects of its practice rather than, say, severing *Dong* from *Still Life* in order to perform an autonomous formal analysis. This strong sense of the two films' connectedness is reinforced by watching them together and thinking about them as the companion pieces Jia intended. Let me start with the apparently simple sense of place, i.e., nation.

China?

Where is this "China" in which these films take place? Literally in a fraught landscape that is the Three Gorges, but also figuratively in a "China" that is increasingly multiple, abstract, and mediated, especially with regard to one of its most contentious representative filmmakers, Jia Zhangke. There is some very good writing on Jia's *oeuvre*, and much of it catalogues the embrace with which Jia is held by greater Asia and the West as a favorite of the festival and arthouse circuit, and the chilly contrast of his reception in mainland China, where his work has received at best mixed blessings. Michael Berry, in his short book on Jia's "hometown trilogy" – *Xiao Wu* (1997), *Platform* (2000), and *Unknown Pleasures* (2002) – suggests that Jia Zhangke's films of the late 1990s and early 2000s were received negatively in the PRC because, in essence, they were deeply critical in their subject matter about everyday life in provincial China as well as formally challenging, playing "to some mainstream audiences as a series of amateur cinematic exercises lacking in tension, plot development and drama."[1] Jia's films did not become either less critical or less boring, at least to some eyes, over the next decade, and so they have continued to challenge Chinese censors who nonetheless clearly understand that Jia attributes turbulent crises in human relations to China's social problems, many of them arising from accelerated development. His achingly violent 2015 film *Touch of Sin* was denied a release in China (where, in that same year, one could freely watch the murder and torture on offer in *Mission Impossible: Rogue Nation* [Christopher McQuarrie], a film partly financed by the Alibaba Pictures Group, a division of the Chinese internet giant Alibaba). Although his most recent feature films, *Mountains May Depart* (2016) and *Ash is Purest White* (2018), were shown publicly in China, Jia sees his lukewarm reception at home as a question of the role of the artist in social critique:

> 'I think the main factor is our different perceptions of the current reality [in China],' says Jia of audiences in China. 'It's whether they can agree with the reality presented in my films. There was a dramatic shift in 2008 when nationalism began to rear its head. [It is promulgated] that China cannot have problems; that artists cannot reflect on China's problems; that China is a happy society without a tinge of sadness.'[2]

In what follows, I will argue that Jia's overwhelming project as a filmmaker is to give materiality and form to that abstract "tinge of sadness." In the work of painter

FIGURE 4.1 The director's signature. *Still Life*
(Jia Zhangke, 2006)

Liu Xiaodong, Jia finds an ally and fellow aesthete to join him in this endeavor. The project is, however, different in the two media of film and painting. In film, Jia confronts the challenge of cinematic realism by representing bodies who have been enfolded into the problems of China's rise: he wants to show laborers, displaced people, everyday folks in relation to those very problems that are denied by Chinese spectators (Figure 4.1).

The very first scene of *Still Life*, in fact, witnesses those laborers, the migrants from Fengjie, duped into a "lesson" in how capital extracts resources. In painting, Liu aligns with a different history of realism in which bodies come to the fore as whole and fleshy subjects (in a rejection of the fragmentation of cubism and other forms of modernist vision). In the tradition of Francis Bacon and Lucian Freud, as I will discuss, he continues the British painters' emphasis on everyday and familiar intimacy while also emphasizing the materiality of paint. In an intriguing study of the connection between the filmmaker and the painter, Aija Laura Zivitere enumerates at least three discrete factors that further link these two figures – and art and cinema – together in China:

> (1) before embarking on cinema studies, Jia Zhangke briefly studied painting at Shanxi University in Taiyuan; (2) the film *Dong* (2006) is a documentary on the painter Liu Xiaodong, where the title refers not only to the part of the name of Liu Xiaodong but also alludes to the painter Dong, a protagonist Liu played in Wang Xiaoshuai's feature film *The Days* (*Dongchun de rizi*, 1993), while literally meaning East; (3) being one of the most visible Chinese oil painters, Liu Xiaodong is also well known for his close ties with the Sixth Generation filmmakers as his different cinematic jobs over the time indicate, i.e. an actor, art director or co-producer.[3]

To the degree, though, that Jia's work travels and is adored by cinephiles around the world, it is not only located through these webs of connection in China but is "global": that is to say, it enjoys widespread arthouse distribution in the West. Above all, his films put global capitalism and its ravages (most significantly, dehumanizing labor, the flesh of capitalist value-production that Marx called "labor-power," the worker's bodily *capacity*) under a microscope, magnifying or miniaturizing processes of alienation, displacement, and exploitation, as well as survival. In his 2004 film *The World*, Jia famously tracks the melodramatic and comedic relations between staff members and performers at the Beijing World Park, a real-life theme park populated by small-scale versions of world monuments (the Eiffel Tower, the World Trade Center pre-9/11, the Taj Mahal, the pyramids of Egypt). What better emblem of a Chinese "worldview" than seeing five continents without leaving Beijing, a literal (even more nationalist) version of what Nietzsche described as "monumental history" or "traditional history," where a metaphysical vision contemplates, as Foucault glosses him, "distances and heights: the noblest periods, the highest forms, the most abstract ideas, the purest individualities."[4] Subjecting such a vision to scathing scrutiny, Jia reveals, again to draw upon Foucault's language, a sense of proximity, intimacy, and systems of subjection – in other words, "the articulation of the body and history" (83) – within this very specifically Chinese moment of history's imprint upon the world stage. Both *Still Life* and *Dong* rehearse this conjunction or articulation. In this specific sense, one could say that Jia is a genealogical filmmaker, stressing the materiality of the body as it is inserted into the largest historical transformations yet witnessed in Asia.

On the other hand, then, Jia works within aggressively local or provincial spaces, precisely to counter the nationalist and monumentalist vision of the Chinese rise that has sought to silence him as an artist at home. Indeed, his own ancestral home is the small city of Fenyang in central Shanxi Province, where coal mining supports the local economy and where the economic reform of the late twentieth century in China seeped in slowly, where the old order of traditional life yields nonetheless to the new harsh social and economic realities. Rather than present a nostalgic version of home that, as in more classical Chinese literature, renders the hometown a strange, unrecognizable place, Jia presents the idea of home (whether his own Fenyang or a river city like Fengjie, where both *Still Life* and *Dong* take place) as undergoing a different temporality, one that stages destruction, stagnation, rapid growth, bizarre change, and also poetic possibility, all at the same time. For Jia, migrant workers and artists alike *come from somewhere* and *end up somewhere*: place marks a process of vision, a posing and staging of everyday life within realities of sensation and location (Figure 4.2). What is "real" in Jia's realism is this emplacement in observed space. Jia's camera certainly creates vision. He takes in Fengjie in both films simply by observing the unfolding of history, a mode akin to sensory documentary but enlivened by a bit more structure: buildings are marked for destruction and torn down, workers rest on the rooftop as Dong paints them, the river slowly and insistently cuts through the mountains.

FIGURE 4.2 Workers' flesh. *Still Life*
(Jia Zhangke, 2006)

I want to insist, however, on the alienating or ontic dimensions of this experience: Jia's characters do not quite know where they are but are thrown or cast into the spaces of capitalist transformation that make "home" and "place" almost meaningless terms. Jia's task is to translate the experience of exile and non-belonging into a story that *takes place*. Dong's task, like Jia's, is to convert that homelessness into form (figure, background, shading, the composition of bodies), then into paint. Neither "global" nor "local" nor a neologism like "glocal" does these processes justice: it is more a sense of art as that which *creates* a suspended or alienated vision of where we are, and where we might be.[5] For Jia, as for Heidegger, place is central to thinking:

> We belong to being, and yet not. We reside in the realm of being and yet are not directly allowed in. We are, as it were, homeless in our ownmost homeland, assuming we may thus name our own essence. We reside in a realm constantly permeated by the casting toward and the casting-away of being. To be sure, we hardly even pay attention to this characteristic of our abode, but we now ask: 'where' are we 'there,' when we are thus placed into such an abode?[6]

Still Life follows the character (who is also the person/actor and Jia's cousin) Han Sanming, a former coal miner from Shanxi Province – that is, from home/Fenyang – who journeys to Fengjie. He seeks out his former wife, who (as the limited diegesis would have it) ran away sixteen years ago, and he must navigate a cartography of impermanence, destruction, and violence that marks the Yangtze region, working as he does as a member of a demolition crew while he anticipates a reunion with his wife and daughter. In a parallel story, Jia follows another Shanxi native, Shen Hong (Zhao Tao), a nurse, who pursues her own husband, Guo Bin (Li Zhubing), who has become a successful businessman in Fengjie and betrays her by having an affair. If the narrative focuses on division, missed connections, betrayal and separation, Jia concentrates his visual and aural attention on how the baffling and brutal transformations of Fengjie serve as a fitting *mise-en-scène* for interpersonal devastation. In the film's structure, Jia asks us to connect marital discord – let us call it figuration, narrative, or representation – to landscape, to the very place where drama unfolds, and its temporal unfolding, so that "still life" describes many things at once: a genre of stagnant vision, a way of holding something in abeyance, a formal treatment of *mise-en-scène*, and a way of looking. In simple terms, one could say that his characters manifest or symbolize certain aspects of the environment in which they incubate, that they function as "landscape allegory."[7] With greater insight, one might try to describe, as I will, both bodies and artistic insight as emerging from a common matter of fact, situation, or circumstance.

Dong records the same environment, the same *mise-en-scène*, of *Still Life*, here with an orientation, although loosely structured, around the experience and perception of Liu Xiaodong. It is vitally important, in other words, to see the two films as emerging together from something like the situation of Fengjie, by which we designate place as the site of death and horror as social products, as well as aesthetico-political responses to them in the form of images. This is the strong sense in which they are companions and illuminate one another. These films-as-urgent-responses do not mitigate the horror, such as casual death of a worker or environmental catastrophe, but they do, importantly, propose a kind of composition of bodies and insight, or what I earlier called flesh and vision, as legitimate rejoinder. Jia made *Dong* first and then generated the narrative world of *Still Life*, but Jia also intended to include Liu's rooftop painting scene in *Still Life*, although he removed it from the final cut (Figure 4.3). The two films share a minimal amount of footage, with Han working on the demolition crew and the sanitation crew disinfecting

FIGURE 4.3 Liu Xiaodong painting Han Sanming. *Dong* (Jia Zhangke, 2006)

the demolition site. Both films were shot in mini-DV, with all of the flattening and homogenization that the resulting image entails, but also, as Zhen Zhang and Angela Zito observe, with the effect of broadening debate and conversation toward a kind of "digital political mimesis," where viewers engage sympathetically with the image.[8] Both films witness the disappearance of the landscape and lifeworld of the Three Gorges: the actual place that Jia recorded for the films barely sustained itself for the period of the films' production, so much so that he raced against time to complete the second film, *Still Life*, before its world literally plunged underwater.[9] Playfully generalizing his subject's given name to an abbreviation, Dong (a word that means "East" in the most general way), Jia both loads symbolic meaning onto Liu, his artwork, and its role in the world, and enfolds "Dong" into the vision that sustains *Still Life* and Jia's own creative practice. Indeed, the worlds of *Dong* and *Still Life* begin to meld in our experience of the two films seen together, as we witness Han Sanming as a documentary subject in *Still Life* and can come to see Liu as a fictional character, especially in moments when we are able to see formal parallels (the early scene that parallels Han's contemplation of the river) or emotional intensity that would befit a fictional character (such as Liu's visit to the dead worker's family). Formally, there is surprisingly little in *Dong* – rife with contemplative scenes of the landscape and everyday interactions of Fengjie as is *Still Life* – that would differentiate it as a documentary, much less an artist's documentary or documentary of Chinese visual arts. Mostly, that is, it just hangs out in Fengjie and then later in Bangkok, sometimes and only sometimes with Liu, and only occasionally when he is painting or talking about art. Indeed, *Dong* is unlike almost all documentaries about artists I have ever seen. In its novel structure, Jia splits the film into two halves that track Liu's *subjects*, rather than the painter himself: in the first, Jia follows the worker who died, as Liu pays his respects to the man's family, and in the second half, Jia himself follows one of Liu's subjects in Bangkok. Jia thereby raises questions about cinematic and artistic presence and agency: Liu follows an absent/dead man, and Jia follows a woman Liu seems unable to understand or track. In its attention to these absences and intermedial aspects, Dong is likewise not a film that conventionally celebrates the accomplishments of a famous Chinese artist (like *Sky Ladder: The Art of Cai Guo-Qiang* [Kevin Macdonald, 2016] or *Ai Weiwei: Never Sorry* [Alison Klayman, 2012]), his/her long-buried talent, or his/her revelation of technique as a "how he does it" intrigue, as in *Gerhard Richter Painting* (Corinna Belz, 2012). *Dong* contains only a few moments of actual painting or the image of the very large paintings executed by Liu. Instead, it accompanies *Still Life* in its efforts to look critically at the body in history, to look at flesh. I will turn to a closer reading of several illustrative sequences in it after encountering both its filmmaker and its artist at greater length.

The filmmaker and the artist: composition in time

Liu Xiaodong is an accomplished painter who, as I have mentioned through Zivitere's essay, has also played a number of roles in China's independent film sector, as an actor in Wang's *The Days* and as art director for Zhang Yuan's punk film of the same year, *Beijing Bastards* (1993). With Jia, these Sixth Generation filmmakers form a network of underground artists whose work emerged in the post-Tiananmen climate of censorship and the commercialization of the state film industry. Shooting on tight budgets due to the lack of state funding, some with digital equipment and others shooting on 16mm, these makers create works with resonances to other historical moments and resulting film cycles, most obviously Italian neorealism. The Sixth Generation shares with neorealism the use of non-professional or not-yet-professional actors, hand-held cameras, quick production, the prominence of ambient sound, and other aesthetic markers of cheap and critical cinema. The politics of Sixth Generation films, like those of neorealist films, are not consistent; some of the critical force of these films derives from youth subcultures, some from their urban environments (prominently, but not only, Beijing, where many of these makers studied art and filmmaking), and some from a reaction to the lush and comparatively expensive undertakings of Fifth Generation luminaries, such as Zhang Yimou and Chen Kaige. Liu and Zhang are exactly my age, born in 1963. Wang is a little bit younger, and Jia is the baby, born in 1970. Molded by historical bookends, these artists came into consciousness during the Cultural Revolution and came into early adulthood after Tiananmen. Their conceptions of the world have been forged through these events in ways that we can assume to be as impactful as they are uneven, just as their art emerged within the complex climate of the 1990s.

Photography, cinema, and digital and new media dominate the Chinese contemporary art scene in ways that are crucial to document. CAFA co-hosted the first Beijing Media Art Biennial in 2016, a show that cemented the importance of digital and new media art in the current climate, but the dominance of the arts of reproduction on the national and global arts landscape dates to the decade of the 1990s. Successful and influential photographers include Zhang Huan Qiu Zhijie, Liu Zheng, Rong Rong, Song Dong, Song Yongping, and others, many of whom turned from careers in printmaking, painting, and other arts to a medium that seemed uniquely appropriate to documenting the rapidly changing world these (also "Sixth Generation") artists were witnessing and often indicting. In the production of images, these artists often emphasized a sense of place, whether observing breakneck urbanization with horrified fascination, coolly observing scales of change in the city, or documenting imperiled relationships in cities that are nonetheless visually malleable and dazzling. The video artist Song Dong laments the loss of his web of relationships in the new city, in a passage cited by Christopher Phillips in his catalog essay for the definitive collection *Between Past and Future: New Photography and Video from China*:

> Regarding the issue of demolishing the old city, I have had contradictory thoughts that have evolved over time. Now, for example, I am learning how to drive, and I see that large streets are much better for automobile traffic. But practical issues are not everything ... The type of relationships I used to entertain with other people living in the same *hutong*, which was probably very similar to those of other people living in other ones, is slowly disappearing. Now, everybody lives in compounds, in high-rise buildings.

> The relationships between family and family, between who is living here and who is living there, have changed.[10]

It is precisely this sense of fragile habitation that Jia Zhangke, too, seeks to record. With regard to his own reputation by comparison to these artists I have just mentioned, it would be difficult to overstate how much of a film celebrity Jia has become in the PRC, precisely because his frame for contemplating place and location is a capacious one. Walter Salles's film *Jia Zhangke: A Guy from Fenyang* (2016) includes footage of an appearance Jia made at CAFA as a guest artist, where the spillover audience overwhelms the lecture hall and documents its own enthusiasm with selfies and WeChat posts.[11] As an artist who has steeped himself in Paris and New York, Jia exemplifies a peculiar blend of local and cosmopolite, never resolved into a unified stance in relation to Chinese politics or globalization, much less provincial life or something as grand as "human nature." Instead, Jia continues to produce slices of life, still lives, or "touches," or "tinges," that are coherent as worldviews even if they are impressionistic and fleeting encounters with flesh. In this pair of Jia's films in particular, rather than delineating characters, figures, or subjects, Jia focuses on embodied labor, the fleshly men whose bodies fuel the breathtaking transformations of the Three Gorges. His camera highlights the contrast between the otherworldly landscape of demolition, its dangers and its violence, and the fragile bodies that do the work (and sometimes do not survive it). In noting the fragility of social bonds, Jia seems reluctant to rely too heavily on conventional notions of character and motivation, favoring instead a way of contemplating human associations in their humdrum conviviality, as in the final moving sequence of the miners in *Still Life*.

In *Dong*, Jia finds a most generative vision that forms a prompt for *Still Life*, insofar as Liu's paintings provide him with analogous, or companion, forms. Liu's commitment not only to painting but to figurative painting in particular (as opposed to abstract or conceptual art, photography, or video) stands as an unspoken or implicit rebuke to the dominance of technological arts, but no art form is inherently conservative or prestigious. Liu's reputation in China is rather due to his singular status as the *only* painter who successfully bridges all three domains of Chinese art: academic, commercial, and state-driven. To be held in esteem in two of them is astonishing; to be an ambassador for all three is just unheard of, and yet Liu has done so because he has moved adroitly from social realist idioms into looser modes of figuration without abandoning the social altogether.[12] Rightly, the published literature on *Dong* compares Liu's figurative work to Lucian Freud's, primarily due to the emphasis by both painters on tones of the flesh (Figure 4.4). Through the writings of Gilles Deleuze, in his book *The Logic of Sensation*, we might test a similar comparison to the work of Francis Bacon, in particular his "ceramic" approach to the coloration of the flesh and to the immensely important relationship between background/structure and figure.[13] It would be wrong – a kind of Orientalism in reverse – to suppose that a Chinese artist is not fully steeped in the Western canon, and it would be just as misguided to presume that the most

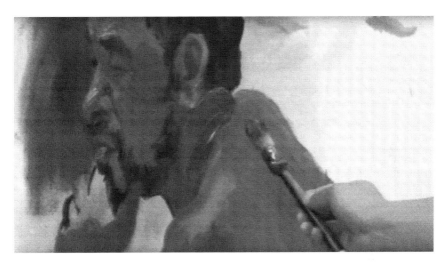

FIGURE 4.4 Detail of painting by Liu Xiaodong. *Dong* (Jia Zhangke, 2006)

important British painters of the twentieth century would not exert *direct* influence on a young artist wielding a brush in Beijing. The question becomes, in my view, how to understand the paintings themselves as generating ways of seeing and then to find concepts adequate to that vision, differentiating as one must. One of the benefits of Deleuze's book is his *specification* of Bacon's vision: Bacon's catalogs of oval forms, his interest in the exact points where subjectivity dissolves, his obsessive attention to techniques of scrubbing, and so on. Although *Dong* the film conjoins the visions of Jia and Liu together, by looking more carefully at Liu's painting, we can begin this process of specification.

In *Dong*, Liu in turn paints two of his *Hotbed* paintings, *Hotbed 1* (a painting in five panels of workmen lounging on a bed mattress), painted on the flat rooftop of a building in a destruction zone overlooking the Yangtze River, and *Hotbed 2* (a painting in five panels of young Thai women likewise lounging on a bed mattress), painted in an interior room in Bangkok. The sitters for both paintings are drawn from the everyday life of the place (demolition workers and bar workers respectively), and the process of the paintings' construction is documented extensively by Liu in his sketchbooks, journals, photographs, and diaries, all of these in addition to Jia's film. Formally, the two paintings share in size (they are about ten meters in length), assembly (five panels each), motif (figures arranged around a bed mattress), and style. A "New Era" painter, Liu abandoned a certain form of social realism in the 1990s in favor of a style that embraced everyday moments, a form I would like to describe further still as that of visual objectivity (without embellishment or detail of scenery or setting), and indifferent to ideas of completeness or balance of composition. Drawn from life (although aided by photographs of his objects taken during the process), Liu interacted with his sitters, arranging them and chatting with them in a process of dialogue that arguably attributes more agency to them than the usual tyranny of painter over model: as a painting *practice*, it is part group portraiture and part immersive documentary, insofar as Liu is recording for us his very experience of making the artwork. As critics have noted, the panels moreover invited a way of viewing the work that has something in common with ancient Chinese scroll paintings (in which Liu is quite interested and from which he derives inspiration): viewers approach each panel as a part of a whole, which remains elusive if not entirely out of sight given the scale of the work. Jia's own filming of the painting in fact mirrors its own fragmentation and incomplete form. What strikes me as most useful about making the connection to scrolls is the issue of temporality: like cinema, Liu's *Hotbeds* unfold in time, they reveal ordinary moments and compositions of flesh in a dispersed perspective. Indeed, let us now turn to the film more closely to see through several key moments precisely *how* flesh and vision conjoin, in the time of cinema *and* painting.

Dong

After a quick introduction of credits and a glimpse of Liu's train travel from Beijing, Jia Zhangke's stationary camera patiently awaits the conjunction of the painter and the landscape of Fengjie.[14] Liu gazes at the mist-covered hills above the Three Gorges and takes a photo from atop a heap of rubble, behind which we observe the sanitation crews in hazmat suits, swarming over piles of brick and broken concrete like aliens. As Liu plays a balancing game with his hand and a piece of brick, the viewer senses that he is already somehow at one, synchronized with this space and its workers, so steeped in the materiality of the site is he as seen through Jia's lens. The palette is quintessentially urban Chinese: grey that envelops the sky and is the peculiar density of smoggy pollution and mist at once. It obstructs vision and yet mystifies the environment by bathing everything that could suggest scale and orientation in a murky white. Against this palette, Liu's painting will suggest another by contrast: the ochre and pink skin tones that reflect strenuous work in the unforgiving sunshine, and the brightly colored Chinese men's shorts/underwear, a kind of loincloth/diaper hybrid that segments the body into two clean halves while pulling the eye to the midsection and genitals. Grey competes with eye-popping browns, pinks, and blues, and the result is less a composition of death *against* life than it is that embodied tinge of sadness I remarked upon earlier.

In the first several minutes of the film, Jia has already set two poles firmly in the ground, filling the frame with the tension between them: dehumanizing labor of physical destruction (in an overall calculus of critique that sees the Three Gorges project as extracting a baffling cost) and a collective massing of bodies that can suggest affinity and care without nostalgia for a world untainted by history, one of the hallmarks that differentiates the Sixth Generation from its Fifth Generation predecessors. It is this collective affinity that Liu paints: the bodies of the guys from Fenyang, the migrant laborers, whose festive and drunken meal shared together serves as the final scene of *Still Life* and whose gathering on the roof of the structure in Fengjie gives Liu a chance to compose *Hotbed 1*. "I have always been fascinated by the growth of human body," Liu remarks to Jia, and one could add that "growth" is also a name for *form*. Following Liu's directions, the guys, Han Sanming significantly in the foreground, pose their torsos and limbs in relation less to Liu's gaze than to the feel of one another's presence; the whole scheme of the painting is about a form that the guys *invent* (to be sure, at Liu's careful insistence, documented and photographed with loving attention) between their bodies.

In the background, both literally and figuratively, we witness the bland and banal death of one of the destruction workers, as a concrete and rebar structure collapses at a distance on his body. It is only as his corpse is carried from the construction site that it is aestheticized, adorned with a kitschy and loud floral (I would guess polyester) blanket: a contrast between still life (lifelessness) and color that Liu's painting both mimics and refutes. By "aestheticized," I mean to emphasize that it is a carefully composed shot, one of the moments in the film where Jia seems to create a fiction staged for his camera. Formally, Liu's painting says: color redeems death, figuration speaks to human potentiality and relationality. Formally, though, the film shot of the dead body says: color cheapens death, figuration is impossible in this horizon of devastation. I love this tension in *Dong*, a tension in part produced by the intermedial relationship between cinema and painting, where Jia and Liu both celebrate the capacity of art to transform *and* find art insufficient to address what it witnesses.

I want to suggest, in other words, that my phrase "flesh and vision" is meant to resist a liberal humanist reading of vision as Enlightenment in Jia's films or in Liu's paintings. Not vision *of* flesh, in which man is revealed to himself as a perceptual or sensorial ground capable itself of insight or empowerment: the Three Gorges films are not "about" labor power. Instead, they constantly push up against the horizons of vision or insight, where bodies and the emplaced lifeworld they inhabit pull insistently back to an unknown ground. When the filmmakers and Liu travel to attend the wake/funeral of the worker killed on the construction site, they are taken to see a car that has been overtaken by the floods, stranded in a culvert about to revert to nature. Here is one among several figures for this pressure: we could call it a return to necessity, or a call for groundedness, or a recognition of chance, or the underside of progress. Whatever we name it, it is, I think, at the revelatory core of Jia's filmmaking practice and Liu's painting. This image captures vicissitude: the car is swept up in history, a victim of environmental degradation and full-throttle capitalist development but also a figure for the dissolution of the now into a time to come.

If we are moved by the careful orchestration of place, vision, and flesh in the first half of the film, we are bound to be disappointed in the second half, in which Jia and Liu travel to Bangkok, where Liu will execute the second large *Hotbed* painting with the young women who work in Bangkok's bars. As aware as we become of the ties that bind Fengjie, Fenyang, Jia, and Liu in the Three Gorges, we get the sense that in Bangkok we are witnesses mostly to the globalization of contemporary Chinese art. This is not a bad thing to see. As I have noted and will amplify below, Liu *is* an internationally recognized figure, showcased in global art-world exhibitions such as the Guggenheim's 2017 *Art and China after 1989: Theater of the World* (which shows Liu's path from Socialist Realism to multi-panel events similar to the *Hotbed* series). Like Jia, he *does* travel all over the world to make and show his art, and he is therefore an ungrounded tourist as much as Jia wants to document the many ties that bind them to the Three Gorges. And so the opening sequence in Bangkok finds Liu at a typical tourist floating market, his voice-over misnaming the river that flows through the capital city as the Mekong, rather than the Chao Praya.

The mistake is telling: it reveals the difference between knowing and not knowing the land and its people, even in a situation in which that very knowledge is alienated and challenged. In Bangkok, both Jia and Liu look upon the city as visitors, travelers, part of the smart set of artist/intellectuals who move from continent to continent to generate value for international markets. I see an abrupt shift in vision here, first to a tourist's gaze that emphasizes familiar exteriors such as Bangkok's notorious traffic, scooters, and tuk-tuks, as well as the night market (on which the film ends with a dirge). Here there are, of course, dragon fruits and pineapples, for local color. Second, by contrast, Jia follows the young women as they move through the city: on trains and subways and on the streets that are pockmarked with global brands like McDonald's and 7-Eleven. Their vision constrained, they offer their bodies for Liu's painting, and he remakes this unknown world into a composition that reflects the attenuated encounter of his own artistic practice.

In documenting the latter – the side of Liu celebrated in global markets – Jia shows us the difficult situation of art in China today, his own and his friend/colleague Liu's. Both artists gravitate toward idioms that are not sanctioned by the state, emphasizing devastating social change, conflict, and exploitation. Both artists nevertheless are located in China, if that China is multiple and contradictory: the CAFA's Beijing, Jia's Fenyang, a shared experience of Fengjie, global travel, and so on. To speak meaningfully, and pointedly, to the layers of that experience: this is the task of both *Still Life* and *Dong*.

Notes

1 Michael Berry, *Xiao Wu, Unknown Pleasures, Platform: Jia Zhangke's Hometown Trilogy* (London: BFI, 2009), 9.
2 Jia Zhangke, "Why My Films Are Received Differently in China and Abroad," *South China Morning Post*, October 25, 2015, www.scmp.com/lifestyle/film-tv/article/1871408/jia-zhangke-why-my-films-are-received-differently-china-and-abroad.
3 Aija Laura Zivitere, "De-framing 'Dong': Liu Xiaodong and Jia Zhangke," *International Journal of the Arts in Society*, 4, no. 6 (2010): 328.
4 Michel Foucault, "Nietzsche, Genealogy, History," in *The Foucault Reader*, ed. Paul Rabinow (New York, NY: Pantheon Books, 1984), 89.
5 Although it is beyond the scope of this chapter, Jia's Fenyang becomes the star of yet a different artist's documentary, Brazilian filmmaker Walter Salles's *Jia Zhangke: A Guy from Fenyang* (2016), a film that is revelatory yet much more conventional than Jia's own *Dong*. In the film, Salles accompanies Jia to his hometown to see how it shaped his worldview.

6 Martin Heidegger, *Basic Concepts*, translated by Gary E. Aylesworth (Bloomington, IN: Indiana University Press, 1993), 75.
7 A term proposed by David Melbye in his book *Landscape Allegory in Cinema: From Wilderness to Wasteland* (London: Palgrave, 2010).
8 Zhen Zhang and Angela Zito, eds., *DV-Made China: Digital Subjects and Social Transformations after Independent Film* (Honolulu, HI: University of Hawai'i Press, 2015), 316.
9 The project flooded thirteen cities, 140 towns, and 1,350 villages, displacing more than one million people. "Three Gorges Dam," International Rivers, accessed May 6, 2019, www.internationalrivers.org/campaigns/three-gorges-dam.
10 Christopher Phillips, "The Great Transition: Artists' Photography and Video in China," in *Between Past and Future: New Photography and Video from China*, eds. Wu Hung and Christopher Phillips (Chicago, IL: Smart Museum of Art, University of Chicago, 2004), 46.
11 WeChat is a Chinese social media mobile application.
12 My sincere thanks to Professor Peng Feng, School of Arts at Peking University, for fruitful conversations about Liu Xiaodong's status within circles of Chinese contemporary artists.
13 Gilles Deleuze, *Francis Bacon: The Logic of Sensation*, trans. Daniel W. Smith (Minneapolis, MN: University of Minnesota Press, 2004), xxxi.
14 Jia Zhangke shares cinematography credit with Chi-sang Chow, Li Tian, and Nelson Lik-wai Yu.

5
GLOBALIZING AI WEIWEI

Luke Robinson

Ai Weiwei is one of the few Chinese artists to have obtained genuine celebrity status both outside the People's Republic of China (PRC) and beyond the art world; he is arguably "the only Chinese artist to have transcended the role of 'Chinese artist' in an international context."[1] Named the most influential artist in the world by *ArtReview* in 2011, the same year he was voted runner-up for *Time*'s Person of the Year, he is the subject of a number of English-language documentaries, both cinematic and televisual, and more media profiles than it is possible to enumerate. In 2017, he co-curated a season of Chinese documentaries at the Guggenheim in New York, while simultaneously releasing his own documentary, *Human Flow*, which addresses the plight of refugees round the world. Few Chinese artists are accorded the possibility to make such high-profile statements. Perhaps as importantly, even if offered, few would probably accept. Yet Ai is also a polarizing figure at home and abroad. His fame overseas increased exponentially following his design for the famous "Bird's Nest" Beijing Olympic Stadium and his subsequent public denouncement of both the building and the sporting event, but this international stature is often dismissed as purely political; his own love of social media means he is sometimes written off as a mere self-publicist. Critically, the role of Western media in generating an image of Ai that is inaccurate and self-serving – both for the artist and for foreign journalists – is often the focus of these criticisms.

This chapter looks in detail at one example of such a Western media image of Ai: *Ai Weiwei: Never Sorry* (2012; hereafter *AWWNS*), a documentary about the artist by the American filmmaker Alison Klayman. My interest is primarily in Ai as documentary filmmaker, though his filmmaking practice cannot easily be separated from his art more broadly. By exploring how Klayman's film represents Ai's filmmaking, I seek to address the question of how the artist's authorship is constructed outside China. Studies of Ai's documentary filmmaking have identified his practices not just as activist, but also as performative and collaborative. I suggest here that Klayman's documentary, and the paratexts surrounding it, place most emphasis on the performative element of Ai's film practice and his art in general. What emerges is therefore a picture of the artist as lone dissident, rather than as a member of a networked collectivity – an image that embodies a particular set of political values. Yet this image is not simply the consequence of political prejudices or preferences. It also emerges as a consequence of market forces, production contexts, and the particular physicality of Ai's filmmaking. All of these combine to make a film about Ai into a particularly attractive prospect for international distribution, and help to explain Klayman's own contribution to the artist's ongoing global celebrity. Ai's awareness of this process, however, means that he, too, contributes to the production of this image. To conclude, I therefore touch on one further example of a documentary about the artist – *Ai Weiwei: The Fake Case* (Andreas Johnsen, 2013) – to consider what it suggests about the relationship between Ai and his documenters, and about the entangled relationship between creative practice and the artist documentary more generally.

Ai Weiwei: performativity, participation, and politics

Ai Weiwei was born in 1957 to the poet Ai Qing and the writer (and former ballerina) Gao Ying. Despite his father's support for the Chinese Communist Party and anti-Nationalist credentials, Ai's family was exiled from Beijing during the Anti-Rightist Campaign of 1957–9. On returning to the city in 1976, Ai enrolled at the Beijing Film Academy and participated in one of the earliest of the avant-garde art groups to form in the late 1970s, the Stars Group (*Xingxing huahui*). He then moved to New York in 1981, where he spent over a decade studying and working. In 1993, he moved back to Beijing, quickly becoming a staple of the art scene.

Although Ai is most famous for his work in the plastic arts, his practice covers both still and moving image work, including documentary filmmaking. Indeed, Ai himself says that he started experimenting with home video while he was in the US, though he never incorporated this everyday footage into his art pieces. From the early 2000s on, he produced a series of videos capturing Beijing's infrastructural changes and their social consequences. However, his more sustained interest in documentary was clearly a response to events that occurred in the run-up to the 2008 Beijing Olympics, particularly the Wenchuan earthquake of May 12 that year. In 2009, he released three pieces – *Little Girl's Cheeks* (*Hua lian ba'er*), *4851*, and *Disturbing the Peace* (*Lao ma ti hua*) – that directly addressed the impact of the earthquake. While *4851* is a moving image gallery piece that memorializes the names of all 4,851 victims, the other two films are both feature-length documentaries. *Little Girl's Cheeks* is a work of citizen journalism focusing on the shoddy building work that contributed to the high number of children killed in the quake. *Disturbing the Peace* tracks the artist and his friends as they travel to Sichuan to testify on behalf of Tan Zuoren, the lawyer on trial for his own investigation of the earthquake. All three works are overtly political, explicitly documenting perceived abuses of power by the Chinese state, whether building code violations in Sichuan or the physical violation of Ai and his companions in their hotel room by Chengdu police. All three also set the tone for the documentaries he has produced since, which have led him to be included in the very small group of prominent independent Chinese filmmakers who can be understood as activists.[2]

How Ai's filmmaking manifests as political extends beyond its obviously sensitive subject matter. It is also a question of form and process. *Little Girl's Cheeks*, *4851*, and *Disturbing the Peace* all function to make visible and memorialize a particular event – to render it public in a manner that counters the official government narrative about the earthquake. As such, they can be understood as attempts to create a counterpublic, a space in which "members of subordinated social groups invent and circulate counterdiscourses, which in turn permit them to formulate oppositional interpretations of their identities, interests, and needs."[3] Critical here is the use of editing and montage, which, according to Ying Qian, allows Chinese activist filmmakers to juxtapose official and unofficial footage, while layering material shot by many different people "to consolidate truth claims of images" without reducing them to a single voice.[4] *Little Girl's Cheeks* follows this format, mixing official TV footage, live footage of the quake shot by locals, and investigative footage shot by Ai and other citizen journalists, to build a multi-faceted picture of the earthquake's impact at different geographical sites. Following naturally from this is the prioritization of the film's participants and subjects over the figure of the filmmaker. For Ai's audio recording *Remembrance* (*Nian*) (2010), produced on the second anniversary of the earthquake, the artist had strangers record the names of students killed in the earthquake and then email him the recordings. These files were then compiled into a single MP3 with all of the dead students' names read out loud. As Bo Zheng notes, "in *Nian*, the artist concerned himself with creating not an object to represent his individual opinion, but a discursive space for other people – strangers, citizens – to make their expressions public."[5] Here, the authorizing figure of Ai becomes only one of many in a more distributed version of authorship, where shared participation in the work produces a new collective identity for those involved, that of the concerned citizen. This mirrors the similar process at work in *Little Girl's Cheeks*, where multiple individuals participated in the filming of raw footage for the finished work, which was edited together by Ai and close colleagues.

But if this participatory and collective model of authorship is one marker of Ai Weiwei's documentary filmmaking style, the other is the performative. In this mode, Ai's individual presence is foregrounded. *Disturbing the Peace* fits this formula most clearly. Although the film was produced collectively, Ai remains the primary focus throughout. Much of the film's footage was shot by the main cameraman, Zhao Zhao, and Ai is present in most of it. Indeed, *Disturbing the Peace*'s single most famous image is probably the artist's camera-phone self-portrait, standing in a lift surrounded by policemen, taken as proof of the beating he had just received from local law enforcement. But just as important are the sequences in which, as Tianqi Yu points out, "Ai's actions are conscious performances of his public image."[6] Throughout the documentary, the artist uses the act of filming as an opportunity to publicly enact the role of citizen; arguably the entire premise of *Disturbing the Peace* is to highlight the inadequacy of rule of law in the PRC by "performing into being otherwise 'invisible' acts of police repressions and brutality" on camera.[7] It is perhaps unsurprising, then, that this has led scholars to compare Ai's on-camera persona to that of Michael Moore, and not always, perhaps, as a compliment.[8]

The question of authority

As this analysis suggests, Ai's performative filmmaking can still be understood as political. Indeed, the relationship between individual and collective here is not necessarily one of opposition, but can be seen as a continuum. It is possible to understand *Disturbing the Peace* as shot from a "first person plural" perspective: a film in which multiple individual subjectivities are brought together to generate the collective subject position of citizen, in which the "I" and the "we" are defined in relation to as much as against one another.[9] However, the balance is a delicate one, and potential tensions between these different modes are obvious. As Ai has become increasingly famous, his profile may both attract more acolytes; at the same time, it threatens to overwhelm his much less famous collaborators. Yu notes this when she points out that "how Ai Weiwei destabilizes and decentralizes his own authority has become a question" both within, but also outside, his work (65).

This pinpoints precisely the issue with media representations of Ai Weiwei outside China: the extent to which they reinforce, or disperse, Ai's authoritative position in relation to his creative practice and the political consequences thereof. Indeed, this problem has been highlighted in relation to his fine art work. The same tension between the collective, the individual, and the performative is obvious here. Meiling Cheng, for example, argues that Ai is the "consummate performance artist," someone who has used this form first "to globally spread good tidings by promoting contemporary Chinese experimental art and his unique position in it," and more recently "to alert his global audience by publicizing China's political ills."[10] The message may be different, but the form remains the same. At the same time, Christian Sorace argues that Ai's compulsive documentation of his own life, whether through blogs, Twitter, or his "Weiwei Cam" – an installation in which he set up four surveillance cameras in his own home, allowing viewers to monitor his every movement online – constitutes "a radical departure from the medium of biography; it is an exposure of how the self is constructed at the intersection of political and social forces."[11] In other words, the "I" here is always shaped by and relative to society, in the same way that a single seed in Ai's famous sunflower seeds installation at Britain's Tate Modern gallery allows us to perceive the connection between the singular and the collective, "the individual and the commons" (410). Yet, in Western media coverage of Ai's art, this ambivalent relationship between the individual and the collective, at the level of both form and message, is often lost. What tends to emerge instead is an image of Ai that re-centers his authority over the artworks discussed. This image misses "the competing forces and multiple ideological systems that shape the content of his expression and to which much of his work responds," and generates a romantic image of the man as "quintessential anti-China dissident," the lone artist single-handedly facing down the state.[12]

This chapter explores these arguments through detailed consideration of Klayman's film. The aim is both to plot what sense of Ai's filmmaking and fine art practice emerges from this English-language documentary, but also to suggest *why* this image emerges. While the film has been positioned as a window onto Ai Weiwei's collaborative filmmaking practice,[13] I argue that, textually and especially paratextually, the documentary actually serves to stabilize Ai's ultimate authority over that practice. The result is an image of the artist that closely fits the caricature of the individual dissident. However, the reasons for this are multiple. Critics of Ai tend to argue that his popularity overseas reflects his oversimplification of the situation in China and his confirmation of a pre-existing sense of ideological difference between the PRC and Euro-American democracy. As such, his image in Western media is the product, in Sorace's forceful words, of "a catastrophic failure of political imagination."[14] But there are other factors at play. First, this imaginary cannot be separated from the demands of the market. Klayman's image of Ai is shaped by expectations of what a commercial documentary release should look like in the twenty-first century, reflecting the role of the Sundance Institute in producing the film. Second, the powerfully affective qualities of Ai's performative media strategies are the perfect basis for a commercial publicity campaign, as analysis of the marketing materials for Klayman's film demonstrates. Using Bishnupriya Ghosh's concept of the global icon as a sensuous image, I therefore suggest that the artist's image in *AWWNS* is best understood as the consequence of the intersection of a number of political, financial, and formal factors.

Ai Weiwei: Never Sorry and the problem of authorship

AWWNS is arguably the highest-profile feature-length documentary about the artist to have been made to date.[15] The film started life in December 2008, in Beijing, as a short assignment Klayman accepted to accompany a display of the photographs taken by Ai during his years in the US. It quickly morphed into a longer project, following Ai at work from late 2008 through to his detention and release by the Chinese authorities in June 2011. Funded through a combination of Kickstarter donations, awards from charitable foundations, and a grant from the Sundance Institute's Cinereach Project, portions of the work were released in 2010 on the *New Yorker* website, to accompany a profile of the artist, and in 2011 as a short segment for the PBS program *Frontline*. The finished documentary, produced in collaboration with MUSE Film and Television, premiered at Sundance in 2012, where it won the Special Jury Prize in the US Documentary Competition, before moving on to other destinations in the international film festival circuit, including the Berlinale and Sheffield Doc/Fest. *AWWNS* subsequently enjoyed theatrical and DVD/Blu-ray releases in multiple international markets.

Klayman's documentary places Ai in the context of his life's work, but necessarily focuses on the period during which the director was shooting. As a result, most of the original footage focuses on the period in the wake of the Olympics and the Wenchuan earthquake, and Ai's response to these events. This necessarily includes some of his documentary film work. Viewers are exposed to this in two ways. First, sequences from Ai's films are directly remediated in the documentary, including footage from *Little Girl's Cheeks* and *Disturbing the Peace*. Second, Klayman accompanies Ai to Sichuan for some of the period depicted in the latter documentary. While there, she captures images of him confronting the local authorities, and of the artist and his team filming these encounters. As one of the multiple filmmakers on location with the artist, her footage provides an additional perspective both on the events in Chengdu, and on the way Ai and his collaborators set about documenting them.

As a consequence of these different techniques, Selmin Kara believes *AWWNS* destabilizes the authorship of both Klayman and Ai. She suggests that Klayman's incorporation into the documentary of footage from different cameras – shot by her, Ai, other members of Ai's studio, TV footage, and surveillance images – effectively decentralizes her own voice, and thus "trouble[s] notions of authorship."[16] At times, she notes, it becomes difficult to tell who exactly has shot the images we are viewing, Klayman or someone else entirely. Even more significantly, Kara contends that the film does the same to our understanding of Ai's art practice. First, she argues that the sequences in *AWWNS* showing the artist "not only filming things by himself but also crowdsourcing, archiving and curating material submitted by his followers and other civil journalists, or tweeting" demonstrate the networked nature of his working habits, a point reinforced by interviews about his art that imply a "collaborative or crowd-sourced aspect" to his gallery work (47). Second, she proposes that in capturing the performative side of Ai's art practice on film – his "hooliganism," to quote him directly – *AWWNS* allows viewers to draw connections between Ai's deliberate transgressions of state authority in the PRC and other similar forms of art activism elsewhere. Through Klayman's film, she argues, "we can revisit hooliganism as a form of contemporary artivist discourse with broader references rather than merely as the embodiment of Ai Weiwei's singular artistic vision" (47). In effect, Kara sees *AWWNS* as a documentary that destabilizes the romantic image of Ai as a lone dissident artist, emphasizing instead issues of "the crowd-oriented nature of contemporary art, activist and documentary practice" (47).

Kara's exposition of *AWWNS* is an effective counter-reading of the documentary, but I would argue that it decontextualizes its material in a number of ways, and in doing so overestimates the extent to which Klayman's documentary undercuts Ai's authorship and authority. In fact, as I will go on to discuss, the film is arguably edited into a structure that foregrounds Ai even when there is an opportunity to step back and consider the bigger picture. But, as importantly, authorship is not simply a textual construct. Contemporary scholarship emphasizes the significance of paratexts (marketing, news coverage, interviews, photographs) in constructing our understanding of the phenomenon. This is as true in documentary as in fiction film. Although Ai is not the director of *AWWNS*, I would argue that the film's paratextual surround is as critical in constructing our understanding of his filmmaking as it is Klayman's. Furthermore, it does so in ways that re-stabilize our understandings of this practice, reasserting an image of Ai as a romantic dissident figure, ultimately through an iconographic representation of the director that is clearly intended to facilitate *AWWNS*'s international circulation and marketing. In order to demonstrate this, after first considering the film's organization of its material, I want to move on to analyze reviews and interviews available on the film's website, and then marketing images associated with both its theatrical and DVD releases.

The textual foregrounding of individual authority

While Kara is correct to note that *AWWNS* incorporates footage of Ai Weiwei that speaks to his collaborative working models as much as his performative political interventions, the organizing logic of Kayman's film is overwhelmingly biographical. As its title suggests, the film's structure is derived from events in Ai Weiwei's life, which start, conclude, and punctuate the narrative at regular intervals. This focus should not be surprising given the Sundance Institute's involvement in funding the film. The China-themed documentaries that Sundance has supported and promoted, such as Fan Lixin's *Last Train Home* (*Guitu lieche*) (2009), Wang Nanfu's *Hooligan Sparrow* (2016) (which was in fact executive produced by Klayman), or Wang Jiuliang's *Plastic China* (*Suliao wangguo*) (2016), have tended to be primarily character-driven, even when also concerned with social or political issues; so too have been the festival's award-winning films, such as Zhou Hao's *The Chinese Mayor* (*Datong*) (2015). This emphasis is hardly unique to Sundance. As Francesco Ragazzi points out, the contemporary funding landscape largely demands marketable documentaries that "reveal" the given truth about their subject rather than question it, and which are thus largely dependent on a "narrative dramaturgy reminiscent of a fiction film."[17] Nevertheless, given the festival's long-established position as the point of entry for much "indie" cinema into the American mainstream, and from there to overseas distribution, it should hardly be surprising that documentaries produced or promoted by Sundance largely adhere to this structure.

The consequence of this logic for the film's exploration of Ai's filmmaking, however, is that it reinscribes his own authority over his art practice at the expense of the more networked relationships that Kara highlights. *AWWNS* does not discuss political events outside the PRC. It largely remains geographically focused on China, and when it does leave – for example, to follow Ai to an exhibition in Germany, or discuss his time in the US – these spaces are clearly connected to his experiences in the PRC. As a result, the documentary makes little direct effort to link Ai's artivism to equivalent trends overseas, instead framing it by default as Ai's personal response to conditions at home. This dynamic is true even of the sections in which the film samples sequences from works such as *Little Girl's Cheeks*, with its multiple sources of footage. Eleven minutes in, *AWWNS* begins to explore the making of this documentary. It starts with remediated footage, possibly shot by Ai himself, though the viewer cannot directly discern that from the initial images of collapsed buildings shot from a moving vehicle. Nevertheless, the title "from Hua Lian Ba'er: Ai Weiwei" is emblazoned on the top-right corner of the screen, marking the documentary as an Ai Weiwei production (Figure 5.1). As the images unfold, a voiceover by *New Yorker* journalist Evan Osnos explains that questions of "transparency" are Ai Weiwei's primary interest. This voiceover clarifies how we should understand the remediated footage: as a product of Ai's drive to publicize images and information hidden by the Chinese state. The implications for the artist are then underlined in a brief clip from an interview with publisher Hung Huang, who says he has thrown away opportunities for personal enrichment to pursue these other, more civic-minded goals. Finally, we move into a direct consideration of the crowd-sourced manner in which *Little Girl's Cheeks* was made, with Klayman interviewing volunteers who worked collating information and footage direct on camera. Yet the section concludes with a return to Ai himself, pictured in his studio at the computer, editing the images that were remediated directly at the beginning of the sequence (Figure 5.2).[18] While the content here points towards collaborative

FIGURE 5.1 *Ai Weiwei: Never Sorry*
(Alison Klayman, 2012)

FIGURE 5.2 *Ai Weiwei: Never Sorry*
(Alison Klayman, 2012)

forms of authorship, the structure returns us again and again to Ai as the primary intelligence behind what we see on screen. Whereas *Little Girl's Cheeks* uses editing in part to distribute authorship across multiple sites and voices, *AWWNS* uses it to contain the documentary's focus and reinforce Ai's centrality to his films and fine art.

Flipping the bird: marketing an icon

If the editing of *AWWNS* positions Ai Weiwei as the ultimate master of his film and art practice, the media paratexts surrounding the film refine this perspective further while also inviting us to associate specific qualities with such authorship. As collaboration becomes subsumed in the image of the individual, so the documentary acquires intimacy; individuality in turn becomes dissident or rebellious. In this sense, the film's media surround functions as a discursive corollary to its character-driven narrative structure; in simplifying Ai Weiwei's image and work, it does so not simply to meet Western preconceptions of the artist, but also to facilitate the documentary's circulation through global markets. Klayman's strategic use of critical reception material on her *AWWNS* website is one example of this dynamic in practice: in the press section, links to (primarily) American reviews of the film are collated, most of which frame the documentary as the story of one man's battle against a repressive state.[19] I would argue, however, that this process reaches its apotheosis in the film's visual marketing, particularly the use of an image from Ai's *Study in Perspective* (1995–2003) series for the theatrical and DVD release of the film.

Study in Perspective is one of Ai's most famous and controversial works. It consists of a series of photographs of the artist flipping the bird at seven famous architectural icons, including the White House, the Eiffel Tower, the Hong Kong waterfront, and the Forbidden City in Beijing (from across Tiananmen Square). Each of the photos is structured in a similar manner: all that is visible of Ai is his hand and finger, in the foreground; in the background is the building being insulted. The series was first publicly exhibited as part of the *Fuck Off/Uncooperative Manner* show that Ai organized with the artist Feng Boyi, which showcased the work of 46 avant-garde artists whose work had been excluded from the government-organized Shanghai Biennale of 2000. A montage of images from the series appears briefly at the beginning of Klayman's documentary (Figure 5.3); later, during TV news footage discussing the Olympics; and finally, during a discussion of the three books, *Black*, *White*, and *Grey*, that Ai edited in the 1990s, in which some of the earliest photographs from this series were included.

While *AWWNS*'s visual marketing does not seem to be standardized across all markets, images from *Study in Perspective* recur in DVD and theatrical marketing materials from a number of different regions. With the exception of the French release, which uses the Eiffel Tower image, all of the others make use of the Tiananmen Square photograph. This appears on all the posters and the DVD cover of the Artificial Eye release in the UK, the Njuta Films release in Sweden, and in German and Australian marketing for the film. There is an American poster for the film that bears the design; it is also the image that serves as wallpaper for the film's

FIGURE 5.3 *Ai Weiwei: Never Sorry*
(Alison Klayman, 2012)

official site. In most of the marketing material the original photo has been adapted slightly. The original image has been cropped and zoomed: Ai's finger is larger, more centered, and the portrait of Mao that adorns the front of the Forbidden City is clearly identifiable. It is obvious that Ai is flipping the bird not just to Tiananmen and the old imperial palace, but to the Great Helmsman as well.

The decision to use this image in the film's marketing has particular implications. First, the selection of one photograph from a series of many affects how the viewer interprets this material. As Lin Zhang and Taj Frazier point out, placing a photo of Tiananmen alongside images of major Western architectural icons served in 2000 to position "Beijing landmarks as sites of cultural cosmopolitanism equivalent to that of the Louvre."[20] In turn, the iconoclasm of the middle finger was directed not specifically at the PRC, but at historical manifestations of wealth, power, and high culture more globally. Isolating the Tiananmen photo strips it of this semiotic range: the image alone is difficult to interpret as anything other than "an overtly … political gesture … a symbol of defiance set against a symbol of power."[21] Furthermore, the defiance is clearly individual and the power is specifically that of the Chinese state. Visually, I would argue, it is the equivalent of describing Ai as a "dissident." But the photo is also endowed with a highly embodied sense of conflict through the man's hand, the solidity of the square and the Forbidden City, and the extremely physical gesture of contempt that positions the two as antagonistic. The image not only suggests a very clear politics to Ai's work, but also emphasizes both its performative aspect and the corporeal underpinnings of this performativity – as with the self-portrait in the lift taken in *Disturbing the Peace*, but to rather different effect.

In her book *Global Icons*, Bishnupriya Ghosh discusses how a person becomes iconified. In part, this requires the public iteration and circulation of a standard image of that individual, one that can be replicated and remediated across different media platforms and formats.[22] But Ghosh argues that the iconic image is also a specific kind of image. An icon "is a physically expressive sign, incorporating as its quality sensations circling between subject and object" (43). In other words, the icon activates certain sensations in the viewer, feelings that appear to belong to the object, to endow it with its distinctive qualities. It is partly this sensuous quality that expedites the public circulation of the icon globally; it is also this quality that makes it highly susceptible to appropriation and repurposing, often for very different political purposes from those it was originally intended to fulfil.

What I am suggesting is that these marketing materials contribute to the articulation of Ai Weiwei as a global icon. The selection of the image from *Study in Perspective* as a key part of *AWWNS*'s marketing material is precisely a standardized image that can be replicated and recirculated, a metonym for the artist, if you like. However, it is also an image that aims to activate particular sensations in the viewer, in turn conferring certain qualities (defiance, resistance, dissidence) on the image itself. These highly embodied feelings draw on the physicality of Ai's performative practices, particularly the manner in which he places his body center stage during filmmaking and photography. As Yingjin Zhang notes, producing embodied knowledge through "political intervention" is a key aim of Ai's performative documentary practice, and explains in part the foregrounding of embodied confrontation in *Disturbing the Peace*.[23] But where these feelings are being directed is quite different. If Ai uses performative interventions to generate a collective sense of citizenship, *AWWNS*'s marketing is aimed at the consumer. Here, Ai, the icon, is clearly being used to sell Klayman's documentary, to lubricate the path of the commodity as it moves out into international markets. The standardization of the artist as heroic individual dissident in *AWWNS*'s visual marketing effect may appeal to a Western audience's expectations of China, the state, and Chinese artists, but it does so primarily in order to sell product.

My point here is not to reject arguments concerning the political appeal of Ai Weiwei to either Western audiences or commissioning editors. Rather, I am noting that these cannot be easily divorced from the commercial imperatives of contemporary theatrical distribution or television programming. The image of Ai that emerges from the text and paratexts of *AWWNS* – the ultimate author of his work, the lone dissident, defender of the rights of the individual against the state – cannot be separated from the demands of the market; indeed, the former is arguably the product of the latter. But if we are to take Ghosh's argument seriously, then the embodied and affectively charged nature of Ai's performative practice is an important component of this market popularity overseas. As the images discussed here suggest, this charge provides the raw material that, amplified and redirected, becomes a key tool in the marketing of *AWWNS*, underpinning the iconification of the artist. Klayman's film is ultimately too complicit with this dynamic to provide the viewer with significant critical distance on it; instead, the documentary becomes part of this process. But I think Ai Weiwei already knows this. Halfway through *AWWNS*,

Klayman captures Ai browsing on the internet, looking at T-shirts screen-printed with his face. "Do you think you're becoming like a brand?" she asks the artist, from off camera. "Yeah … I happen to be," he responds. "A brand for liberal thinking and individualism."

Conclusion

Released the year after *AWWNS*, Andreas Johnsen's *Ai Weiwei: The Fake Case* (2013) is, in some ways, quite different. This Danish–British co-production picks up from where Klayman's film concludes, following Ai in the immediate aftermath of his release from detention, while under house arrest awaiting tax evasion charges (the "fake case" of the title). Unlike *AWWNS*, it is also mostly shot in the observational mode. Yet the image of the artist that emerges is very similar. This is partly a question of narrative form: more so even than in Klayman's film, Ai is presented as a lone dissident, facing down the might of the state. But it is also an issue of visual style. As with *AWWNS*, the filmmaker was invited by Ai to shoot the artist at home and in the studio; there is a certain consistency to these interior sequences in both films, both in terms of the activities captured and their framing by the camera. Certain cinematic tropes of transparency also re-occur: filming Ai filming the filmmaker, for example, itself identifiable from Ai's documentaries, particularly during his encounters with law enforcement. Dependent as both films are upon personal access to Ai, it is clear that each film is in turn shaped by this access, traces of which are visible onscreen.

This interplay suggests how the awareness Ai demonstrates of his own iconification may feed back into his relationship with those filming him. Just as directors such as Klayman make use of Ai, his art, and his image to sell their product globally, so the artist, through a (carefully managed) performance of transparency and access, uses Western filmmakers to help publicize his image outside the PRC. This resembles the ways Ai exploits the webcam to connect directly to overseas audiences or utilizes interventionist filmmaking to make visible the public secrets of contemporary Chinese state–society relations. The relationship between the artist and his documenters is thus symbiotic and mutually beneficial. In addition, it is potentially dialogical; here, we get a sense of Ai adapting to the needs and expectations of the overseas media, even as he is also curating what he reveals to them. But these parallels also underline the extent to which we should view films about Ai Weiwei in relation to his creative practice. This is not just a question of marketing. *AWWNS* and *Ai Weiwei: The Fake Case* are, in a sense, both non-fiction commentaries on, and extensions of, Ai's art and filmmaking, and thus cannot be understood entirely distinct from them. In their allusions both to each other and to Ai's own work, these films highlight what we might see as a problem acute to documentaries about artists generally: where, in this complex intermedial entanglement, do we locate creative authority, and does it matter?

Notes

1 Philip Tinari, "A Kind of True Living: The Art of Ai Weiwei," *Artforum International* 45, no.10 (June 2007): 455.
2 Documentaries that Ai has produced since *Disturbing the Peace* on similarly sensitive subjects include, amongst others, *One Recluse* (*Yige gupi de ren*) (2010), *Hua hao yueyuan* (2010), *So Sorry* (*Shenbiao yihan*) (2011), *San hua* (2013), *Ping'an yueqing* (2011), and *Stay Home* (*Ximei*) (2013).
3 Nancy Fraser, "Rethinking the Public Sphere: A Contribution to the Critique of Actually Existing Democracy," *Social Text* 25/26 (1990): 67.
4 Ying Qian, "Working with Rubble: Montage, Tweets, and the Reconstruction of an Activist Cinema," in *China's I-Generation: Cinema and Moving-image Culture in the Twenty-first Century*, eds. Matthew D. Johnson, Keith Wagner, Luke Vulpiani, and Tianqi Yu (London: Bloomsbury Academic, 2014), 189. Ai's guerilla distribution methods (free online uploads and DVDs mailed through the Chinese postal system) are also arguably an attempt to constitute an inclusive public through the exploitation of digital technology and accessible infrastructure. See Luke Robinson, "Documenting Dissent: Political Documentary in the People's Republic of China," in *The Routledge Companion to Cinema and Politics*, eds. Yannis Tzioumakis and Clare Molloy (Abingdon and New York, NY: Routledge, 2016), 458–468.
5 Bo Zheng, "From *Gongren* to *Gongmin*: A Comparative Analysis of Ai Weiwei's *Sunflower Seeds* and *Nian*," *Journal of Visual Art Practice* 11, no.2–3 (2012): 130.
6 Tianqi Yu, "Camera Activism in Contemporary People's Republic of China: Provocative Documentation, First Person Confrontation, and Collective Force in Ai Weiwei's Lao Ma Ti Hua," *Studies in Documentary Film* 9, no.1 (2012): 65.
7 Yingjin Zhang, "Who's Afraid of the Documentary Camera?: Refiguring Reality, Memory, and Power in Chinese Independent Documentary," in *Filming the Everyday: Independent Documentaries in Twenty-first Century China*, eds. Yingjin Zhang and Paul Pickowicz (Lanham, MD: Rowman & Littlefield, 2017), 26.
8 See, for example, Yu, "Camera Activism," 64; Selmin Kara, "Rebels Without Regret: Documentary Artivism in the Digital Age," *Studies in Documentary Film* 9, no.1 (2015): 42–54.
9 Yu, "Camera Activism," 61.
10 Meiling Cheng, "Ai Weiwei: Acting is Believing," *TDR: The Drama Review* 55, no.4 (2011): 10–11.
11 Cristian Sorace, "China's Last Communist: Ai Weiwei," *Critical Inquiry* 40, no.2 (2014): 408.
12 Lin Zhang and Taj Frazier, " 'Playing the Chinese Card': Globalization and the Aesthetic Strategies of Contemporary Chinese Artists," *International Journal of Cultural Studies* 20, no.6 (2017): 574.
13 Kara, "Rebels Without Regret."
14 Sorace, "China's Last Communist," 398.
15 In addition to the documentaries by Klayman and Johnsen (which received both international theatrical distribution and public television broadcasts), the BBC's *Imagine* series also produced an hour-long documentary feature, *Ai Weiwei: Without Fear or Favour* (Matthew Springford, 2010).
16 Kara, "Rebels Without Regret," 48.
17 Francesco Ragazzi, "Your Film in Seven Minutes: Neo-liberalism and the Field of Documentary Film Production," in *Documenting World Politics: A Critical Companion to*

IR and Non-fiction Film, eds. Rens Van Munster and Casper Sylvest (Abingdon and New York, NY: Routledge, 2015), 24.
18 The implicit point of comparison for Western viewers, and one that arguably shadows the entire documentary, is that of Andy Warhol. Warhol is sometimes invoked more directly in American reviews of the film. See, for example, David D'Arcy, "'Ai Weiwei: Never Sorry,' review of *Ai Weiwei: Never Sorry*," *Screen Daily*, January 25, 2012, www.screendaily.com/reviews/the-latest/ai-weiwei-never-sorry/5037647.article.
19 "Press," *Ai Weiwei: Never Sorry*, accessed August 5, 2018, www.aiweiweineversorry.com/press.html.
20 Zhang and Frazier, "'Playing the Chinese Card'," 577.
21 Jason Miller, "Beyond the Middle Finger: Plato, Schiller, and the Political Aesthetics of Ai Weiwei," *Critical Horizons* 17, no. 3–4 (2016): 312.
22 Bishnupriya Ghosh, *Global Icons: Apertures to the Popular* (Durham, NC: Duke University Press, 2012), 148–9.
23 Zhang, "Who's Afraid of the Documentary Camera?" 26.

PART III
Questions of documentation

6

FILM AND THE PERFORMANCE OF MARINA ABRAMOVIĆ

Documentary as documentation

Chanda Laine Carey

Since 2013, a series of conferences, monographs, and edited collections have highlighted the importance of documentary across the spectrum of art practice and film representing a variety of perspectives, politics, and applications without any significant emphasis on its role in performance art.[1] Notably, documentaries about Marina Abramović, one of contemporary art's best-known practitioners, have eluded sustained attention. In four documentaries, filmmakers have communicated the clarity of her artistic vision through observation of the artist at work. Documentary films about Abramović blur the lines between the products of mass media and performance art documentation. These films observe her diplomatic contacts cross-culturally, and document her groundbreaking performances, creative process, and audiences inside and outside the museum. From China to Brazil, the Guggenheim to the Museum of Modern Art (MoMA), documentary film has followed Abramović as her art practice intervenes in the most important discourses around performance art. As this body of work has developed, the genre of documentary film has entwined with Abramović's performance, participating in her institutionalization.

Beginning in 1989 with *The Great Wall of China: Lovers at the Brink* (Murray Grigor), Marina Abramović has been the subject of numerous documentaries. Grigor's documentary captured her last collaborative performance with her partner of twelve years, Ulay. In the new millennium, Abramović has returned to the center of art discourse through her decades-long commitment to performance. Babette Mangolte's *Seven Easy Pieces* (2007) closely observes the artist during a series of performances at the Guggenheim in New York over seven consecutive nights. *Marina Abramović: The Artist Is Present* (Matthew Akers, 2012) brought together her past work and her triumphant performance at MoMA, during her first major retrospective exhibition. The year 2016 saw the debut of *The Space In Between: Marina Abramović in Brazil* (Marco del Fiol), which follows the artist during a journey of spiritual tourism through the country while she also developed new work. These works can be situated in different genres of documentary, but what distinguishes them is the many ways in which they challenge and redefine the performance document in the context of performance studies and art history.[2]

This chapter addresses the crucial and increasing significance of documentary films to performance art, its histories, and theories of documentation through the subject of Marina Abramović. At the roots of the theory of the document in relationship to art is Walter Benjamin's "Thirteen Theses Against Snobs," in which he systematically differentiates the work of art from the document. In thesis II, he states, "The work of art is only incidentally a document. No document is, as such, a work of art."[3] In thesis IV, he separates the artist from the public through taxonomic differentiation: "With artworks, artists learn their craft. With documents, a public is educated" (458). The didactic power of artworks notwithstanding, the grey areas between document and art in the contemporary abound, from the creative identity of the documentarian to the aesthetic strategies of artists. Benjamin neatly separates the artwork from the document with language and assumptions about mediation that are at times both dated and resilient, giving rise to an opportunity to observe their synthesis in the case of Marina Abramović. Following the model established by gallerist Sean Kelly for Abramović, the marketability of editioned performance documentation complicates the distinctions between artwork, document, and the documentation of the work of performance. The slippage between these three things in Abramović's practice highlights her role as a pioneer of performance and its commodification, as well as the contributions her controversial fame have made to the types of performance documents available to scholars and the public.

In the field of performance studies and discipline of art history, performance art holds a unique position as an embodied, live, and ephemeral event in complex relation to its mediation. Peggy Phelan's seminal essay "The Ontology of Performance" theorizes performance art as a practice that depends on the unique experience of artist and audience co-presence for the political integrity of its performance.[4] As a context that eludes forces of mediation, and thus, commodification, its inability to be fully captured by recording and other forms of documentation is essential. Through mediation, Phelan argues, the experience of presence that defines performance becomes something else. Presence is an obstacle for the art historian, who seeks to define and interpret performance in an intellectual context that is often inaccessible, except through documentation. Amelia Jones establishes a counter narrative to the prevailing oral histories of performance art, in her essay "'Presence' in Absentia: Experiencing Performance as Documentation," by arguing that the phenomenological intersubjective relationship between performer and spectator is equally intersubjective as the "documentary exchange" between a viewer/reader and a text or image.[5] She draws on Derrida's theory of the supplement to establish a relationship of lack between the body and the recording of an event that instantiates "an infinite chain, ineluctably multiplying the supplementary mediations that produce a sense of the very thing they defer."[6] Jones's work has proven influential in the field of art history, establishing definitive approaches to mediation and the work of the scholar that foreground the importance of documentation to research and interpretation as equal to and for some methods, superior to artists' narratives.

Performance scholar Philip Auslander theorizes two categories of performance art documentation: the *documentary* and the *theatrical*. *Documentary* images have an ontological relationship to events presented for spectators or listeners, while the *theatrical* may be performed, or staged specifically for the camera, without the presence of an audience.[7] In the theatrical, "the space of the document (whether audio or visual) thus becomes the only space in which the performance occurs" (2). Through J.L. Austin's theory of the performative utterance, Auslander argues that documenting a performance is a performative rather than constative action, "*the act of documenting an event as a performance is what constitutes it as such*" (5, original emphasis). Auslander thus develops a theory of documentation that rejects Phelan's ontology of performance in favor of a focus on phenomenological study of the relationship between the audience and the document: "the process by which the event, whether a performance or an exhibition, discloses itself to us through our engagement with its artifacts."[8]

For Auslander, the performance document is not a mere secondary representation, but a presentational space, where the event takes place for the viewer. By bringing the focus on the event to the phenomenology of its reception across recording media, Auslander opens an increasingly wide field of mediation to consider as documentation of performance art. His approach relies on his reading of Hans-Georg Gadamer's hermeneutic understanding of a work's contemporaneity with the present through its aesthetic relationship with a receiver. This is not an innate mode of consciousness, but Gadamer's definition of contemporaneity as a "task for consciousness," enacted by the viewer of works of art.[9] For Auslander, aesthetic works that are receptive to contemporaneity include performance documentation. Although most performance art is intended to be experienced by a live audience, much of its audience experiences it through the written scores, narratives, photography, or film or video recordings that are intentionally made to disseminate, preserve, and authenticate the artist's work. Marina Abramović, a pioneer of performance art and its documentation, offers an ideal example of the resilience of documentary film as an increasingly important form of performance documentation, as well as a flexible one that produces a multimodal phenomenology of reception. From the museum to the cinema, the text to the image, her *oeuvre* marks out a terrain of performance art documentation that has expanded its traditional forms of photographic, filmic, and audio recording to the adapted documentary film and other modes of transmission. Abramović's early adoption of video, as well as photography, to document her performances since the 1970s has resulted in a near-complete archive of her performances, which in Auslander's terminology includes both documentary and theatrical documentation. An excellent example of the theatrical document is Abramović's early work *Art Must Be Beautiful, Artist Must Be Beautiful* (1975), where she performs for the camera alone. In this, her first performance for video, the cameraperson was zooming in and out, thus continually changing the viewer's point of view. Dissatisfied with the result, Abramović had him leave the room after setting up a single shot that framed only her bust. Her extensive use of scores, photography, and video since that work have established an immense archive of performance documentation.

In 1988, Marina Abramović and Ulay, her partner in life and art, began the last of their collaborative works together, *The Lovers: The Great Wall Walk*, which ritualized an act of coming together a final time before ending their professional and intimate relationship. Once intended to conclude with a marriage, rather than the dissolution of their relationship, the artists walked towards each other from opposite ends of the Great Wall of China over a period of three months, meeting at Mount Erlang in Shaanxi province. Their relationship and performative charisma had developed in a series of multiple performances known as the *Relation Works* (1976–9), which explored the tensions and conflicts of male–female relationships through the medium of the body. With their visceral exploration of human relationships, the *Relation Works* are now recognized for their pioneering historical import, while *The Lovers: The Great Wall Walk* holds similar status, operating on the same principles of movement as the iconic *Relation in Space* (1976), the first of their *Relation Works* together. The epic scale of the performance in *The Lovers* required extensive negotiations with the Chinese government, and support from art institutions and diplomatic authorities in the Netherlands. The unusual nature of the long-duration performance eliminated the observation of art audiences and the conventional context of live reception. Primary documentation of the performance came through first-person observations in a catalog essay by Thomas McEvilley, a *Village Voice* article by Cynthia Carr, and photographs later exhibited in museums.[10] The artists walked accompanied at differing times by writers, Chinese nationals, and their respective translator/guides. A documentary film crew directed by Murray Grigor filmed elements of the performance, culminating in a 64-minute documentary titled *The Great Wall of China: Lovers at the Brink*, which screened at the International Festival of Films on Art in Montreal and was broadcast on the UK's Channel Four.

A producer and director of arts documentaries, Grigor collaborated with Abramović on the script, which departed from strict documentary and framed the event through a narrator, voiceover, and other scripted scenes including Chinese nationals. Some of these people appear in the storytelling and dream-like sequences of an Orientalist China that punctuate the film. The narrator, an elderly Chinese woman, introduces the walk in the mode of a nomadic storyteller who travels with a projector and screens films along her route. In voiceover, she identifies as a filmmaker who has gone blind, yet most wanted to make a film about strangers, "two aliens." Unable to make the film she intended, she envisions it in her mind while retracing the steps of the lovers; her vision introduces the artists. The film weaves the performance of the artists into mythological frames of Chinese folklore, adding aspects of the artists' Orientalist imagination as well as ethnographic research Abramović had conducted along the way. The scripted elements frame the film as a performative documentary, which is further underscored by fact that the footage is not of the performance, but elements of the walk reperformed for

Grigor's cameras. In this way, the documentary fits into Auslander's definition of theatrical performance documentation. While the unique circumstances of the walk along the wall precluded the spectatorship of a conventional art audience, the event was observed by officials and citizens along the way, rendering it documentary performance documentation. In response to the complexity of the question of audience and event, the film can be understood as both documentary and theatrical performance documentation. I define this emerging body of performance documents as *cinematic documentation*, where the performance is embedded within a documentary film. Unlike prior forms of documentation that lack specific qualities beyond their function as documents, cinematic documentation presents the work of art as the subject of another creative work that circulates in the cultural sphere of film and video. Unlike Auslander's forms of documentary or theatrical documentation, cinematic documentation often includes diegetic elements that establish a larger narrative around the documented performance or ephemeral artwork.

The film includes other scripted sequences of the artists' narrative voiceover of their walk, which aestheticize their individual interests and encounters with villagers along the way.[11] Ulay's preoccupation with his relationship to the land and people as a foreigner contrasts markedly with Abramović's interest in folklore, translated narratives on ethnographic subjects, and staged encounters with costumed performers acting out stories that she gathered during the walk. These performative aspects of the documentary heightened the mythological aspects of the work and its Orientalist image of ancient Chinese culture. As documentary, these highly performative elements of the film did not migrate into documentation of the performance within exhibition contexts, where the anti-theatrical approach to institutional and gallery performance art that defined Abramović and Ulay's practice continued to prevail. It was only in 2010 that Grigor's film was remastered and reedited for screening in the gallery space of Abramović's MoMA retrospective, *The Artist Is Present*. In its translation into an exhibition installation format edited from 16mm film and transferred to digital video, the 15-minute dual-channel installation of the work refines the film into a silent meditation on two bodies in a vast landscape. This newly created documentation from a documentary film heightens the dualistic and symmetrical aesthetic that defines many of the most important *Relation Works*. Grigor's film had itself emphasized this element of their work with a montage surveying selected *Relation Works* at the conclusion of the film. Other than selected scenes of Marina walking the wall surrounded by Chinese people in the touristy area of Badaling outside Beijing, no other people appear in 2010 documentation.

Ulay, in blue, and Marina, in red, traverse different climates and landscapes linking their performance to the sublime landscape and the architectural marvel that ranges across mainland China. From the eroding tamarisk and clay wall in the deserts of the Qin Dynasty wall in Gansu Province to the massive stone engineering of the Ming Dynasty wall surrounding Beijing, the document contrasts the bodies of the artists and their surroundings, while ranging across the same long stretch of earth, linked by the wall. As in Grigor's film, the installation eschews any semblance of contiguous geography or chronology in its organization of the landscape. The walks do not unfold over time and space, but are edited, recycled, and reorganized into formal harmonies, creating a symmetrical visual experience of the artists, rather than any real sense of their progress. The atemporality of the document's presentation of *The Lovers*, as documentary film, or installation as performance documentation, highlights the performative nature of the documentary approach, further underscored by the fact that the film itself is a reenactment of the walk for Grigor's cameras at selected locations in October of 1988, months after the conclusion of the original performance.[12] The dual-channel installation transforms Grigor's narrative into a contemporary multiscreen spectacle for the museum. Installed in the gallery high on the wall more than ten feet above the ground, the public engaged the work in a vastly different format than the original television documentary, where improved picture quality and editorial intervention have produced documentation that reflects Abramović's aesthetic in the twenty-first century.

The atemporality of documentary film as performance art documentation is a part of the challenge and accomplishment of director Babette Mangolte's *Seven Easy Pieces*, a ninety-minute film distilling Abramović's forty-nine-hour, seven-night performance at the Guggenheim Museum in New York City. Each night for seven hours, the artist performed one of five historical works by other artists she esteemed, one of her own past works, and a new performance as a part of the 2005 edition of the performance biennial, Performa.[13] A filmmaker especially well known for her cinematography for Chantal Akerman and Michael Snow, Mangolte is a major figure in performance documentation, having filmed and photographed important works by Trisha Brown, Yvonne Rainer, and Joan Jonas.[14] Mangolte's approach to the performance is linear, precise, detailed, and condensed. She intended to show the artist's body living the strictures of each piece "with details that outline the body's fragility, versatility, tenacity, and unlimited endurance."[15] The long duration of Abramović's performed interpretations of works by Bruce Nauman, Vito Acconci, Valie Export, Gina Pane, and Joseph Beuys required extreme endurance and physical testing of the body's limits, which are defining features of the artist's own *oeuvre*. The works involved attenuated use of the body in many different challenging actions, including pressing the body with force against a solid object, masturbation, full-frontal display of her genitals while holding a gun, lying in fireproof clothing on a bed of iron above lit candles, and intimate contact with a dead hare. Her recreation of these well-known performances constelled a number of important issues in the history of performance since they were based on performed events with limited documentation.

The question of document and documentary have polarized scholars and critics with regard to the film *Seven Easy Pieces*. Iain Millar's review declared Mangolte's film neither document nor documentary, occupying the position that, "to perceive the real power of Abramović's work, there is no alternative to actually being there."[16] Robert Blackson deploys the vocabulary of re-performance and reenactment to argue a strong counterpoint, acknowledging Mangolte as a "famed" documentarian.[17] His work recognizes the role the event has in affirming Auslander's phenomenology and refuting Phelan's ontology. As document, he assesses the strength of Mangolte's expert camera work as "slick color films that could eventually stand in for the original works," known mainly through black-and-white photographs, text, and oral histories (39). Nancy Spector's curation of the event involved immediate presentation of Mangolte's footage, situating documentary and its role in the institutionalization of performance from the outset. Blackson observes the image-making dimension of Abramović's performance in the flat screens positioned behind the stage displaying recordings of the previous nights' performances (39).

The direct-to-exhibition cycle of Mangolte's footage in the museum added a technological presence during the original performance not included in Mangolte's film. Her intense focus on the ritualistic repetition of Abramović's performance resonates in image and sound, with audience reaction and close attention to the artist's body, resulting in an intimate view of the event as strictly embodied. Views of Frank Lloyd Wright's rotunda emphasize site-specificity and throngs of visitors, while maintaining focal awareness of the artist as the center of the document. The exquisite clarity of the documentation of sound from a microphone hung in the center of the performance space reverberated through the architecture, establishing a rich, multisensory experience of the event rarely accomplished in performance documentation.[18] Such subtleties receded as the institutionalization of Abramović proceeded at her MoMA retrospective. Klaus Beisenbach's curation of the retrospective presented all seven performances simultaneously in the last gallery of the exhibition, allowing the performances to compete, as much as coexist in the space. The force of Abramović's own work was observable in the gallery as the public crowded with rapt attention around the screen showing her re-performance of her own *Lips of Thomas* (1975/2005). In one of her most harrowing performances, she cuts a five-pointed star on her abdomen with a razor blade, self-flagellates with an imposing leather cat-o'-nine-tails, and lays on a bed of ice in the form of a crucifix (Figure 6.1).

FIGURE 6.1 *Seven Easy Pieces*
(Babette Mangolte, 2007)

106 Chanda Laine Carey

Mangolte's film condenses the grueling seven-hour performance to twenty-seven minutes of rhythmic repetition, following Abramović through the cycles of action that become bloodier with each iteration. The nude body of the artist holds the space in the museum and lens of the camera with charismatic magnetism, confidence, bare emotion, mastery of dramatic tension, and a penetrating, yet distant, gaze. The imagery of indelible moments of the violence of the blade, freezing ice, and the whip circulate around the emotional center of the performance when Abramović occupies the front of the stage, picks up a razor blade, and carefully cuts a single line on her belly. This cycle of actions repeats eight times during the seven-hour performance, condensed, but not softened, by Mangolte's editing. Under the watchful eye of the camera, Mangolte closely observes as Abramović spreads the skin to draw dripping blood to the surface, dabs the drops on a white flag she ties to her walking stick from *The Lovers*, and waves it as a religious-patriotic song of her native Yugoslavia plays. During the performance, the camera follows Abramović's face, the form of her body, and the precision of her gestures to capture much of the experience of presence. Rather than the fixed frame of Abramović's earlier video documentation, Mangolte's direction reproduces the details of a roving eye. Her close-ups bring the viewer as close as if they were using the telescope Abramović has installed in multiple exhibitions.

After Mangolte's close observation of each cut that Abramović makes in her belly, the patriotic song of national sacrifice to which she listens accentuates the camera's focus on her concurrent facial expressions. The act of cutting and listening to the music is the center of a repeating cycle that gains emotional force as the five cuts that make up the form of a star are completed. The agonizing spectacle is not over, and the camera documents the repetitive precision of Abramović's performance and Mangolte's direction through the end of the performance. As hours passed, Abramović used a new blade for each cut, and the performance closes with a close up of eight used blades carefully lined up at the front of the stage. As document and documentary in an exhibition context, Mangolte's film of *Lips of Thomas* pulled the crowd more strongly than any others, underscoring the differences between experiencing film in theatrical and gallery contexts, which Mangolte theorizes in her essay "Black Box, White Cube: Installations and the Film Experience."[19] The filmmaker distills the experience to one factor: choice. In the gallery, the viewer chooses what to look at and for how long, while the theater is a commitment to the full narrative of the work and undivided attention for its duration. Recognizing the varied and portable access of the digital age and its devices, she notes the changing experience of film and fragmentation of its narrative or fundamental temporal structure (186). The fragmentation of the narrative structure of a film provides one of the best-known documents of Abramović's performance.

Two former lovers sit across from each other, reenacting a tableau they performed together ninety times two decades earlier (Figure 6.2). The striking woman in a long red gown gazes impassively, holding her expression steady until overwhelmed by emotion. As tears stream down her cheeks, Abramović reaches across the table to grasp the hands of Ulay, breaking the strictures of her performance and recognizing

FIGURE 6.2 *The Artist is Present*
(Matthew Akers, 2012)

the affective and professional enormity of the moment. This scene from the documentary film *Marina Abramović: The Artist Is Present* has been viewed more than sixteen million times on YouTube and used as a music video viewed more than thirty-four million times.[20] It has also been reposted and linked to myriad internet stories romanticizing the reunion of the former collaborators and life partners in performance art. By comparison, the MoMA Flickr photostream of the exhibition has logged fewer than 1.8 million views to date.[21] While the clip was not intended as documentation of the work of art and has not been exhibited in galleries or museum contexts, this snippet of documentary film may be the most indelible and well-known document of Abramović's monumental performance. It enters the realm of *cinematic* documentation through the internet, rather than through curatorial strategy.

Marina Abramović: The Artist Is Present, Abramović's retrospective exhibition and concurrent 716.5-hour performance at MoMA, confirmed her importance to the history of art and catapulted her to a global level of fame. The Abramović phenomenon of long-duration performance art, blockbuster exhibition, viral internet sensation, and massive media exposure were followed in 2012 with Akers's documentary film, also titled *Marina Abramović: The Artist Is Present,* and filmed during Abramović's preparation for the exhibition and landmark performance. The success of Akers's film on the international film festival circuit, subsequent theatrical release, and wide distribution on HBO and streaming services placed performance art at the center of the robust genre of documentary films about contemporary artists. The polyvalent reception of the Marina and Ulay documentary film clip alters the taxonomy of performance art documentation, as defined by Auslander's innovative framework: "Performance art documentation participates in the fine art tradition of the reproduction of *works* rather than the ethnographic tradition of capturing *events*."[22] Documentary films about art often situate works of art with in a context of ethnographic events, conflating the discrete forms. The simultaneity of event and work in a context of fine art and ethnography demonstrates the increasing importance of documentary film to ephemeral contemporary art and its documentation, necessitating the new category of *cinematic* documentation. Cinematic documentation acknowledges the coexistence of these two types of documentary subject through narrative structure and editing.

Akers's documentary captures several poignant moments in the long-duration performance *The Artist Is Present*. It anchors documentary film in the museum as not only its subject, but the documentary film as an object of the main exhibition. Six floors above the Marron Atrium where Akers filmed Abramović, eight major performances captured by moving-image documentarians were exhibited to the public as her art. Theoretically, the difference between performance art document and documentary film is wide enough that they do not intersect. Films of performance made by artists like Mangolte focus on the work of art, while documentarians of narrative films invest heavily in the production and events that precede and surround a work of art. Yet at MoMA, documents and documentary film occupied the same exhibition context. They coexisted within that groundbreaking exhibition that constellated numerous debates in performance and exhibition strategies including re-performance. Through Abramović, documentary film has migrated out of the space of adjunct event to the exhibition and into the main galleries.

The fragmentation of the digital audience by the viewing choices of the individual prevails in the era of Netflix and YouTube, where documentaries about artists proliferate under the aegis of multifarious production companies. As Mangolte observes, audience attention and the experience of film is fragmented outside of the black box. Remarkably, *The Artist Is Present* garnered a wide audience in several contexts, including streaming digital video, where films, including *As Is by Nick Cave* (Evan Falbaum, 2016) and the Netflix-produced *Sky Ladder: The Art of Cai Guo-Qiang* (Kevin Macdonald, 2016), use the prevailing model of the contemporary art documentary, giving it the title of the artwork it records and following the artist through the development and completion of that work. All three films reflect the current interest of documentarians in contemporary art manifested as ephemeral event. The interpersonal and dramatic narratives created by the filmmakers in these works depend on musical soundtracks at the climax of each film, the realization of the subject's work of art. This insertion of music superimposes emotive cues that contrast with the artist's intentions, foregrounding the filmmaker's perception of a lack in the work of art that requires supplementation, or covering the sound of the natural space altogether. Unlike Mangolte's documentation strategy as a filmmaker, the experience of ambient sound is overwhelmed, when not completely cancelled, by music that is at times dissonant with the artists' aesthetic and the events being displayed. Editing techniques also introduce the prevalence of the heavy hand of some filmmakers with dependence on quick cutting, slow motion, and other effects that superimpose the narrative concerns and aesthetic of the filmmaker to the detriment of the artwork and its cohesiveness.

Presumptions about the attention span of the audience may be significant factors in the differences between some documentarians' encounters with the work of art. As a temporal experience of a different sort of attenuated attention, the importance of long duration to Abramović's performance works can in some ways be more clearly conveyed by still photography than the montage of participant faces favored by Akers at the end of *The Artist Is Present*. Still photography is a mainstay of Abramović's approach to mediating and commodifying her increasingly marketable work. *The Artist Is Present* was officially photographed by Marco Anelli, whose portraits were widely seen through the MoMA Flickr photostream, increasing awareness of the performance during its seventy-two-day length. Akers's montage of sitters in the documentary differs significantly from Anelli's photographic work, favoring engaging smiles rather than the complex and frequently tearful engagements captured by the photographer. Anelli's presence matched the entire length of Abramović's performance, while Akers shot most of the footage of sitters in the documentary over a few days with great emphasis on the first and last days of the performance. Anelli's contributions to Abramović photography reaches into numerous contexts, including another documentary about the artist.

The importance of Anelli to Abramović's recent work is hardly visible in Marco del Fiol's documentary *The Space In Between: Marina Abramović in Brazil*. The feature-length documentary follows Abramović on a journey of spiritual tourism through Brazil. She visits world famous faith healer João de Deus, a syncretic religious community at Vale do Amanhecer, 108-year-old Candomble leader and traditional herbalist Mãe Filhinha, and partakes of ayahuasca, not once but twice. Abramović's excruciating bad trip during her first experience with the powerful psychoactive drink did not deter the intrepid artist, who demonstrated her penchant for facing fears and testing her limits by repeating the exploration of ayahuasca a second time with a shamanic guide. She is documented at the center of private nude rituals that involved being covered in verdant flora, smeared with healing mud, bathed with water, then rubbed all over with raw eggs – finally breaking them with her bare hands.

Interspersed with these visits are Abramović's expeditions into the Brazilian landscape, enacting her idealization of contact with nature. The artist contrasts nature with urban life as a place of wholeness that does not need art. During the documentary, the viewer accompanies Abramović to massive caves, dramatic vistas, freshwater pools, and lush waterfalls where she performs for the camera. Only at one location does Anelli appear in his role as photographer, at Chapada dos Veadeiros National Park in Goiás state (Figure 6.3). Del Fiol includes him within the frame as the photographer directs the artist's gestures, while she is drenched in the immense, roaring falls while wearing a long, thin white gown. This dramatic shot cuts to Abramović alone in the falls in slow motion, with her hands slowly sweeping over her face. Muted water sounds and an ambient score accompany the shot, which ends with her hands poised on each side of her head – a brief performative moment attenuated for film. This vignette and others in the built environment are, in fact, alternative documents to those Abramović presents as art in the photographic series *Places of Power* (2013–15) and *The Current* (2013), resulting in a body of work that

FIGURE 6.3 *The Space In Between: Marina Abramović in Brazil*
(Marco del Fiol, 2016)

fits Auslander's definition of *theatrical* documentation but was created in a context of *cinematic* documentation. While the secondary purpose of the trip is never detailed, Abramović's travel is similar to other journeys to far-flung parts of the globe in search of the experience that inspires much of her art. While no footage from del Fiol's film has been presented in exhibition contexts, the similarity of his shots with Anelli's photographs for the gallery gives access to Abramović's performance in other varied contexts governed by the selective and fragmented conditions of the digital sphere.[23]

The range of performance captured by documentarians has been complicated by its migration into the gallery and onto the internet. Performance without a conventional audience has gone beyond the performances Auslander referred to when he wrote,

> the identity of documented performances as performances is not dependent on the presence of an initial audience ... we cannot dismiss studio fabrications of one sort from another category of performance because they were not performed for a physically present audience.[24]

The site-specificity of Abramović's performances and other ephemeral contemporary art events result in performance documents that benefit from the participation of the film documentarian as an alternative audience with a highly sophisticated approach to time-based media. When documentary follows the contemporary artist, the sense of place as both local and global comes to the fore as expanded access and distribution increase art audiences.

Phenomenologically, the circulation of documentary films about contemporary art beyond the festival circuit, through such disparate contexts as social media and streaming services mark the use of Abramović documentaries in museum galleries as distinctive. The gallery raises the film into the circles of high art, while digital media democratize and fragment their images. The use of film in the gallery expands the recognized forms of performance art documentation, and reframes documentary film as a central element in curatorial practice. As both exhibition and documented performance, *The Artist Is Present* stands as a landmark moment in the relationship of documentary film to performance documentation, when exhibition and production converged in the first retrospective of a performance artist at MoMA. When documentary film in the museum emerges from its usual place in special programs and adjuncts to main exhibition, opportunity arises to look more critically at the strategies documentarians use to narrate and interpret the production and history of art. Through the eye of the editor and the curator a sustainable relationship is emerging that may continue to bring film out of the collateral events to exhibitions and increase the visibility of documentary film in the gallery as *cinematic* documentation.

Notes

1 Julian Stallabrass, ed., *Documentary* (London: Whitechapel Gallery; Cambridge, MA: MIT Press, 2013); T.J. Demos, *The Migrant Image: The Art and Politics of Documentary during Global Crisis* (Durham, NC: Duke University Press, 2013); Jill Daniels, ed., *Truth, Dare or Promise: Art and Documentary Revisited* (Newcastle upon Tyne: Cambridge Scholars Publishing, 2013).
2 Abramović documentaries have also exceeded the realm of performance art, including an intimate portrait for German television in the early 1990s and *Bob Wilson's the Life & Death of Marina Abramović* (Giada Colagrande, 2012), a documentary focused on the production of an opera about Abramović's life.
3 Walter Benjamin, "Thirteen Theses against Snobs," in *Walter Benjamin: Selected Writings*, vol. 1, 1913–26, ed. Walter Benjamin and Michael W. Jennings (Cambridge, MA: Belknap Press, 1996), 459.
4 Peggy Phelan, "The Ontology of Performance: Representation without Reproduction," in *Unmarked: The Politics of Performance* (London: Routledge, 1993), 146–66.
5 Amelia Jones, "'Presence' in Absentia: Experiencing Performance as Documentation," *Art Journal* 56, no. 4 (1997): 12.
6 Cited in Jones, 14.
7 Philip Auslander, "The Performativity of Performance Documentation," *PAJ: A Journal of Performance and Art* 28, no. 3 (2006): 1–2.
8 Philip Auslander, "Pictures of an Exhibition," in *Between Zones: On the Representation of the Performative and the Notation of Movement*, ed. Raphael Gygax and Heike Munder (Zurich : JRP/Ringier, 2010), 271.
9 Hans-Georg Gadamer, *Truth and Method*, 2nd ed., trans. Joel Weinsheimer and Donald G. Marshall (London: Continuum, 2004), 123–4.
10 Thomas McEvilley, "Great Walk Talk," in *The Lovers*, ed. Marina Abramović and Ulay (Amsterdam: Stedelijk Museum, 1989); Cynthia Carr, "A Great Wall," in *On Edge: Performance at the End of the Twentieth Century*, rev. ed (Middletown, CT: Wesleyan University Press, 2008), 25–48.
11 James Westcott, *When Marina Abramović Dies: A Biography* (Cambridge, MA: MIT Press, 2010), 212.

12 Westcott, *When Marina Abramović Dies*, 209.
13 Marina Abramović, *Seven Easy Pieces* (Milan; New York, NY: Charta, 2007).
14 Barbara Clausen, "Babette Mangolte: Performing Histories: Why the Point Is Not to Make a Point …, " *Afterall* no. 23 (2010): 35, 41.
15 Babette Mangolte, "Director's Statement," in *Seven Easy Pieces*, DVD (Houston, TX: Microcinema International, 2010).
16 Iain Millar, "Abramović Passes Latest Endurance Test," *Art Newspaper* 21, no. 236 (2012): 63.
17 Robert Blackson, "Once More … With Feeling: Reenactment in Contemporary Art and Culture," *Art Journal* 66, no. 1 (Spring 2007): 39.
18 The use of microphones to amplify and record sound in the *Relation Works* is important to their aesthetic, yet not accomplished with the quality of Mangolte's production.
19 Babette Mangolte, "Black Box, White Cube: Installations and the Film Experience," in *Truth, Dare or Promise*, 197.
20 MiticoMazz, "Marina Abramović E Ulay – MoMA 2010," accessed December 15, 2012, www.youtube.com/watch?v=OS0Tg0IjCp4; How I Became The Bomb, "How I Became The Bomb – Ulay, Oh | Music Video," accessed October 8, 2017, www.youtube.com/watch?v=CAID_2iKO5Y.
21 "Marina Abramović: The Artist Is Present – Portraits," Flickr, accessed May 15, 2019, www.flickr.com/photos/themuseumofmodernart/sets/72157623741486824.
22 Auslander, "The Performativity of Performance Documentation," 6.
23 The distribution of the film differs from past Abramović documentaries. After selective screenings and a tour of the festival circuit, the film has only been available for purchase or rental in the US and Europe through Vimeo or iTunes (Australia was the only territory with a DVD release).
24 Auslander, "The Performativity of Performance Documentation," 7.

7
GAINED IN TRANSLATION

Site-specificity in recent documentaries

Vera Brunner-Sung

Visual documentation has been a vital component of site-specific art since its inception as a contemporary practice in the late 1960s. At the time, artists were leaving their urban studios and gallery spaces behind to create work in the dramatic landscapes of the American West. Land art or Earthworks, as it came to be known, required the physical presence of the viewer, yet was often ephemeral or difficult to access, and thus relied on images to corroborate its existence. Early films on site-specific work were often personal or experimental in nature: Robert Smithson's *Spiral Jetty* (1970), which brings viewers into a poetic interweaving of the concept and process behind his eponymous earthwork; Nancy Holt's *Sun Tunnels* (1978), an observation of the process and installation of her eponymous project; the made-for-German-television *Land Art* (Gerry Schum, 1969), which staged the creation of a series of projects for the camera to produce a kind of televised *vernissage*.

Site-specificity as a practice has continued to develop, and in recent years a growing number of documentaries have been made on site-specific artworks and artist practices, shown in theatrical settings and geared toward audiences beyond the art world who may be less familiar with the form. This chapter examines the formal and narrative strategies utilized by these filmmakers, myself included, to interpret notions of site-specificity in artists' work. It finds that filmmakers operate not only as observers, but may serve an important collaborative function for certain types of projects. In addition, while they generally strive to bring the viewer to a more proximate understanding of an artist's intent as in the case of most art documentaries, their films occasionally challenge intent by reframing the nature of an artwork's site.

Models of site-specificity

Site-specific art as practiced today is richly complex, and not informed solely by the land art movement. Around the same time that some were abandoning art world spaces, others chose to examine them more closely. In an approach that came to be known as institutional critique, artists used sculpture, performance, and other means to expose the hidden social, political, and economic conditions of exhibition venues. Today, the notion of "site" has expanded further, with artists creating work in a wide variety of locations beyond the art world to engage with social issues, popular culture, and political and academic discourses. Art historian Miwon Kwon has defined three models of site-specificity that provide useful guidance in discussing this wide-ranging form.[1] She identifies the practice of the land artists and others who assert an inherent bond between the artwork and its location as *phenomenological*. This work also requires the viewer's physical presence for its completion and presumes a "universal viewing subject" inherited from modernism (13). Institutional critique falls under the *social/institutional* model, which takes into account not only the physical attributes of a site, but its cultural context. The spectator in this case is recognized as a subjective being in possession of a specific social identity based on gender, race, class, sexuality, etc. The third practice is what Kwon terms the *discursive* model. She observes that in their triangulation between place, culture, and theory, such works are no longer exclusively bound to a physical site. Rather, they are located in "a field of knowledge, intellectual exchange, or cultural debate" (26). Additionally, Kwon notes that phenomenological, social/institutional, and discursive site-specificity are not mutually exclusive; an artist's practice may engage with one, all, or some (3–4).

Documentaries on British sculptor Andy Goldsworthy and German artist Anselm Kiefer provide insight into techniques used by filmmakers to represent phenomenological site-specific works. *Rivers and Tides* (Thomas Riedelsheimer, 2000) documents Goldsworthy's practice of working in natural landscapes, where he constructs what are often ephemeral sculptures out of site-specific materials such as ice, rocks, and leaves. *Over Your Cities Grass Will Grow* (Sophie Fiennes, 2010) captures Kiefer's creation of a mysterious, massive complex of structures, tunnels, and cells at an abandoned factory in southern France. Both films are "pure" artist-centered films, guided or structured around the artist's on-camera interview and/or voiceover; neither includes interviews with outside experts. And while we see Kiefer addressing his assistants in *Over Your Cities*, both films offer no more than a cursory acknowledgement (through a brief interview or silent presence within the frame) of any facilitators or collaborators on their work. In other words, the artists are shown to work in relative isolation, ensconced in a kind of private universe indicative of their socially hermetic practices.

As with their land artist forebears, Goldsworthy's and Kiefer's sites are so remote that, aside from creating a record of their projects' existence and their personal creative visions, the films provide an audience with a basic level of access to both the artists and the work itself. Accompanied by avant-garde musical scores imparting a meditative or brooding tone, both films are heavily observational and rely on long takes and slow camera movements. Steven Jacobs has discussed the vital function of camera movement to animate static sculpture and allow the audience visual access to all sides of a three-dimensional work;[2] indeed, movement as applied by Riedelsheimer and Fiennes serves primarily to simulate a physical encounter with the work. In addition, the use of duration and movement help to convey the physical labor and concentration of the artists as they manipulate or struggle in real time with their materials.

With its *vérité* approach, Albert Maysles and Antonio Ferrera's *The Gates* (2007) is a stark contrast in form: a hand-held camera and brisk editing are used to chronicle the over-twenty-year process of realizing Christo and Jeanne-Claude's eponymous two-week installation of thousands of saffron-colored fabric panels along paths in New York's Central Park. These artists are not isolated geniuses; rather, we witness them about in the world, having discussions with city bureaucrats, attending contentious public meetings, and performing site visits; fabricating materials; participating in press conferences; and connecting with the collaborators integral to the execution their project. The pacing is lively; occasional musical interludes add energy and excitement. Throughout, we observe and encounter members of the public in the park; their day-to-day activities and reactions to the project develop a sense of both physical and social "site" for the viewer. But once the artists' structures are installed and unveiled, the energy and tone of the film become more tranquil. The artists' presence recedes, making space for the finished work and the public's engagement. The camera is more often set on a tripod, using strategically executed moves to capture shifting light, weather conditions, and human activity in and around the installation – similar to the phenomenological strategies cited above. The soundscape remains primarily ambient, heightening the awareness of wind, rain, and spectators' voices.

While the film does not rely exclusively on Christo and Jeanne-Claude's narration, its attention to both the social/institutional and phenomenological aspects of their project is largely in accordance with their artistic intent. The pair often face bureaucratic and political obstacles due to the ambitious scale and public context of their projects, and thus they consider this encounter with state and society an important aspect of their practice.[3] The artists have mounted several "documentation exhibitions" over the years which display the chronology of their efforts and that of their collaborators. The moving image, of course, is able to capture this aspect of their work with more immediacy, and the pair developed a long-term relationship with Maysles (and his brother David) to create short films documenting previous projects.[4] And yet the self-described phenomenological dimension of their work remains vitally important. As Christo states in the film:

> We live in a terrible century of banalization and trivialization. Of repetitious things. [...] And we, the humans, like to experience something unique. Once in a lifetime, if never again. All our projects have this type of quality, that if you missed them, you will never see them.

Their investment in the social/institutional aspect of their work notwithstanding, Christo and Jeanne-Claude ultimately seek to create transcendent, ephemeral experiences for anyone and everyone, regardless of background – the kind of "universal subject" posited by Kwon's phenomenological model. The sequences documenting *The Gates* in its completed form honor this sensory encounter with the work, just as Riedelsheimer and Fiennes do in their films. The one point of tension to emerge relates to Jeanne-Claude's somewhat surprising assertion that she and Christo do not care about audience response. Regardless, the filmmakers diligently document the opinions of members of the public. This cacophony of voices contributes to the development of the social/institutional site of the park, while also capturing the work's discursivity: the debate it generates on the value of art to society. The filmmakers' inclusion of this otherwise invisible and unacknowledged (by the artists) "site" in the film is a small act of rebellion that expands the artwork beyond the boundaries defined by the artists.

Lucy Walker's film *Waste Land* (co-directed by João Jardim and Karen Harley, 2010) documents *Pictures of Garbage*, a project by Brazilian artist Vik Muniz. Though consisting in part of photographic art objects, the project is most accurately described as a social/institutional and discursive site-specific work. Celebrated for his photographs of images created out of sugar, dirt, and other unusual materials, Muniz embarked on the project to make portraits of *catadores*, workers who scavenge recyclable items from Rio de Janeiro's largest landfill. His goal from the outset went beyond photography: he invited his subjects to become active collaborators in the construction of their images, not only posing for his camera but also being paid to collect and arrange waste materials to recreate these portraits at a massive scale, which Muniz then re-photographed. At the outset of the film, Muniz says of his intent, "What I really want to do is to be able to change the lives of a group of people." He continues, "It wouldn't just be an experience in how art could change people, but also, can it change people? Can it, can this be done, and what would be the effect of this?" For the artist, then, *Pictures of Garbage* consists not just of the final photographs, but also of the effect that the process has on its participants and the latter's ramifications for the power of art.

True to the discursive model, Muniz has chosen a site outside the art world – the landfill – not to create a transcendent experience for viewers in the phenomenological mode, but to impact the lives of its workers, who are among the most destitute members of Brazilian society. Muniz, who grew up poor in São Paulo, is shown to be motivated by an earnest critique of social hierarchy in his home country. "It's horrible how people really believe – and I am talking about educated people – they really believe they are better than other people," he tells the camera with evident disgust. In an extension of the project's site into the social/institutional realm of what he describes as the "very exclusive, very restrictive" art world, Muniz sells the finished images at auction and donates the proceeds back to the workers. The sale of the workers' portraits (constructed out of waste materials) functions as an implicit critique of how value is assigned to both objects and people in capitalist society.

With its preponderance of observational footage, *Waste Land* finds kinship with *The Gates*. A hand-held camera follows the artist, his assistants, and the project participants as they navigate the site of the landfill, their homes and neighborhoods, the artist's studio, and the auction house in London. But Walker deviates from orthodox *vérité* with the incorporation of talking-head interviews, slow motion, and time-lapse (used to capture the creation of the images); her approach is in fact closer to Bill Nichols' more broadly defined "participatory mode."[5] Ultimately, it is *Waste Land*'s narrative strategy that translates the discursive nature of Muniz's project: the interweaving of sequences where individual participants discuss their lives and, later on, articulate the project's impact on their outlook and sense of self-worth. Shot mostly in close-up, these moments, the longest just over five minutes, transform them from object to subject. Positioned as protagonists in their own right, overcoming obstacles and transforming in significant ways, they temporarily eclipse Muniz's presence in the film and affirm his inquiry into the power and value of art. The fact that the project's fundamental discursive site is imperceptible to viewers of the photographs speaks to the vital role of the filmmaker here. She is not merely an observer, but like Maysles and Ferrara, a collaborative agent helping to make visible the full scope of the work of art.

A filmmaker's perspective: *Fallen Star*

From the beginning, *Fallen Star: Finding Home* (2016), which I directed and produced with Valerie Stadler, was aligned with this notion of the filmmaker as artist's collaborator. Renowned for his architectural fabric sculptures, Do Ho Suh has been making work about home, displacement, and personal space since he came to the US from South Korea in the 1990s. When he approached us about filming *Fallen Star* (2012), his ambitious new installation for the Stuart Collection on the campus of the University of California, San Diego (UCSD), he was undergoing a dramatic shift in his practice, coming to see the often complex process behind his projects as more important than the resulting objects. Suh had already been working with videographers to create short pieces documenting the fabrication of his works, which he would present on monitors or project in gallery spaces alongside the finished objects during exhibitions. Until recently, these videos hewed closely to the formal strictures of the phenomenological mode cited above. The project at UCSD, however, was far greater in scope than any of his previous undertakings and Suh was interested in both documentation for his archives as well as the potential for a longer, more complex film. Beyond requesting that we capture his process, he was largely hands-off regarding the documentary's shape; he considered it a "commission" for us under his auspices as executive producer.

Years in development, Suh's *Fallen Star* touches on all three models of site-specificity. Physically, it consists of a functional cottage and garden perched at an angle on the edge of a campus building. Its pale-blue structure is a scaled replica of a house from Suh's memory of his time studying in New England; inside, the furnishings and décor are quaint and cozy, but in a phenomenological manifestation of the unease of displacement, there are no plumb lines or right angles. It brings Suh's creative interests into dialogue with the social/institutional site of the campus, an "artificial environment" wherein people have to generate their own sense of belonging. Still, with Suh's reprioritization of process, his interest with *Fallen Star* was not just to bring viewers into the physical site of the work, but to generate unique and perhaps even transformative opportunities for those involved behind the scenes. An exceptional feat of engineering and construction, the project required that the cottage be built on the ground and lifted by crane to a seventh-story roof; he needed the assistance of, among others, a project supervisor, an architect, a structural engineer, a construction crew, and crane specialists to complete it. "I was just a catalyst or conduit to give them an opportunity to do something like this," he says in the film of his collaborators. "Often I think that this art, work of art, is some kind of excuse," he continues, "and that the more important thing is how you reach that goal." In locating the most important part of the project in a field of knowledge or exchange between individuals, Suh indicates the primacy of the project's discursivity.

Understanding the discursive qualities of Suh's practice helped us determine that our film would center not just on the finished installation and Suh's voice, but on process and collaborators' perspectives. We also decided that, just as the artwork itself touches laypeople's lives, the audience for the film, too, should extend beyond the art world. With these aims in mind, it became apparent that the overarching question we ought to answer was: what made this crazy project possible? Over several years, we filmed interviews with key collaborators, students, administrators, and staff at the university, and documented the evolution of the house and garden. As we pored over our footage with our editor, Tamara Maloney, collaborators' identification with the themes of Suh's project, their professionalism, and their sense of camaraderie were evident, thus enabling us to answer the "how" and "why" of the project's realization. We used a wide array of camera angles (and cameras) to capture the construction, lift, landscaping, decorating, and maintenance of the project. Attentive to the odd proportions and mind-bending position of the structure, we used Steadicam and aerial drone footage to convey a sense of its dramatic spatial orientation.

We encountered a key manifestation of Suh's discursive interests while seeking sources of narrative tension to generate excitement in the storytelling. While most of our interview subjects were art world insiders or white-collar elites, one, construction superintendent Don Franken, was a relative outsider who initially spoke skeptically about the value of the artwork even as he worked overtime for its successful realization. Franken was also at the center of the most obvious moment of tension in the film: the dramatic hoisting of the cottage. Following a sequence that demonstrates the elegance and apparent ease of the cottage lift (Figure 7.1), we show it again from Franken's point of view. Although Suh's voice dominates much of the film, we give over narration here to Franken. Observational and body-camera footage accompany his description of the immense pressure he felt, working with the crane operator to get the thirty-five-ton, odd-angled cottage up to the roof safely, and then fitted into its bearings, which he had designed. Accompanied

FIGURE 7.1 *Fallen Star: Finding Home* (Vera Brunner-Sung and Valerie Stadler, 2016). Courtesy of the Artist and Stuart Collection, University of California, San Diego. © Do Ho Suh

by suspenseful music, this section functions as the climax of the film, resolving with the successful landing of the cottage and Franken, observed on the rooftop just moments afterward, recounting to crew members how he told his wife he would either be "a hero or a zero" on this day (Figure 7.2). He adds, "[T]here's certain days in your career where you either shine or you don't. This was one of them." His self-described heroic turn demonstrates how *Fallen Star* gave him an unprecedented opportunity to prove his tenacity and skill.

When Franken surprised us in a later interview with a revelation on the meaning of art, we knew immediately that this was a vital transformation to include in our film. Interviewed prior to the lift in his on-site office trailer, Franken says,

> Most people just think it's a waste of money. I mean, it's over a million dollars for something that, it's this house that, like, nobody can live in it […] I mean, what is it really doing for humanity? Take that million dollars and go feed the homeless.

But in an interview following the project's completion, Franken, now seated inside the finished artwork, says:

> You know, I just think that this place, this house is going to serve many purposes that will probably never be fully understood. And that's what makes it different. You know, it's unspecific. Maybe that's what art is, unspecific. See, I'm a very specific guy. When I build a hospital it's to heal people, right. There's no, there's no two meanings about that hospital […] This here was unique. Because it means something different to different people.

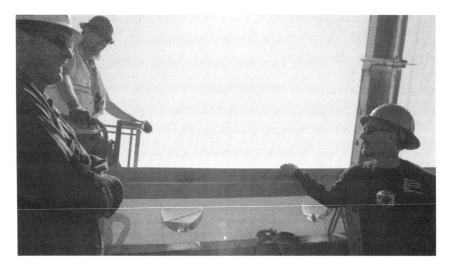

FIGURE 7.2 *Fallen Star: Finding Home* (Vera Brunner-Sung and Valerie Stadler, 2016). Courtesy of the Artist and Stuart Collection, University of California, San Diego. © Do Ho Suh

Here, Franken harkens back to his initial skepticism – which he attributed to "most people" but quickly became personal ("I mean, what is it really doing for humanity?") – and articulates a newfound appreciation not only for *Fallen Star*, but for art in general. For us as filmmakers, Franken's epiphany was a profound discovery, the kind of meaningful transformation one always hopes to encounter. It is an intangible iteration of the *Fallen Star* project captured by the film, and perhaps even made possible by it.

In documenting the making of *Fallen Star*, Stadler and I were able to go beyond the nuts and bolts of how the project was created to demonstrate *where* the work exists. Franken's and other individuals' experiences and reflections on their involvement speak to a site that is not physical, but located within the challenges, thoughts, and ideas generated by people's participation. Without our film, as in the case of *Waste Land* and Muniz's *Pictures of Garbage*, this would remain largely invisible.

Site reimagined in *Levitated Mass*

Across a variety of practices and models of site, the films discussed thus far demonstrate a general adherence to the artist's intent, asserting the value of the work of art in accordance with the vision of its creator(s). *Rivers and Tides* and *Over Your Cities Grass Will Grow* provide intimate access to their artists' process and concepts. The inclusion of public comment notwithstanding, the bifurcated structure of *The Gates* that honors process and result aligns with Christo and Jeanne-Claude's conception of their practice; in *Waste Land* and *Fallen Star: Finding Home*, the attention to project participants' voices reflects the artists' discursive aims. But what if the site of most interest to the filmmaker diverges from that defined by the artist? What are the implications of looking beyond the artist's intent? These questions are prompted by Doug Pray's film *Levitated Mass* (2013), which documents a large-scale permanent installation at the Los Angeles County Museum of Art (LACMA) by land art pioneer Michael Heizer.

Renowned for his so-called negative sculptures, Heizer's monumental marks in and upon the landscape shift the viewer's perception of time and space, characteristic of a practice firmly rooted in Kwon's phenomenological model of site-specificity. His project *Double Negative* (1969–70) involved the excavation of two massive trenches on the edge of a high desert mesa; *Circular Surface Planar Displacement Drawing* (1970) consists of tracks made with a motorcycle in a Nevada dry lake. In 2012, Heizer completed *Levitated Mass*, a project he first conceived of in the late 1960s. It consists of a massive boulder positioned atop a graded man-made trench that also allows people to pass beneath the rock.

Pray's film tells the story of the project at LACMA, but the majority of the film focuses not on the completed work as the artist intended it to be experienced, nor on its reception, but rather on its material – the rock – which was delivered from a quarry over one hundred miles away. The director of several documentaries exploring subcultures and iconoclasts, Pray was initially drawn to the project for the sheer spectacle of the transport and knew little about Heizer.[6] His populist perspective informs the look and feel of the film: the upbeat tempo of the editing, broad range of camera coverage, and emotive use of music (rock, naturally). As in *Fallen Star: Finding Home*, information is predominantly communicated via on-camera interviews with the many collaborators, workers, and officials who contributed to the project, as well as members of the public who turn out to witness the rock pass through their neighborhoods. Experts speak to the meaning and historical significance of Heizer's work; they are especially necessary because, despite approving of the making of the film, Heizer himself did not want to speak about his work on camera.[7] Indeed, aside from a few clips of archival footage, Heizer appears only in the last thirteen minutes. In his absence, Pray, who both directed and edited the film, structures his story into three identifiable sections, or acts: (I) the lead-up to the rock's move; (II) the rock's transport; (III) its final installation at the museum. The proportional dominance of the first two acts and their emphasis on collaborative labor and public response, in effect, expands the artwork's site from the purely phenomenological intent of the artist to the social/institutional and discursive realms.

Pray establishes the work's social/institutional site in the first act by showing the many individuals involved in the realization of the project, along with the obstacles, pressures, and stresses they face as they attempt to work together toward a common goal. LACMA director Michael Govan emerges as a key protagonist in his championing of the project and shepherding it through financial, logistical, and bureaucratic obstacles. A brief sequence addressing his broader plan for the museum and an interview with a trustee lend Govan the air of a visionary leader. "I immediately got it," he tells the camera, recounting his reaction when Heizer first contacted him about the work. "I knew exactly what to do with this and how it would work at the museum. And of course, then I stepped back and said, 'Is anybody going to understand this, is anybody going to *let me* do this?'"[8] Govan tells of choosing a donor to approach, and a subsequent interview with him illustrates the workings of the upper-echelon of the art world. At the close of the act, he states,

> Everything – the millions of dollars, the ambitions, a life of an artist's work, all that I had hoped for the museum, the donors – everything rested on the shoulders of a few part-time city officials who were having trouble grappling with this.

We see him alone in his office, a wide-angle lens rendering the space as if the walls and ceiling are closing in. In Heizer's absence, it is Govan who has the most at stake for the project's success or failure.

Three additional sequences establish the seemingly insurmountable task at hand and the individuals outside the art world who are involved. First, a two-minute section brings together the concerns of the construction and engineering team as they design and execute the trench needed to support the 340-ton boulder. Excerpts of interviews and meeting discussions are cut together emphasizing the unconventional and unpredictable nature of the project: "It's not logical"; "not what you'd think in the world of fine art, which is pretty out there"; "how are we going to build it, how are we going to make it straight"; "The city doesn't accept anything … with that kind of approach you might kill the project." Reams of paper with computer visualizations, data, charts, text, and diagrams are juxtaposed with people's expressions of incredulity and anxiety; the construction company's project coordinator states that they have been discussing the project for years.

Next, another sequence reinforces the difficulty faced by those working on the transport side of the project. As workers at the quarry assemble a massive steel trailer, an executive calls the move "a big logistical nightmare." We cut to the side of a road where the transport company's director of operations measures the clearance beneath an overpass. He explains their timeline for the move, with the caveat that municipal approval is not guaranteed; we then follow him to the office of the overweight load permit service, observing as he updates the owner. "Jeez, I was up late last night. Working through this stuff," he confides. The permit service owner then shows the camera the vast amount of paperwork needed for the approval process of both the route and load, which, he explains, must be signed off on by the state, county, and each city they pass through, as well as every utility company affected.

A third sequence shifts to the public sector. A variance load coordinator for the California Highway Patrol discusses his fear that the vehicle might break down at the one significant hill on the route; we then move to the county building where, after two shots establishing the abundance of plans and files in the office, a lateral camera move reveals the transportation permit unit supervisor inside his cubicle. He speaks to the challenge of the project's original timeline, and is backed up a moment later by a deputy in the county supervisor's office. "I'm thinking, this is impossible," she recalls. In two more interviews, local officials state their reluctance to cooperate due to their concerns about their cities' infrastructure. Finally, in a progressively rapid montage set to tension-inducing music, we cut between the overweight load permit company owner and deputy county supervisor as they rattle off names of the twenty-two cities and towns that must provide approval for the transport. "It's been a pain in the neck, that's what it's been," the deputy county supervisor states. "It's been one of the biggest challenges I've had in this office, and I've been in government for 36 years."

The first act thus establishes the players, logistical challenges, and bureaucratic hurdles faced by the private and public entities tasked with working together to realize Heizer's project. In several cases, subjects describe the work as personally straining. Implicit is the dramatic question of *will they pull it off?* Can these private–public, art world–workaday world partnerships succeed for this art project? In an echo of Muniz's query in *Waste Land*, Pray shows how *Levitated Mass* is an experiment in not just *how* art can get different people to work together, but whether it *can* at all.

These questions are answered at the opening of the second act, with local and national media coverage confirming that the rock's transport has been greenlighted. A montage of news clips sets up the dauntingly complex journey, establishing a new dramatic question: *will the rock arrive safely?* For the next 40 minutes (with occasional breaks to learn more about seismic engineering and Heizer's past works), we witness the slow but steady transit of the rock. Pray assembles an immense amount of coverage to depict the caravan as it moves through urban, suburban, and industrial landscapes (Figure 7.3). We are shown images of the workers, but the details of their activities and identities are mostly unspecified; Govan himself recedes as a character and no single individual emerges to take his place.

Instead, thanks to the incorporation of a number of sequences of interviews with bystanders along the rock's route, a collective character emerges: the vox populi (Figure 7.4). It is with the inclusion of these voices – unidentified individuals of diverse racial, ethnic, and class backgrounds from all over the Los Angeles basin,

FIGURE 7.3 *Levitated Mass*
(Doug Pray, 2013)

124 Vera Brunner-Sung

FIGURE 7.4 Interview subjects in multiple shots from *Levitated Mass* (Doug Pray, 2013)

on the sidewalk or in their front yards, at work, or patronizing local businesses – that Pray demonstrates the discursive site of *Levitated Mass*. The editing organizes people's thoughts and feelings around several central themes: technical awe, paranoid suspicion (is it really what they say it is?), the purpose of the artwork, the thrill of the spectacle, the significance of the artist's intent, and the project's cost. In each of these sections, voices are juxtaposed to create a sense of conversation. A few excerpts are discussed below; in the first, a group of people grapple with the nature and purpose of Heizer's project:

Older white-haired woman: A rock? Sounds kinda dumb.

Man in T-shirt: So it's a rock. It's not art, it came from nature. Now if he carved it and made something, and we could see the sculpture, then that's different. You can't say 'I'm an artist and this is my rock.' Nah, you didn't create that, bro.

Man with gray ponytail: It takes a while to try to comprehend it as an art piece. Part of art is in the presentation, and part of that presentation is what's surrounding it. And so, I can't imagine what the artist is saying.

Boy with long bangs: They're planning on just putting it on two concrete beams and having a ditch under it about 15 feet under the ground where you can just walk under the rock. I think it would be pretty cool, but, I think if it was sculpted it might be a little more interesting to see.

Here the second person helps develop the first one's idea (why the project is "dumb"), while the third gently reasons with them ("It takes a while to try to comprehend …"). The fourth has more information on the complete work of art, but remains somewhat skeptical, like the first two. Other people cannot get past the price tag. Following an archival interview where Heizer addresses the anti-capitalist nature of his practice – he is not creating objects that can be traded as commodities as they are "not worth anything" – Pray incorporates a section on the subject of the project's $10 million cost.

Young man in Raiders jersey:	That's a lot of money, a lot of money. That's like an impossible calculation. That's too much money.
Older man in Harley hat:	It's a waste, it's a waste of money. There's a lot of people who could use the money.
Young woman with infant:	If you got billions and billions of dollars to burn, do what you want.
Older man in Harley hat:	It's a rock. What's a rock do? Nothing.
Woman in big sunglasses:	Even though I understand that it's privately funded, it just seems a little bit excessive being that there's so many people out of work.
Woman on custom trike:	Yeah, I heard it was $10 million. But it was through somebody's, other private party, so you can't complain, really. If they would have said the city footed the $10 million, oh, then I think we would have protested.

With its vehement rhetoric and cutting back and forth between the young woman and older biker, the sequence is constructed as a debate about the just allocation of resources. Some feel the discrepancy between economic need and a cultural value determined by elites ("What's a rock do? Nothing") cannot be countenanced ("waste," "too much," "excessive"). Others back a private individual's right to spend how they choose ("you can't complain, really").

People on the street also have positive, sometimes deeply emotional, responses to the rock. Just as the transport crew, having survived a transmission breakdown, is about to reach the biggest challenge on their route, Pray cuts to a man standing on a sidewalk:

> I definitely feel emotional when I think about it. Everyone, you know, has this journey that we're all on, but it seems impossible when you're facing it, and to, like, know that if you just take it one day at a time, you always end up somehow on the other side and looking back and saying, 'That was difficult, but it shaped me into who I am.'

This interview – followed by shots of crew members horse-playing set to a soaring, hopeful melody – demonstrates one of the ways the rock serves as a catalyst for philosophical and even spiritual reflection.

Finally, as the caravan nears the museum and the end of its journey, Pray turns to the matter of intent and addresses Heizer's apparent indifference to public response:

Young man with messenger bag:	I don't think that it necessarily matters that they're looking at the work in progress of some great artist's work. […] there's still kind of an artistic effect taking place. And I heard the artist didn't intend that at all.
Young woman in beanie:	Speaks to the kind of introverted artist that he is, and he's all about the art. […] He's out to convey a message.
Older woman in wheelchair:	I would hope that he would stop and see it, because it's his dream and his vision that's having this effect on everyone.
Middle-aged woman in glasses:	It's our rock now, it doesn't matter what he thinks!

Pray concludes this discussion on an unambiguous note. Indeed, he demonstrates that the project has taken on a life of its own, activating reflection, debate, and a range of emotions across the city. Even as individual speakers may disagree, the editing works to create a sense of social cohesion, with people from different communities defending or helping to articulate one another's points of view. The film's emphasis on the social and cultural experience generated by the rock's transport insists that *Levitated Mass* exists not just in its completed state, but in the discourse inspired by its process.

In this way, Pray embeds a larger debate regarding the significance of artistic intent into the structure of *Levitated Mass*: how to reconcile the social/institutional and discursive impact of a project with the indifference of its phenomenologically-minded artist. At the start of the third act, following the climactic arrival of the rock at the museum, Pray gives Heizer the opportunity to reassert his control of the narrative. "What art? There is no art," he states, inscrutable in wraparound sunglasses and a cowboy hat. "It's not built yet. Just moving some of the components around." In the next eight minutes, the work is completed, and several brief, phenomenologically-oriented sequences showcase the finished sculpture. But situated as they are in the final minutes of the film, these moments are anticlimactic, dwarfed by the emotional and dramatic outpouring of the first two acts. The unresolved contradiction provides Pray with powerful narrative conflict, and, in another extension of the work's discursive site, encourages its viewers to consider not only the value and meaning of art, but its very definition.

Conclusion: observer, collaborator, provocateur

The films discussed in this chapter share the common goal of providing access to site-specific works of art, but how that manifests depends a great deal on the practice of the artist. Sculptures that are physically grounded in a place, that seek to generate a (meta)physical experience for its viewers, are well served by the slow movement and long takes of films such as *Rivers and Tides* and *Over Your Cities Grass Will Grow*. These films position the filmmaker as a close observer, a kind of proxy for viewers who are unable to encounter the remote site or ephemeral object in person. Works with more social and collaborative dimensions, such as *The Gates*, *Pictures of Garbage*, and *Fallen Star* are aptly represented through interviews and *vérité* techniques that capture the intangible elements their artists have declared equally, if not more, essential than any physical object. In these documentaries, the filmmaker functions as a kind of collaborator, extracting, compiling, and arranging the thoughts and feelings of human beings that might otherwise be forgotten. They exist not just as an accompaniment or a response to the work of art, but as an extension of it.

Interestingly, the documentaries discussed here also mirror the positionality of their artworks' ideal viewer: *Rivers and Tides* and *Over Your Cities* pursuing an objectivity in line with the phenomenologically-defined universal spectator, with the others tending toward a subjective perspective as in the social/institutional model. The exception, of course, is *Levitated Mass*, which diverges from the artist's phenomenological orientation to take a predominantly social and discursive point of view. Here the filmmaker is less an observer or collaborator than a provocateur as he challenges the nature of the artwork's site-specificity. The consequences are not insignificant: as Rebecca Fortnum and Chris Smith have noted, documents of the creative process "mediate between the artist and posterity and in doing so wield enormous (cultural and fiscal) power."[9] Intermedial translation does not occur in a vacuum, for the filmmaker is one artist interpreting another.

Notes

1. Miwon Kwon, *One Place after Another: Site-specific Art and Locational Identity* (Cambridge: MIT Press, 2002).
2. Steven Jacobs, *Framing Pictures: Film and the Visual Arts* (Edinburgh: University of Edinburgh Press, 2011), 1.
3. See discussion of "software" and "hardware" on the artists' website under "Common Errors: General Information," accessed October 12, 2018, http://christojeanneclaude.net/common-errors.
4. These other films include *Christo's Valley Curtain* (1974), *Running Fence* (1978), *Islands* (1986), *Christo in Paris* (1990), and *Umbrellas* (1994).
5. Bill Nichols, *Introduction to Documentary* (Bloomington: Indiana University Press, 2001), 115–23.
6. Stephen Saito, "L.A. Film Fest '13 Interview: Doug Pray on His Transfixing Diamond in the Rough Doc 'Levitated Mass,'" *Moveable Fest*, 24 June 2013, http://moveablefest.com/levitated-mass-doug-pray.
7. Saito, "L.A. Film Fest."
8. Emphasis added.
9. Rebecca Fortnum and Chris Smith, "The Problem of Documenting Fine Art Practices and Processes," *Journal of Visual Arts Practice* 6 (2007): 173.

8
THE WAGES OF *!W.A.R.*
Activist historiography and the feminist art movement

Theresa L. Geller

Lynn Hershman Leeson's *!Women Art Revolution* (a.k.a. *!W.A.R.*, 2010) documents both the feminist art movement, which exploded on the scene in the late 1960s and early 1970s, and its continuing legacy and influence on today's art world. With over 12,000 minutes of footage compiled from forty years of interviews, Hershman Leeson crafts a documentary film that provides one of the most important historiographies of the feminist art movement to date. She also turned the film into an archival media project, with "!W.A.R.: Voices of a Movement," providing an extensive online archive of videos, transcripts, and over 1,000 scanned images of artwork by women, and inviting contemporary women artists to upload their work as well. *!W.A.R.* documents four decades of feminist interventions in, and reinventions of, Art History, while also working as a continuation of that project by challenging the usual, often patriarchal, tropes of visual arts documentaries. By focusing on the historical context out of which the movement emerged, the film refutes the "great man" – or even "great artist" – paradigm that dominates the genre. This is consistent with Hershman Leeson's *oeuvre* as a feminist artist – one that has only received substantial recognition in the art world in recent years. She herself has stated that she has more than a vested interest in the recuperation of the feminist art movement:

> 'People say I've gotten rediscovered,' Hershman Leeson told me, 'but there's no *re-*. I was never discovered before two and a half years ago.' Since then, she has been retrofitted back into history as a pioneer of feminist art and an essential figure in the evolution of art and technology.[1]

To this extent, Hershman Leeson's documentary does the work the art world would not do for fifty years – to acknowledge and value women artists like the director herself. This begins to suggest the complex synecdochic relationship of *!W.A.R.* to the larger feminist art movement and the career of Hershman Leeson as part and parcel of it. In other words, !W.A.R. is a history of the movement *and* a significant part of its expansive archive, both metonymic and metaphoric of the feminist art movement it documents.

While on the most obvious level the film introduces decades of artwork to entirely new audiences, it also stands as a synecdoche of the feminist art movement on several levels. Like the feminist art it represents, the film moves across disciplines to incorporate not only a wide range of art production, but also political actions, such as the direct action taken by Faith Ringgold and others who hid eggs and sanitary napkins around the Whitney Museum in 1970 to protest the lack of representation of women and people of color in the museum. !W.A.R. is a document not just of the artistic contributions of women but of the battles waged to force the art world to recognize this work, demanding their place in galleries, museums, performance spaces, classrooms, and textbooks. Indeed, its expansive approach includes women's painting, photography, performance art, video, ephemeral artwork, and new media, alongside the work of feminist art scholars and curators who helped create the intellectual and physical spaces for the reception of such works. The film is not just "about" feminist activism in the art world, it is itself feminist art activism.

Akin to the once-incendiary artwork *The Dinner Party* (1974–9) by Judy Chicago, who is a central figure in the documentary, !W.A.R. reclaims women's centrality to history, specifically Art History. Furthermore, it makes a place for younger generations of women to sit at the table by including more contemporary women artists at the film's conclusion, and inviting others to add to the archive. Indeed, its broad transmedia project sets it apart from other documentaries of the feminist art movement.[2] !W.A.R. generated numerous paratexts, from its original score composed by Carrie Brownstein (highlighting its links to the feminist cultural

FIGURE 8.1 *!Women Art Revolution*
(Lynn Hershman Leeson, 2010)

movements that followed; in this case, Riot Grrl music) to its published graphic novel (connecting it to more recent feminist grassroots politics and art found in zine culture), and the traveling interactive art exhibit, *RAW/WAR*. Gabriella Giannachi elaborates on the significance of *!W.A.R.* as a work of transmedia, discussing at length its different platforms, especially the online archive, "!W.A.R. Voices of a Movement," housed at Stanford University. Made up of the film's raw footage, shot mostly by Hershman Leeson between 1990–2008, including sixty-eight video tapes, along with transcripts and biographies of the interviewees, Giannachi avers, "The archive not only captures [revolutionary] transformations in the words of those who witnessed them at the time, but also, in doing so, facilitates their multiplication at the present time."[3] Of course it is the film itself that initiates this work of facilitating feminist transformation in the present, reaching a broader audience in its traditional form of a documentary film, with its concomitant exhibition routes of the film festival, the classroom, and streaming services, such as Netflix and Kanopy.

Such transmedial innovation and experimentation with form, in this case with the boundaries of the documentary, is precisely what makes the film part and parcel of the feminist art movement it records. Hershman Leeson is today recognized as a forerunner in transmedia art: "At a time when young artists are exploring how we construct identity through technology, Hershman Leeson's work in all her different media has proven remarkably ahead of its time."[4] The director originally picked up the video recorder forty years previously, not with the intent of making a documentary film four decades later, but rather as part of her own artistic practice, one centered on temporal media, new technologies, and the exploration of women's lives. Much of Hershman Leeson's art employs new technologies precisely to archive lives both real and fictional, working with various recording technologies to explore the personal and experiential, most famously with her alter ego Roberta Breitmore (1973–8), and continuing with even more complex technologies (e.g., a tape recorder in *Breathing Machines* [1966], LaserDiscs with *Lorna* [1979–82], and pioneering the use of touch screen in *Deep Contact* [1984]). Her work has long been one of documenting otherwise unrepresented (if invented) lives in order to produce feminist counter-history, from Breitmore's sessions at Weight Watchers and EST to her time-traveling fiction film, *Conceiving Ada* (1997), which reclaims the woman who invented the first computer algorithm, Ada Lovelace, from historical obscurity. *!W.A.R.* makes explicit such aims of her work, and of feminist art practice in general: to bring to light women's experiences and the counter-knowledge to which such experiences give rise.

!W.A.R. illuminates subjugated knowledge, as defined by Michel Foucault, by excavating the "historical contents" of women's art production and their substantial contributions to culture that have been "buried or masked" by the "formal systematization" of official Art History.[5] Foucault suggests that subjugated knowledge is made up of "a whole series of knowledges that have been disqualified as nonconceptual knowledges, as insufficiently elaborated knowledges, naïve knowledges, hierarchically inferior knowledges" and the like – the very terms by which women's art has been marginalized and suppressed (7–8). *!W.A.R.*

challenges these terms by embodying the very feminist methodology it documents in its archive of art and interviews, that of consciousness-raising (C-R). As Catherine MacKinnon defines it,

> Consciousness-raising is the major technique of analysis, structure of organization, method of practice, and theory of social change of the women's movement. In consciousness-raising, often in groups, the impact of male dominance is correctly uncovered and analyzed through the *collective speaking of women's experience*, from the perspective of that experience.[6]

Hershman Leeson documents the role of C-R in the feminist art movement, but the film is also a form of C-R, formally structured to revivify C-R's historically revolutionary work.[7]

Yet the fact that *!W.A.R.* is itself part of the long line of art (and media) by women that has systematically been ignored by the male-centered art world makes the parenthetical aside at the end of Penelope Andrew's *Huffington Post* review all the more concerning: "*!W.A.R.* will always be a work in progress (but never forgotten nor excluded from history)."[8] But will it not? The film documents only too well that women artists continue to be forgotten; in 2006, few could name three, as Hershman Leeson demonstrates at the start of her film in a short set of interviews of visitors to the San Francisco Museum of Modern Art and the Whitney Museum of American Art in New York City. Moreover, the exclusionary practices of the film industry are well-established, which begins to explain why women documentarians outnumber women in narrative film production today while still being woefully underrepresented in the field of documentary.[9] Hershman Leeson's documentary, lacking the support of major distributors (as opposed to, for example, the many companies involved in the global distribution of Wim Wenders' *Pina*), was not widely released, and was already in the process of being forgotten in the year of its release, like the works of the artists it curates and records.[10] In the lists of best documentaries from 2011, Hershman Leeson's work is sadly absent; indeed, women directors are nearly entirely absent from these "best of" lists.[11]

This chapter seeks to engage and extend Hershman Leeson's project, which counters the willful forgetting of women's art production and activism, a willful forgetting to which Hershman Leeson's documentary is not itself immune, since it is well documented how all of Hershman Leeson's work has been ignored, or worse, over the intervening years; for example, her film *Teknolust* (2002) earned only $29,000 at the box office.[12] This disappearance is already underway with the death of the "live" online archive developed with the film, *RAW/WAR*, a platform for interactive user-generated content to develop and extend the project of the film into the future. Does not the defunct status of *RAW/WAR* figure the loss of spaces open to women artists that *!W.A.R.* itself decries? *!W.A.R.* rejects the very grounds on which such erasure is often premised, as Linda Nochlin famously summarized it: "the naïve idea that art is the direct, personal expression of individual emotional experience, a translation of personal life into visual terms."[13] Thus, the film does not focus on a singular woman artist (like *Pina*), but rather refuses to subscribe to the "great man" paradigm, premised on Enlightenment ideologies of the individual (demanded by capitalism, and the logic underlying the billion-dollar art market). Hershman Leeson's film breaks with the "great artist" tradition, which makes up the majority of visual arts documentaries, and situates itself in an altogether different tradition – that of feminist documentary and its conscious-raising practice. "The making and screening of women's documentaries," Janice Welsch argues,

> provide a climate and a situation in which women can focus on their experiences and achievements without pressure to conform to the expectations or dictates of patriarchal authority. [...] The conversational, woman-centered contexts set up, even precipitate, responses oriented toward feminist consciousness.[14]

In *!W.A.R.*, form truly follows function, employing the cinematic techniques that emerged in the feminist documentaries of the late sixties and early seventies, which were thoroughly dialogic, not simply because they utilize interviews and conversations "to name our oppression, define our concerns, confirm our creativity, celebrate our accomplishments, establish our place in history, share our experiences, and explore our values," but also "by virtue of their juxtaposition of feminist perspectives with patriarchal perceptions" (169).

!W.A.R. only briefly begins by questioning museum visitors about their knowledge of women artists, but it works to frame all that follows with the question: did the feminist art movement – a movement many say was the most important movement in the arts in the twentieth century – have any lasting impact?[15] How is it that the most important movement is also the most readily forgotten? Hershman Leeson hints at this demoralizing paradox in the complex opening in which we see most visitors fail to come up with a single woman artist's name, while Hershman Leeson herself addresses her audience directly, stating that this film has been forty years in the making, starting with the formation of Women Artists in Revolution in 1968. It begins with a historical dialectic; those questioned in 2006 are immediately juxtaposed with Hannah Wilke and Rachel Rosenthal speaking of the silence and invisibility of women in the art world, as well as the complete absence from textbooks and the art institutions that they confronted as women artists. This provides the thesis for the film, which Hershman Leeson promptly brings to the fore in her cut to direct address.

She commits further to this rupture by rejecting the authority endowed to her as a disembodied narrator, putting herself physically in the film, shown in her living room (notably not an art gallery, but the space of domesticity to which women were confined) where she tells us, in a direct address, that she began her interviews thirty-five years ago. These formal choices allow Hershman Leeson to reconstruct the history of the feminist art movement through lived experience, opting for autobiographical inscription in place of supposed "objectivity." More to the point, by refusing to "invoke the power of disembodied knowledge and abstract conceptualization in favor of the enabling power stemming from situated knowledge and the subjectivities of corporeal experience," she rejects the historical referent expected of conventional documentary form in order to make space for an alternative feminist history, one that is both dialectical and dialogic.[16] Such a departure from the unacknowledged filmmaker behind the camera is fundamental to the heteroglossic practices of feminist documentary elaborated by Welsch:

> For women making, participating in, or viewing women's documentaries, dialogue can occur between filmmakers and participants or viewers, among the film participants or between them and viewers ... filmmaking practices are chosen with dialogue in mind. For instance, rather than relying on the seemingly omniscient voice-over of many traditional documentaries, feminist documentarists have often favored interviews and on-screen discussions.[17]

Such dialogical aims are evident as viewers are invited into the same living room as the many artists who visited Hershman Leeson there over the decades.

For Hershman Leeson, this is a subversive filmic strategy, reflecting the principles of feminist C-R, principles that shape *!W.A.R.* in both content and form, but it is also something more. She breaks documentary rules by acknowledging her role as narrator but also by putting herself, albeit hesitantly, into the story from the beginning as a constitutive member of the movement. At times, her interlocutors acknowledge her by name, or she talks about the liminal spaces in which she filmed her interviews, like bathrooms of universities, as we see in her early interview with Judy Chicago. In this way, Hershman Leeson foregrounds the film's low-tech and unfunded origins and contexts, demonstrating its core argument about the liminality of women in the art world and the material effects this has on their artwork. While *!W.A.R.* shares with other feminist documentaries certain radical techniques that question the truth-claims endemic to the form, such as

> direct address to the audience by the filmmaker ..., the filmmaker's visual or verbal interaction with her subjects, and shots reminding viewers, either through images, printed text, or sound, that the film is constructed and offers neither a comprehensive nor completely objective treatment,

the filmmaker's presence in the film transforms the documentary into a constitutive piece in Hershman Leeson's video art opus.[18] This inclusion of her history as a woman artist – rejected by art dealers and willfully neglected by art critics – is more than just another voice numbered among the women artists, critics, and curators represented.[19] Rather *!W.A.R.* is part of a larger body of autobiographical work for which the artist is known, as David E. James explains:

> As a video artist, she subsequently [after *The Electronic Diaries*] made tapes about people other than herself, but while the autobiographical component seemed to diminish, in fact, it massively proliferated. [...] Her autobiography

is discovered to have been a social story, for other [women's] lives are found to reenact her own ... just as her own plurality figures the multiplicity of other women's selves. But since all are artists, the original disjunction between the autobiographical subject and the subject of autobiography (the speaking subject who makes the videos and the subject of speech presented in them) ... become correspondingly more complex.[20]

The filmmaker has long worked in new media, and was among the early artists to adopt video as a medium, exploring the technology at least a decade before its popularization.[21] Therefore, videotaping the early interventions of feminist activists in the art world cannot be understood apart from her broader body of work.

From the autobiographical video series *First Person Plural: The Electronic Diaries of Lynn Hershman Leeson 1984–1996* to her experimental documentary films about visual artists persecuted by their governments, including Steve Kurtz (*Strange Culture*, 2009) and Tania Bruguera (*Tania Libre*, 2017), her work repeatedly addresses the artist in conflict with the wider culture. Moreover, Hershman Leeson's *oeuvre* is known for its interrogation of the social norms (and constraints) of gender and sexuality. Filmmaker and performance artist Valie Export observes:

Lyn [sic] Hershman ... and others, connected persona and performance, not merely to adjust images of women or show the attitudes inflicted on them by culture and mass media. Rather, they deconstructed the cultural coding of women, from art history to mass media. For example, in photographs, films, performances, and even life itself, Lyn Hershman played on images of women's roles ... shatter[ing] different socially coded female identities.[22]

!W.A.R. was filmed during the decades Hershman Leeson was producing these other works, documenting the community and context out of which they emerged. While she was introduced to activist art in 1974 when she worked as associate director for Christo and Jeanne-Claude's *Running Fence*, she was already asking feminist questions in her own art projects, and "along with other artists of the 1970s, Hershman began to envision a history of art that included women ... [in a video project] she set up a conversation between herself and Marcel Duchamp, figuratively inserting herself into art history."[23] Hershman Leeson not only commented on women's general absence from Art History, but on her own invisibility in art criticism. Notoriously, Bay Area art critics would not cover her art openings in her hometown: "Her outspokenness – and the fact she's a woman – slowed down her career, especially in the 1990s and 2000s, when the *San Francisco Chronicle* virtually ignored her exhibits, and the paper's art critic, Kenneth Baker, dismissed her art, she says."[24] She was never mentioned, even when the exhibitions in which her work appeared were reviewed, for over thirty years. Early in her career, the only way her art was reviewed was when she did it herself, writing art reviews and essays under the pseudonyms Prudence Juris, Herbert Goode, and Gay Abandon. She says, "I assumed the identity of three fictional critics who wrote ... about the work of

Lynn Hershman … With tangible reviews in hand, I was able to garner my first exhibitions and legitimate critical evaluations."[25]

She began this intervention in art criticism as part of her Master's thesis in 1968, with the belief that "historical relevance is part of the process of completing a work" (17). That same year, Valerie Solanas wrote in her *SCUM Manifesto*: "The true artist is every self-confident, healthy female, and in a female society, the only Art, the only Culture, will be conceited, kookie, funkie females grooving on each other and on everything else in the universe."[26] Certainly, Hershman Leeson grooves on funkie females, seeing herself as part of a community of women artists who refused to believe their irrelevance. While Solanas published her manifesto, in part a response to her involvement with Andy Warhol's Factory, Hershman Leeson videotaped hers over several decades, from her early piece on Duchamp and *Cut Piece: A Video Homage to Yoko Ono* (VHS, 1993), with its discussion of the significance of the work, to the multimedia project that is *!W.A.R.* If her *Electronic Diaries* aimed to document Hershman Leeson's shifting self-perception through her video confessions on everything from her battle with food (*Binge*, 1987) to her experiences of childhood sexual abuse (*Confessions of a Chameleon*, 1986), then *!W.A.R.* takes on social perceptions of women as a group, rewriting Art History by providing a powerful counter-story decades in the making. Many of the founders of the feminist art movement were part of the broader revolutionary politics of the time – the anti-war movement, Black Panther Party, Civil Rights, the free speech movement, Students for a Democratic Society, the Student Nonviolent Coordinating Committee, and the anti-colonial struggle, among others – but became increasingly aware of the ways their fight for justice alongside the men in these various leftist groups did nothing to alter the sexism they faced in society or by the very men with whom they worked for change. This formed the backdrop for the emergence of second-wave feminism, with its radical, liberal, and socialist schools of thought, which impelled women artists like Rachel Rosenthal, Faith Ringgold, Judy Chicago, Miriam Shapiro, Howardena Pindell, and so many others, including Hershman Leeson herself, to make art and feminist activism co-constitutive practices.

!W.A.R. situates the origins of the feminist art movement in 1968, although it acknowledges individual works that came before, such as Ono's, that laid the groundwork for the artist-activists that followed. The year 1968 provides the historical context of the "subterranean" political struggles that followed, like the anti-war movement, Civil Rights, and the free speech movement at Berkeley, to which Hershman Leeson belonged. Yet, this heightened moment in world history, connoting uprisings and anti-colonial struggles all over the globe, is not simply a frame for the feminist art movement but the content and form of its expression. The film displays the expected montage of archival images from the period, such as Black Panther rallies, the protests of the Vietnam War, and the beginnings of the Women's Liberation Movement, particularly the direct actions taken at the Miss America Pageant in 1968, but the accompanying narration provided by women artists grounds these (by now) cliché news clips in lived experience. Adrian Piper,

for instance, describes the origins of her performance art as a response to President Nixon's escalation of the Vietnam War, with the video of her work showing Piper rolling on the floor under superimposed images of the still body of Kent State victim Jeffrey Miller, and set against Nixon's political speeches. It was, in fact, the way artists responded to the war that served as an early catalyst for the first feminist actions in the art world. Carl Andre and other artists at the time pulled out of the Venice Biennale, opting to curate an art show in protest at the Vietnam War, but, for all their leftist fervor, they only included work by white men, exposing all too well the profound misogyny and racism of even leftist men in the art world. Leading the charge against such hypocrisy was African American artist Faith Ringgold, who called out the show for its racism and sexism and threatened the activist male artists who organized this "Biennale in Exile." Many interventions followed around the country demanding integrated showings beginning in 1970 (and the decades that followed), including the famous demonstrations against the Whitney Annual Show, with slides of women's art projected against the building, and eggs placed inside representing the absence of women artists, with Ringgold painting her eggs black to signal the absence of black artists.

Central to !W.A.R.'s genealogical project is its responsibility to these raw memories of the feminist art movement, memories that reveal the founding intersectionality of the movement, with key figures such as Howardena Pindell, Faith Ringgold, Adrian Piper, Lowery Stokes Sims, and Judith Baca having dominant voices and leading roles in the film's feminist art historiography. For Foucault, genealogy is "both a meticulous rediscovery of struggles, and the raw memory of these fights … a combination of erudite knowledge and what people know," reclaiming both buried and disqualified knowledges to "allow us to constitute a historical knowledge of struggles and to make use of that knowledge in contemporary tactics."[27] !W.A.R. details these many battles against a hegemonic white male art world, while also documenting the creation of separate spaces established to foster the "scholarly erudition" needed to recover disqualified knowledge, such as the AIR Gallery women's art cooperative, the Women's Art Program at Cal State University in Fresno, and the Cal Arts Conference that was itself a genealogical "insurrection of knowledge," providing a history (and valuing) of women's art production. Such intellectual and academic spaces represented, as Foucault describes it, "the removal of the tyranny of overall [art historical] discourses … an insurrection against the centralizing power-effects that are bound up with institutionalization" (8–9); in this case, the hierarchizing discourses of Art History, and the several art schools and academies that have centralized their power to disqualify women's art production for centuries.

Hershman Leeson is explicit about the methodology that made the feminist art movement possible: C-R. Armed with the ethos that the personal is political, women confronted the lived experience of oppression, a process that Martha Rosler explains in her interview as enabling "women to face up to the micropolitics of power within the family, and how they have shaped women and their responses." Several interviews detail the effects of C-R on the lives of women, including experiences of rape and battery that were transformed into art and politics. This is because, as

FIGURE 8.2 *!Women Art Revolution*
(Lynn Hershman Leeson, 2010)

MacKinnon notes, "Consciousness-raising ... inquires into an intrinsically social situation, into that mixture of thought and materiality which is women's sexuality in the most generic sense."[28] Notably, Hershman Leeson follows Arlene Raven's disclosure of the "politicizing" experience of rape with her own story of being a survivor of sexual assault (a traumatic experience she transformed into art in *The Electronic Diaries*), demonstrating in the film how subjugated knowledge becomes historical knowledge when it is shared and legitimated.

As Hershman Leeson narrates, "the personal became the political, and the very personal became art ... we were living covert lives beneath the surface of visibility." This works to segue to the discussion of the politics of performance art, which allowed women to bring their subjugated knowledges into the public realm of art. She speaks of her own invention of identities, transitioning to the politics of social identities, as explored by women of color and lesbian artists. Piper and Pindell confront the experience of racism in their performance art, epitomized in Pindell's video piece *Free, White, and 21* (1980), and both artists attest to the angry reactions their insurgent work received from a racist art world. Inviting differences between and among women into the film provides a transition to a lengthy section on the conflicts and vulnerabilities within the feminist art movement (with Judy Chicago often at the center). The film does not shy away from the painful and divisive conflicts within the movement, many of which remain to this day. These conflicts are presented in the film not only synchronically, within the community, but also diachronically, as women process events of the movement at different historical junctures. For example, the creation of Womanhouse,[29] in 1972, led to the Woman's Building,[30] both powerful symbols of the feminist art movement and what it could build, but also precariously situated outside of (and resistant to) institutionalization. By dialectically interviewing Sheila Levrant de Bretteville in 1990, when she is still optimistic and confident as a co-founder of the Woman's Building (1973–91), and then again in 2008, when she is nearly inconsolable in her grief at the loss of the creatively supportive space for women (due to lack of funding to sustain it), the stakes of the feminist art movement become painfully clear. Moreover, Hershman Leeson uses this technique as a form of feminist historical materialism, contrasting interpretations from different points in time to produce understandings of the workings of history itself, and the power that subtends it, in the viewer. Foregrounding shifts not just in perspective but in affect as well, this explicit address of the role of temporality, of history, in the feminist art movement implicitly implores the viewer to see themselves as shapers of that history, and of the (feminist) history to come. Such feminist dialectics encourage the viewer to ask: what are the conditions of possibility for the next feminist art movement?

The film documents the splintering of the movement in various directions, creating more alternative art spaces, producing activist and community art, developing independent feminist art journals, as well as integrating into the academy and museums. By 1984, in the midst of the national conservative backlash, particularly against women, the feminist art movement came full circle with the rise of the Guerilla Girls, and later, the Women's Action Coalition – activist groups tasked with holding institutions in the art world accountable for their racist and sexist exclusionary practices. And yet, even these groups were rife with conflict when faced with the logical outcome of misogyny and violence against women's bodies in very concrete terms, as in the suspected murder of Ana Mendieta by her husband, artist Carl Andre. The male art community rallied around Andre (who was tried for second-degree murder but subsequently acquitted), paying his steep legal expenses, and many women also came to his defense. While Mendieta's alleged murder stands apart in the film as an unassimilable trauma, the conflicts around her death invites Hershman Leeson to orchestrate several voices to speak about how the movement imploded, with women turning against one another in the internal battles waged over the principles of the movement, which was never unified or coherent from the outset. In this way, Mendieta's death takes on deeper significance, figuring the loss of the feminist movement she helped lead (curating some of its most important shows) and her own work embodied – quite literally.[31] Importantly, however, the film pulls back from the "end of the movement" narrative, signaled in the death of Mendieta – the death of the artist stands as a common concluding trope for many visual arts documentaries. Instead, Hershman Leeson's voiceover invites the spectator to rethink the habits of teleological history; "history is fragile," she announces to introduce the final "chapter," titled "Time." This meta-narration draws our attention to the film as an instance of its archive. Driving this point home, the last artwork discussed is the film itself, with the director's voiceover admitting how much has been left out. She insists the work is "patched together," and directs the viewer to consider: "what questions are asked in determining history? More importantly, what questions aren't asked?" True to form, these queries are dialogical, providing analysis of the documentary *in the film itself*: "the film," art historian Krista Lynes responds, "opens up a set of problems the 1970s raised without solving them, and that is one of the important parts of feminist

FIGURE 8.3 !Women Art Revolution
(Lynn Hershman Leeson, 2010)

practice, is not to shut down the questions." She concludes the film with some of the successes, if not answers, made possible by the feminist art movement, including Marcia Tucker's opening of the New Museum and the *WACK!: Art and the Feminist Revolution* exhibition of 2007 that traveled around the country.

The post-millennial legitimation of feminist art the film details, in fact, made the film itself possible. Hershman Leeson makes this relationship clear by providing a "slide" of the "timeline for this film," which she says is also her "own timeline." Images are given the sound effect of a slide projector, that crucial technology to the dissemination of women's art, from the protest projections onto the side of the Whitney to the reproduced slides from the early Cal Arts Conference. Bringing her own living relationship to the movement to the fore, she describes how she sold some of her artwork in 1975, but when the buyer discovered she was a woman, he returned the work, telling her "buying women artists is a bad investment," and she sold nothing for seventeen years. She could not even donate her work to a local museum, which threatened to destroy her art if she did not take it back. Thirty-five years later, she says, that same work was appraised at 9,000 times the original sales price, and "it was that sale ... that enabled the completion of this film," providing, too, narrative closure for the filmmaker: "I've been waiting all this time for the right ending." Because of the battles won (and lost) by the feminist art movement, women's art is now valued, making the film's completion possible – a film that in turn further legitimates art produced by women, and thereby continues its legacy.[32]

!W.A.R. does not simply revive alternative memories of the feminist art movement to present a corrective history. Rather, Hershman Leeson's genealogical approach aims to resurrect counter-memories to re-energize forms of resistance, ones very much in need today, as the means by which women have been driven from the visual arts (and elsewhere) are becoming increasingly more apparent. The

#MeToo and Time's Up movements have exposed the culture of sexual predation endemic to the art world (film world, journalism, politics, and everywhere else), proving only too well Griselda Pollack's assertion:

> It is not a question of merely overcoming the neglect of women artists by art historians […] Investigating the nature of the obstacles women faced, listing the diverse forms of discrimination, though necessary, is not a complete answer … 'It is not the obstacles … that really count, but the rules of the game that demand scrutiny,'

and those "rules" include, but are certainly not limited to, "a particular order of socio-sexual relationships and powers."[33] *!W.A.R.* plumbs the subjugated knowledges circulated by the feminist art movement precisely to scrutinize these rules of the game and open up the playing field; or, as Hershman Leeson describes it in the film itself, the documentary is a testimony to her "absolute resolve to preserve an enduring future." Building on women's experiences and memories well outside official Art History, *!W.A.R.*'s feminist genealogy develops an art and activist counter-history – a concept Foucault directly associated with revolutionary practice.[34] Counter-history aptly describes what sets *!W.A.R.* apart from so many visual arts documentaries, because it identifies a historical project that sets out to "disinter something that has been hidden, and which has been hidden not only because it has been neglected, but because it has been carefully, deliberately, and wickedly misrepresented" (78). Hershman Leeson's visual arts documentary is thus, in my reading, something much more than a filmed history of the feminist art movement; it is itself activist praxis, rekindling the revolutionary *frisson* that mobilized the movement by making women's history visible in the service of their future.

Notes

1. Alex Greenberger, "A New Future from the Passed: Lynn Hershman Leeson Comes into Her Own After 50 Years of Prophetic Work." *ArtNews*, March 28, 2017. www.artnews.com/2017/03/28/a-new-future-from-the-passed-lynn-hershman-leeson-comes-into-her-own-after-50-years-of-prophetic-work/.
2. I am grateful to Roger Hallas for bringing these films to my attention. See Joan Braderman's *The Heretics* (2009), *Reclaiming the Body: Feminist Art in America* (Michael Blackwood, 1995), and *Rebel Women: The Great Art Fightback* (Clare Tavernor, 2018), which was commissioned for BBC Four.
3. Gabriella Giannachi, *Archive Everything: Mapping the Everyday* (Cambridge, MA: MIT Press, 2016), 44.
4. Greenberger, "A New Future."
5. Michel Foucault, *Society Must Be Defended*, trans. David Macey (New York, NY: Picador, 1997), 7.
6. Catherine MacKinnon, "Feminism, Marxism, Method, and the State: An Agenda for Theory," *Signs* 7, no. 3 (1982): 519–20; emphasis added.

7 In an influential 1978 essay, Julia Lesage argued that C-R provided the methodological foundation for feminist documentary film in the 1970s. See "The Political Aesthetics of the Feminist Documentary Film," *Quarterly Review of Film Studies* 3, no. 4 (Fall 1978): 507–23.

8 Penelope Andrew, "*!W.A.R.: Fighting the Politics of Exclusion by Documenting a History of Women's Art (and Much More).*" *Huffington Post*, July 31, 2011, www.huffingtonpost.com/penelope-andrew/war-fighting-the-politics_b_868995.html.

9 In fact, the numbers of women in the film industry dropped in 2017 from previous years, averaging about 18% of all positions behind the camera. See Derek Thompson, "The Brutal Math of Inequality in Hollywood," *The Atlantic*, January 11, 2018, www.theatlantic.com/business/archive/2018/01/the-brutal-math-of-gender-inequality-in-hollywood/550232/.

10 *!W.A.R.* was released in the US by the small independent distributor, Zeitgeist Films, which also distributes Yvonne Rainer's work and a number of art documentaries about women artists, including *What Remains: The Life and Work of Sally Mann* (Steven Cantor, 2006), *Louise Bourgeois: The Spider, The Mistress and the Tangerine* (Marion Cajori and Amei Wallach, 2008), and *Eva Hesse* (Marcie Begleiter, 2016).

11 When the occasional mixed-gender co-directed films appear (e.g., *Semper Fi: Always Faithful*), or even when one or two documentaries directed by women directors are represented on various lists (Cindy Meehl, Gemma Atwal, Natalia Almada, Heather Courtney, Pamela Yates, Liz Garbus), nearly all of them take as their subject matter *men's lives*. See Roger Ebert, "The Best Documentaries of 2011," *Roger Ebert Journal*, December 25, 2011, www.rogerebert.com/rogers-journal/the-best-documentaries-of-2011; Michael Dunaway, "The 20 Best Documentaries of 2011," *Paste*, December 14, 2011, www.pastemagazine.com/blogs/lists/2011/12/the-20-best-documentaries-of-2011.html?p=4; Scott Tobias, "2011 in Film: Five Breakthrough Documentaries," *NPR*, December 28, 2011, www.npr.org/2011/12/16/143840227/2011-in-film-five-breakthrough-documentaries.

12 Greenberger, "A New Future."

13 Linda Nochlin, "Why Have There Been No Great Women Artists?" in *Feminism-Art-Theory: An Anthology 1968–2014*, ed. Hilary Robinson (Malden, MA: Wiley Blackwell, 2015), 137. Originally published in *Artnews*, January 1971: 22–39.

14 Janice R. Welsch, "Bakhtin, Language, and Women's Documentary Filmmaking," in *Multiple Voices in Feminist Film Criticism*, eds. Diane Carson, Linda Dittmar, and Janice R. Welsch (Minneapolis, MN: University of Minnesota Press, 1994), 165. I can personally attest to the impact of *!W.A.R.* as a tool for C-R. After screening this film for my undergraduates at Grinnell College, they were inspired to start their own feminist art collective, one that continues to thrive years later: https://songhankyeol.wixsite.com/work/ana-cha-art-collective.

15 For a summary of these claims, see Blake Gopnick, "What is Feminist Art?" *Washington Post*, April 22, 2007, www.washingtonpost.com/wp-dyn/content/article/2007/04/20/AR2007042000400.html.

16 Bill Nichols, "'Getting to Know You …': Knowledge, Power, and the Body," in *Theorizing Documentary*, ed. Michael Renov (New York, NY: Routledge, 1993), 188.

17 Welsch, "Bakhtin," 166.

18 Welsch, "Bakhtin," 167.

19 The complete list of interviewees is available on the *!W.A.R.* website: www.womenartrevolution.com/about_interviews.php.

20 David E. James, "Lynn Hershman: The Subject of Autobiography," in *Hershmanlandia: The Art and Films of Lynn Hershman Leeson*, ed. Meredith Tromble (Seattle, WA: Henry Art Gallery/University of Washington, 2005), 203.

21 Hershman Leeson has published on the topic of interactive video, addressing ideas that would later shape the *RAW/WAR* project, in "The Fantasy Beyond Control," in *Illuminating Video: An Essential Guide to Video Art,* eds. Doug Hall and Sally Jo Fifer (New York, NY: Aperature/Bay Area Video Coalition, 1990), 267–74.
22 Valie Export, "Aspects of Feminist Actionism," *New German Critique* 47 (1989): 89–90.
23 Meredith Tromble, "Double Talk: The Counterstory of Lynn Hershman," in *Hershmanlandia*, 203. Many writers use the name attributed to her early works, before she legally changed her name to Leeson.
24 Jonathan Curiel, "A Retrospective of One's Own, For Lynn Hershman Leeson," *SF Weekly*, February 22, 2017, www.sfweekly.com/culture/art/a-retrospective-of-ones-own-for-lynn-hershman-leeson.
25 Lynn Hershman, "Private I: An Investigator's Timeline," in *Hershmanlandia*, 17.
26 Valerie Solanas, "Scum Manifesto," in *Feminism-Art-Theory*, 13. Originally published in *SCUM Manifesto* (Paris: Olympia Press, 1968; self-published in 1967).
27 Foucault, "Society," 8.
28 MacKinnon, "Feminism," 77.
29 See Judy Chicago and Miriam Schapiro, "Womanhouse Catalog Essay," www.womanhouse.net/statement/.
30 See "The Woman's Building: A Brief History," http://thewomansbuilding.org/history.html.
31 Unlike the Guerilla Girls, Hershman Leeson, with Carolee Schneemann and Yvonne Rainer, did protest the politics surrounding Mendieta's death in their short video, *Conspiracy of Silence* (1991), interrogating "the sexual politics of the art world, and the racial, class, and gender inequities of the judicial system," Hershman, "Private I," 74.
32 Hershman Leeson has had large retrospectives in recent years, particularly *Civic Radar*, held in 2014 at ZKM: Museum of Contemporary Art in Karlsruhe, Germany, and later brought to the Yerba Buena Center for the Arts in San Francisco. She also has works included in *Net Art Anthology*, https://anthology.rhizome.org/.
33 Griselda Pollock, citing Rozsika Parker's review of Germaine Greer's work, "Women, Art, and Ideology: Questions for Feminist Art Historians," *Women's Art Journal* 4, no. 1 (1983): 40, 43.
34 Foucault, "Society," 79.

Acknowledgements

This chapter is dedicated to Dr. Linda Nochlin (1931–2017). This research was supported in part by the Beatrice Bain Research Group at the University of California, Berkeley. I would like to thank Roger Hallas, Nicole Archer, and David Maynard for their thoughtful suggestions and editorial advice.

PART IV
Museum gazing

9
WHEN ART EXHIBITION MET CINEMA EXHIBITION

Live documentary and the remediation of the museum experience

Annabelle Honess Roe

Event cinema, termed "alternative content" within the film exhibition industry,[1] was spearheaded in 2006 by the "Met Live" season, which capitalized on recent technological developments in digital film exhibition and satellite technology to broadcast performances from the Metropolitan Opera in New York live to cinemas around the world. Other arts institutions, including the National Theatre in London and the Paris Opera Ballet, followed suit and the event cinema market in the UK doubled year-on-year between 2008 and 2011, from approximately £3m to £13m.[2] This chapter explores a brief-lived, UK-based, phenomenon that appeared at the peak of this period of rapid growth – the live broadcast of museum exhibitions in cinemas between 2011 and 2014. Following the National Gallery in London's successful broadcast of their blockbuster exhibition *Leonardo da Vinci: Painter at the Court of Milan* in 2011,[3] dubbed *Leonardo Live*, another London-based institution, the British Museum, subsequently produced live broadcasts of two of their exhibitions with *Pompeii Live* (2013) and *Vikings Live* (2014).[4] Also in 2014, London's Tate Modern, in collaboration with New York's Museum of Modern Art, broadcast *Matisse Live*.[5] This chapter explores these films as live broadcast documentaries that remediate both the objects contained in their exhibitions – works of art and historical artifacts – and the museum-going experience.

These exhibition broadcasts sought to appeal to the growing audience that was drawn to live event cinema and the opportunity to experience major cultural events from the comfort (and relative lower cost) of the local cinema.[6] In line with the democratizing motivations expressed by producers of event cinema,[7] the National Gallery's press release for *Leonardo Live* conveyed the desire for "the widest audience possible" to "experience this once in a lifetime exhibition."[8] This accessibility for viewers who might otherwise not be able to see the exhibition in person (due to geographical location or other physical or financial constraints) is echoed in the British Museum's press release for *Pompeii Live* two years later in which Tim Richards, CEO of the Vue Cinema chain, talks about the broadcast's reach to "regional audiences."[9] In addition to this rhetoric of democratic access and inclusivity, however, the British Museum press release in particular promotes the contradictory idea of exclusivity. The broadcast is described as an "exclusive private tour" that is "unique" and "intimate," where audiences will be able to see exhibits "close up."[10] In this way, the promotional material surrounding these films is to a certain extent conflicting, promising both democratic and exclusive access, where everyone can be a VIP at a private view that is open to the public. This contradictoriness is, as will be explored below, reflected in the broadcasts themselves.

Another overriding theme in the press releases for both *Leonardo Live* and *Pompeii Live* was the broadcasts' added value. The broadcasts borrow from other forms of exhibition supplementation, such as the exhibition catalogue, audio guides, and even curator tours that are offered to museum visitors as a way to enhance their visit. This type of special insight is offered in the broadcast films via the expert guides and presenters who lead the audience's live "personal tour."[11] However, the broadcasts also promise more than the conventional exhibition add-ons. As with other event cinema, in which audiences get to see material not available to those watching the performance in person, such as interviews with performers and backstage footage, the exhibition films offered something in addition to what the viewer might experience if they physically visited the exhibition, even with the aid of an audio guide. This might include "behind the scenes" footage of the exhibition's creation or contextualizing information about the topic of the exhibition. Additionally, the exhibition broadcasts offer the "best seat in the house" promise of live performance on screen (in this case, the chance, although not explicitly stated, to see the artworks and artifacts without jostling for a closer look in a crowded museum), as well as the cinematic attraction of scale (the opportunity to see precious exhibits up-close on the big screen).

Here, the incongruity of the broadcasts is once again signaled in the promotional material. Unlike the live broadcast of opera, ballet, and theater, which quite closely mirrors the typical experience of being an audience member of the actual live performance (that is, sitting in a seat in a darkened auditorium with a group of mostly strangers and watching a performance take place in front of you), a museum exhibition is not usually experienced as an individual tour with expert and in some cases famous guides, who dictate how long we spend looking at each item on display. Instead, in their desire to tap into the audience for "live" event cinema, these exhibition broadcasts emulate other, quite unrelated, live events, such as television broadcasts of major cultural, sporting, or national events.

Leonardo Live was a live broadcast recorded during the exhibition's opening private gala on November 8, 2011. The ninety-minute broadcast screened in cinemas and simultaneously on Sky Arts, a UK niche satellite-television channel, the night before the much-anticipated exhibition opened to the public. The broadcast featured art historian Tim Marlow as an expert guide, leading the audience through the various rooms of the exhibition, pausing on individual exhibits in the company of a changing roster of special, and often celebrity, guests. For example, Marlow and actress Fiona Shaw discuss the recently restored painting *Salvator Mundi* (c. 1500), making rather tenuous connections between religious and stage "presence." Intercut with this, TV presenter Mariella Frostrup interviewed other guests, ranging from the National Gallery's director Nicholas Penny to musician Nitin Sawney, outside the space of the exhibition on sofas in the gallery's lobby area. This live material, which is at times breathless as guests are rushed through their contributions in order to keep to schedule, was interspersed with pre-recorded material on da Vinci's life and work and on the museum's preparation for the exhibition. The result is a film that the *New York Times* described as "strangely hectic" in its rapid cuts between inside and outside the exhibition,[12] live and recorded material, and multiple guests offering opinions of variable relevance on the significance of da Vinci and his work.

The subject of *Pompeii Live* was a similarly sell-out-success exhibition: the British Museum's *Life and Death in Pompeii and Herculaneum*, which ran from March to September 2013. The broadcast took place mid-way through the exhibition, screening live in 281 cinemas in UK and Ireland on June 18, 2013. Helmed by TV presenter Peter Snow and television historian Bettany Hughes, *Pompeii Live* took a similar approach to *Leonardo Live* in its inclusion of both live and pre-recorded material. Although, in this case the pre-recorded material is limited to the history and events that took place in Pompeii and Herculaneum, rather than any insight into the production and preparation of the exhibition. This later broadcast is less frantic in its pacing, eschewing the rapid cutting back and forth between different spaces within the museum in favor of lingering longer over each segment. *Pompeii Live* also adopts a different approach to special guests. Instead of a large roster of personalities, it features a far smaller number of experts who impart their relevant knowledge in dialogue with the presenters, often pausing for extended periods in different areas of the exhibition. Mary Beard, the eminent British classicist, who has a well-established public profile through various UK television appearances and newspaper columns, features heavily, along with the Michelin-starred, London-based Italian chef Giorgio Locatelli and Rachel de Thame, a gardener and previous presenter of the popular BBC television program *Gardeners' World*. The remainder of the guests are less high-profile and unlikely to be familiar to audiences, cast instead for their expertise on ancient Roman life or their involvement in curating the exhibition.

The following year, the British Museum broadcast *Vikings Live* on April 24, 2014, to 400 cinemas across the UK, which took place halfway through their blockbuster *Vikings: Life and Legend* exhibition. The 2014 broadcast took a similar approach to the previous year's *Pompeii Live* and combined two presenters (Bettany Hughes again, this time with Michael Wood, another historian and broadcaster) with expert guests (including the exhibition curator Gareth Williams), pre-recorded material and live events taking place elsewhere in the museum (such as Viking boat building). The tone of this broadcast is even more populist and accessible than *Pompeii Live*; for example, at one point Williams appears dressed up in Viking armor. *Matisse Live*, broadcast from the Tate Modern's *Henri Matisse: The Cut-Outs* exhibition on June 3, 2014, to 200 cinemas in the UK, was made by the same production team as *Leonardo Live*, but feels very different to that earlier broadcast.

There is one host – Francine Stock, a less high-profile public figure than in previous broadcasts – and the celebrity guests have been axed in favor of insider experts, such as Tate Modern director Nicholas Serota, who appears frequently with Stock in the live segments. The broadcast is much more sedately paced and features less live material in comparison to the earlier broadcasts. The live material, recorded inside the Tate Modern exhibition, which was closed to the public at the time, is highly planned – Stock has notes in her hand and the responses from guests are measured and prepared – to the extent that the live material is less distinguishable from the pre-recorded elements than in the other live exhibition broadcasts.

The short-lived existence of live exhibition on screen means that while much has been said about documentary *as* art and documentary in the gallery space, little consideration has been given to the idea that the gallery can infiltrate the space of the cinema.[13] The live broadcast exhibition films under examination here provide an opportunity to think about the remediation of the museum space and the museum-going experience on film.[14] Studies of event cinema have predominantly focused on theater and opera on screen.[15] The writing that does exist on exhibition on screen tends to be from a museological perspective and concerned with what exhibition on screen can do for museums.[16] Yet, these curious films, part arts documentary, part promotion for their respective museums and exhibitions, deserve further reflection because they can tell us much about the relationship and differences between cinematic space and the museum space and how these, in turn, sit awkwardly with the temporal dynamics and immediacy of live broadcast.

In this chapter, I am going to suggest that these films are awkward, and at times confusing, objects, in and of themselves, in part because of having to negotiate the intermedial tension between two different types of visual regimes or experiences – that of the exhibition and that of cinema. This is a tension that is further brought to bear by their presentation as live broadcasts. This is one way in which exhibition event cinema is unlike opera, theater, and ballet event cinema, which Martin Barker has argued are not intermedial because audiences do not persist in "perceiving each medium as a distinguishable 'system' whose conventions can be separately identified."[17] The awkwardness of exhibition event cinema makes it clear that (museum) exhibition and cinema remain distinct media that, while fundamentally visual, operate in potentially incompatible ways. Furthermore, the format of live broadcast offers a further element of complication that highlights the differences between the experience of visiting a museum exhibition in person and watching a film at the cinema. In what follows, I will suggest that this awkwardness and modal confusion is evident in two key characteristics of these broadcasts: their (im)mobility and their liveness.

Space and mobility

In his review of the cinema broadcast of *David Bowie Is Happening Now*, produced for the Bowie exhibition at London's Victoria and Albert Museum in 2013, Charles Gant in *Sight and Sound* expressed his surprise at the burgeoning popularity of exhibition on screen. Whereas theater and opera performances, he suggests, "naturally lend themselves to the cinema space," he describes exhibitions as "events that by their very nature are presumed to be static," and thus, by implication, less adaptable to the moving image.[18] It is quite clear, however, that while artworks and artifacts displayed in an exhibition are usually static, we experience exhibitions as bodies moving through the gallery space and that the museum-going experience is, as such, an inherently mobile one for the museum visitor. Similarly, while motion pictures are moving images, they are usually experienced by a static, most often sitting, viewer. One of the challenges for exhibition on screen comes in trying to remediate a mobile experience of static objects via a static experience of the moving image, or, in other words, in trying to negotiate the difference between being a museum visitor and a cinema-goer. Trying to turn a fundamentally spatial experience (moving through an exhibition at your own pace) into a fundamentally temporal one (sitting in a cinema for a specific durational period) is a challenge that is demonstrated by the cinematography, and in particular the mobile camera, in the films under discussion here.

Very early on in *Leonardo Live*, Tim Marlow walks through the exhibition, explaining its organization and the focus of each of its seven rooms. Marlow talks directly into a Steadicam, which tracks backwards as he walks, often quickly panning between paintings as he mentions them, thus giving a sense of how the objects are arranged in relation to each other. At the same time, Marlow is providing an outline of the structure of the film to come, indicating that the film's temporal organization closely follows the exhibition's spatial organization. The paintings that are featured in the film will be discussed in the order they would be encountered by the exhibition-goer. Further spatial knowledge is inferred in a later discussion between Marlow, exhibition curator Luke Syson, and artist Michael Craig-Martin, who are situated in the seating area outside of the exhibition, looking at a scale 3-D model of the exhibition space that sits on the coffee table between them (see Figure 9.1). While ostensibly illuminating the discussion about the show's inception and planning (Syson explains that he uses such models to help determine where paintings will hang), this brief bird's-eye view of the exhibition space enhances the viewer's spatial understanding of how the exhibition is organized and its function might be thought of as comparable to the gallery map available to exhibition visitors.

In *Matisse Live*, spatial knowledge of the exhibition space is conferred not by the broadcast's host, but by long Steadicam tracking shots that move through the galleries. This occurs at three points throughout the film, acting as punctuation points to separate the film into sections that are dictated by the contents of the exhibition. In the first of these shots, the camera starts at the entrance to the exhibition, and then moves into the first room. There is no voiceover and the shots are labelled with superimposed subtitles: "room 1" and so on. The camera remains at eye level, but often pans around to highlight a particular exhibit or to give a 360-degree view of the contents of a room. Similarly, in *Leonardo Live*, the cinematography frequently works in conjunction with the editing to emulate the sense of moving through an exhibition. This first, and most noticeably, happens about a minute into the broadcast (prior to Marlow's walkthrough) in a brief montage sequence of short mobile shots

FIGURE 9.1 Presenter Tim Marlow discusses the exhibition's layout with curator Luke Syson *Leonardo Live*
(Phil Grabsky, 2011)

within the empty exhibition space. In these shots, the camera moves in different directions and at a range of distances from the paintings on display. The camera roams into rooms, pans across groups of paintings, pushes into the detail of pictures and so on. In this way, the mobile, free-roaming camera is working to overcome the intermedial dissonance between exhibition- and cinema-going through simulating the spatial and visual experience of walking through the exhibition.

However, in other ways, the camerawork and editing in *Leonardo Live* are not necessarily or straightforwardly reconstructing the physical experience of walking through the exhibition. Fleeting moments of almost ghostlike movement, in which a disembodied camera seems to float unaided through an exhibition space devoid of visitors, reoccur throughout the film. Unlike the brief tour with Marlow and the tracking shots in *Matisse Live*, these moments of mobile camera are unlabeled and disconnected – that is, it is not necessarily clear how the spaces being revealed in each quite short shot relate to each other. The lack of spatial continuity from one shot to another contributes to this sense of ambiguous mobility (for example, the camera will be panning left-to-right in one shot and then right-to-left in the next one). In *Leonardo Live*, in particular, the camera's disembodied status means that it is not simply our avatar. Instead, it often moves through the space of the exhibition in a way that few of us are likely to experience it (not least, empty of other visitors). By freeing the camera from the restrictions of embodied movement and vision, these broadcasts also offer moments of spatial experience that could not be emulated by the physical visitor to the exhibition.

At the start of *Pompeii Live*, there is an indication that it will be privileging the moving camera and will give viewers a clear sense of the museum space in which the exhibition takes place. The broadcast opens with a shot panning up the railings outside the museum's famous façade. It then cuts to a very high-angled crane shot that floats down to a medium shot of presenter Peter Snow, who welcomes viewers to their "private view" of the exhibition as he walks up the steps towards the museum's entrance. Another cut takes us into the museum to a shot showing the architecturally-celebrated ceiling of the museum's Great Hall, before tilting down and tracking Bettany Hughes as she walks down the spiral staircase that surrounds the museum's reading room to meet Snow at the foot of the stairs. The mobile camera of these opening shots establishes the space and place of the exhibition and works in some way to recreate the experience of a visitor entering the British Museum. However, from this point on, and unlike *Leonardo Live*, *Pompeii Live* almost completely elides the spatiality of its exhibition via a remediation that privileges the temporal over the spatial.

After the presenters' introduction, *Pompeii Live* settles into a discussion between Hughes, Snow, and British Museum director Neil MacGregor, who sit on high stools in one of the exhibition's rooms – a space designed to resemble a Roman atrium. In this segment, MacGregor alludes to one of the exhibition's most celebrated aspects – its reconstruction of Roman life through a spatial organization that took visitors from the public arenas of a Roman street into the private spaces of a wealthy Roman family house (areas of the exhibition were arranged to reflect a floor plan of the House of the Tragic Poet from Pompeii as an exemplar of such a home).[19] From the atrium, visitors could enter the various inner spaces of the house, including bedroom, garden, and kitchen and the "emphasis lied on creating the illusion of a single, fully preserved Roman house."[20] But, unlike *Leonardo Live*, which at a comparable point in its broadcast walks viewers through the exhibition space, *Pompeii Live* cuts to a pre-recorded video that gives an overview of the history and archaeological significance of Pompeii and Herculaneum over which Snow, in voiceover, explains that the film will "follow the people of Pompeii and Herculaneum through their last two days." Here the film signals, at least to those familiar with the spatial organization of the exhibition, that *Pompeii Live* is taking a different approach to the events that took place in Pompeii and Herculaneum – one that is temporally, rather than spatially, driven and that, much like mainstream commercial cinema, prioritizes narrative storytelling.[21]

(Im)mobility, detail, and materiality

While *Pompeii Live* adopts a different spatial and temporal approach to the other films, most notably to *Leonardo Live*, there are similarities in the way all four use the camera, both moving and static, as a way of overcoming one of the other fundamental differences between exhibition-going and cinema-viewing – physical proximity to the artworks and objects on display. Although much as the mobile camera allows an occasional privileged view of an empty gallery space, the camera also enables the audience to be in closer visual proximity to exhibits than they might have been if they were physically present at the exhibition, either because of the placement of the item in a glass case or due to the number of other visitors similarly craning for a look. A slowly moving camera often zooms into or pans across paintings and larger artifacts in close-up in order to draw attention to particular details, often in conjunction with discussion between presenter and guest or voiceover material. In *Matisse Live*, for example, the camera roves gently across various close-ups of the 1952 cut-out *The Parakeet and the Mermaid*, accompanied by extracts from Matisse's diaries read in voiceover by actor Simon Russell Beale. The voiceover and close-ups work in conjunction to illuminate aspects of the artwork, such as when Matisse (Beale) says "look at this large composition: the foliage, fruits, scissors – a garden" at the same time as these different aspects are seen in close-up. In *Pompeii Live*, the camera moves in close-up across various parts of a statue depicting the god Pan copulating with a goat while Bettany Hughes and Mary Beard, who are standing next to the display case, discuss the "unsettling" nature of the sculpture for modern audiences. In this way, the live broadcasts often draw audience attention to aspects of the exhibition that might not have been apparent or emphasized to the exhibition-goer. Similarly, Lorna Cruickshanks has noted that the close-ups on objects in *Pompeii Live* often enabled different, sometimes superior, views and angles than encouraged by their placement in the actual exhibition and, as a result, revealed details that the exhibition visitor would most likely have missed.[22]

A notable feature of both *Pompeii Live* and *Vikings Live*, whose exhibitions feature a large number of artifacts and objects rather than artworks, is their use of static close-ups to give the audience a privileged visual proximity to materials that work to not only compensate for the lack of physical proximity of the exhibition-goer, but also to offer something in addition. For example, Hughes handles Roman jewelry in *Pompeii Live* and a cup found as part of a large hoard in Yorkshire in *Vikings Live*. In both instances, the preciousness and the materiality of the objects are emphasized by Hughes's physical reaction to holding them (gasping, mentioning that her heart is racing, commenting on their unexpected weight), combined with close-ups showing the objects in detail. While Hughes is given rare physical access to touch these objects that no normal visitor to the exhibition would be permitted, the viewer is seeing them in closer visual proximity and greater detail than they would be able to do if they viewed them directly at the exhibition. Cruickshanks's research with audiences of *Pompeii Live* revealed that these moments of object-handling were "highly evocative" for viewers who described the experience as a "sensory" one that brought the objects to life in a way that might not have happened for someone seeing them behind a glass case at the exhibition (449).

The guided gaze and curatorial intent

The aspects of cinematography discussed here – the moving camera, the close-ups, and the privileged angles – govern the viewers' experience of the exhibition in a way that the exhibition itself would not. In this way, the exhibition films are more akin to exhibition audio guides than other examples of event cinema. But more than audio guides, the close-ups discussed above highlight the significance of certain objects in the exhibition at the expense of others that might not be featured at all. Furthermore, audiences are instructed not only on how to think about these objects by the presenters, curators, and guests on screen, but also which objects are important, by the film's off-screen producers through the decisions they make about the selection, organization, and presentation of objects in the broadcast film. In this way, these broadcasts run counter to the move towards curatorial practice in museums and galleries, such as the use of interactive displays, which have freed "visitors from the tutelary grip of earlier, more directive forms of curatorial authority."[23] Furthermore, in this remediation of the "spatial syntax" of the gallery,[24] they also run counter to the "individual visiting culture" that Kali Tzortzi suggests is characteristic of most contemporary museums.[25] Even though museums, according to their spatial and architectural organization, offer different levels of individual exploration (as indicated by Tzortzi), any in-person museum experience will offer high levels of individual exploration of the space. Even audio guides offer the capacity to be tailored to individual preference and interest by allowing random access to the recorded material through the numbering of exhibits and the guides' keypads. No such individual exploration of the space is available, of course, to the exhibition film audience, whose passage through the exhibition space is entirely dictated and limited in both time and space.

Tzortzi suggests that museums and galleries with more restricted movement choice due to their spatial layout "reinforce[s] the curatorial reading of the display" (346). In a way then, the live exhibition broadcasts under discussion here could be thought of as a way of addressing a key question facing museum curators – whether the museum's "intended address" actually works.[26] This is perhaps most evident in *Vikings Live*. The British Museum's Viking exhibition was not as enthusiastically received as the previous year's Pompeii offering. The *Guardian*'s Jonathan Jones describes it as a "pedantic exercise in pure archaeology that fails to shape its subject into a stimulating narrative."[27] Similarly, Mark Hudson in the *Telegraph* suggested that the "presentation will hardly set your Nordic viscera surging" because the exhibition was a dry "exercise in academic debunking."[28] The exhibition broadcast can be read as an attempt to respond to those criticisms by making the exhibition's contents, and the stories behind them, more engaging. Strategies such as the live reenactments (of ship building and the burial ceremony), the appearance of the curator in Viking garb as a way of demonstrating his passion for his subject (he is a Viking reenactor in his spare time), and the enthusiasm displayed by the presenters at the objects on display counteract criticism of the exhibition as dull and failing to bring the story of the Vikings to life.

Incongruous liveness

The liveness of *Vikings Live* is a key way in which the broadcast makes the exhibition seem engaging. However, their liveness is also the aspect of these exhibition films that seems most incongruous in terms of their remediation of the exhibition experience. Whereas the elements of cinematography try to emulate, to a certain degree, the spatial experience of an exhibition, the live element has no actual relation to the exhibition-going experience. Instead, their liveness was a way to position the broadcasts within the then growing market for live event cinema. However, whereas ballet, opera, and theater are typically experienced as live performances, exhibitions are not. As a result, the "live" aspect of the films under discussion here feels strange and often at odds with their other characteristics, such as the privileging of the spectatorial gaze through cinematography choices. In this way, the live exhibition films seem to move further away from an attempt to capture the exhibition experience by instead offering a kind of immediacy and presence that is overt to the extent of being obtrusive.

This is most apparent in *Leonardo Live*, with its fast-paced transitions between live guests inside and outside the gallery space, the inclusion of live and pre-recorded material that had to be mixed live, and the seemingly unrehearsed contributions from the guests. This gives the broadcast a sense of spontaneity and energy that Philip Auslander describes as an often highly valued aspect of liveness.[29] The fact that it was filmed during the private opening, whereas the other broadcasts under discussion here were filmed in closed galleries, and the invited visitors can be seen milling around in the background, adds to this feeling of spontaneity, and also presence, another valued aspect of liveness, albeit, in this case, between the presenters and guests and the invited public, rather than between performer and audience.

While *Pompeii Live* felt less spontaneous, mostly thanks to its more measured pace, liveness was still a highly promoted aspect of the broadcast. In the run-up to the transmission, the British Museum posted regular messages on their Twitter account to emphasize the preparation taking place and to generate excitement prior to going live (see Figure 9.2). They then live-tweeted the broadcast, although, given that it was only viewable at cinemas, the public response was muted until the screenings were over. Three days later, the museum also hosted a live Twitter Q&A session that followed up on the broadcast. In the broadcast itself, various nods were given to the typical format of live television events, such as a closing segment in which the hosts put to Mary Beard and curator Paul Roberts questions previously sent in by the public. While these questions were not submitted live, it is reminiscent of the "call in" engagement with the viewer/listener of live television and radio events. Liveness felt more integral to *Vikings Live*, which included various simultaneous live events taking place in the museum's external plaza, such as boat building and a burial reenactment. Moreover, at the end of this broadcast, co-presenter Michael Wood put questions to curator Gareth Williams which did seem to have been received via messages from the public during the broadcast. However, *Matisse Live* drops all but the most basic nod to liveness; other than the heavily pre-planned material recorded live in the exhibition space, hosted by Francine Stock, the rest of the broadcast is pre-recorded.

The difference in terms of liveness between *Leonardo Live* and *Matisse Live* and the British Museum's decision not to produce further live broadcasts following *Vikings Live* is an indication of the awkwardness of the marriage of exhibition documentary and live broadcast. For Phil Grabsky, the director of *Leonardo Live* and *Matisse Live*, who went on to establish the Exhibition on Screen brand via his

When art exhibition met cinema exhibition   155

FIGURE 9.2   The British Museum's Twitter feed emphasizes the liveness of their forthcoming *Pompeii Live* broadcast on June 18, 2013.

production company Seventh Art, the live broadcasts were the "Trojan horse to get arts documentaries in the cinema."[30] He would subsequently direct many more pre-recorded, exhibition-based documentaries that have been screened in cinemas as one-off events. Although it was Grabsky who had approached the National Gallery with the idea for the *Leonardo* film, he was resistant to the live aspect because it was more expensive (approximately an additional £75,000), required a massive crew of 60–70 people, and also negatively effects the quality of the final film, which cannot, for example, be color-graded if it is going out live. However, it was the cinemas in which the film would be exhibited, namely the independent Picturehouse chain, that insisted on it being broadcast live, reflecting the "consensus," as Benjamin Doty describes it, "about liveness in event cinema from distributors and exhibitors."[31]

Grabsky's lack of enthusiasm for live exhibition cinema was also based on his instinct that audiences who are interested in the arts are "interested in content and hearing intelligent people saying things about them" rather than an "overly enthusiastic presenter bounding from one room to another." This preference was ultimately recognized by the distributors and exhibitors of event exhibition cinema. In a 2014 interview, Christine Costello, the managing director of More2Screen, the company which distributed both of the British Museum broadcast films, acknowledges feedback from audiences saying they wanted "more lingering and close-up shots of the key artefacts" and that they "appreciated the authoritative expert view more than general tv 'banter.'"[32]

Conclusion

The recognition that audiences did not necessarily require the accoutrements of liveness to appreciate event exhibition cinema and that liveness, in the case of *Pompeii Live*, "did not seem to have a great impact on audience experience of the exhibition" is one explanation for why live broadcasts,[33] despite their commercial success, were not pursued by museums beyond 2014. Generally, box office figures for event cinema are harder to obtain than for other cinema releases. *Pompeii Live*, however, is known to have sold more than 50,000 tickets, grossing more than £450,000 at the UK box office, an achievement that trade press *Screen Daily* describes as "enviable to some smaller indie film releases."[34] Indeed, the film was tenth in that week's UK box office chart, despite only being shown once,[35] and the second highest-ranking film on its day of release.[36] The majority of the Twitter response from audiences was highly positive (as it was too for *Vikings Live*) and it won several awards at the 2014 Event Cinema Association Awards. However, several of the reviews of the broadcast are not as celebratory. The *Telegraph* is quite supercilious in tone,[37] echoing its rather scathing and snooty review of *Leonardo Live*.[38] While this may betray more about that newspaper than the broadcasts, it is an indication of the lower cultural value attributed to the cinema experience of an exhibition in comparison to the actual exhibitions which, in the case of Pompeii and Leonardo, were almost universally lauded by the critics. It also indicates a resistance to the "democratising" potential and rhetoric surrounding event cinema, at least in the case of museum exhibitions.[39]

Ultimately, however, the demise of the live exhibition cinema broadcast reflects the impossibility of overcoming the intermedial disjuncture of the experiences of exhibition, cinema, and live broadcast. The continuing and successful Exhibition on Screen cinema documentaries produced by Phil Grabsky have entirely rejected liveness in favor of pre-recorded and therefore highly controlled material. Unlike other cinematic arts documentaries, such as *Gerhard Richter Painting* (Corinna Belz, 2011), Grabsky's films continue to use specific exhibitions or collections as the conduit to exploring an artist's life and work. For example, 2013's *Manet* was based on London's Royal Academy of Arts exhibition of his portraiture, and 2016's *Renoir: Revered and Reviled* highlights the collection at the Barnes Foundation in

Philadelphia. However, the exhibitions are no longer the central focus and Grabsky instead sees them as a "springboard to broader biography" films about the artists. The continuing audience for the cinematic exhibition of these films, albeit a more modest audience than exists for live performance broadcasts of theater, ballet, and opera, means that Grabsky can continue make films that are large in scale and not beholden to the variable demands of television commissioning editors.[40]

Following the success of their two live broadcasts, the British Museum produced a pre-recorded event exhibition film for their Hokusai exhibition in 2017. However, the resource-heavy nature of such productions means that the museum has also actively pursued alternative ways to engage a wider audience with their exhibitions, primarily through social media outlets such as Facebook Live and the Twitter app Periscope.[41] Both developments are different responses to the challenge of remediating the museum exhibition via cinematic exhibition. While Grabsky has prioritized the cinematic, the British Museum's social media offerings privilege the exhibition. Whereas live event cinema has become established as a regular part of the program at local cinemas, live exhibition cinema's life was cut short by the intermedial incompatibility of museum exhibition, cinema exhibition, and liveness.

Notes

1. In the US, the term "alternative content" is used more broadly than "event cinema." See Fiona Tuck and Mitra Abrahams, *Understanding the Impact of Event Cinema: An Evidence Review* (London: Arts Council England and BFI, 2015), 5, www.artscouncil.org.uk/publication/understanding-impact-event-cinema.
2. See Martin Barker, *Live to Your Local Cinema: The Remarkable Rise of Livecasting* (London: Palgrave, 2013), 8; and Stephen Follows, "How Big is the UK 'Event Cinema' Market?" October 8, 2018, https://stephenfollows.com/uk-event-cinema/. According to Follows, there was another big spike in the market between 2012 and 2014, at which point the market levelled off at around £33m. Trade paper *Screen Daily* suggested in early 2018 that the event cinema market in the UK is now close to saturation. See Tom Grater, "Event Cinema Close to Saturation in the UK, but International Opportunities Remains, Says ECA Panel," *Screendaily.com*, February 7, 2018, www.screendaily.com/news/event-cinema-close-to-saturation-in-the-uk-but-international-opportunity-remains-say-eca-panel/5126353.article.
3. The idea for this broadcast originated with its director, Phil Grabsky, who approached several London-based museums, including the National Gallery, with the proposal of making a cinema film about an exhibition.
4. Both of the British Museum broadcasts had subsequent live broadcasts aimed specifically at school children.
5. Additionally, during this period the Victoria and Albert Museum in London released a live broadcast of their "David Bowie Is" exhibition in 2013: *David Bowie Is Happening Now*. This live exhibition broadcast falls outside the scope of this book, given the focus of the exhibition on the life and memorabilia of a pop music icon.
6. Although, unlike opera, ballet, and theater, the price differential between tickets for the exhibitions and tickets for the exhibition broadcasts in cinema was much smaller. For example, full-price tickets for the National Gallery's Leonardo exhibition cost £16, not significantly more than the cost of a cinema ticket.

7 Tuck and Abrahams, *Understanding the Impact*, 7.
8 National Gallery, "Leonardo Live," press release, May 2011, www.nationalgallery.org.uk/about-us/press-and-media/press-releases/leonardo-live.
9 Whether the broadcast achieved this regional reach is debatable, given the data showing that the majority of live arts broadcast audiences live in cities in the South East of England, i.e., in relatively close geographical proximity to the exhibition location compared to other parts of the country. See Tuck and Abrams, *Understanding the Impact*, 23–4.
10 British Museum, "Pompeii Live from the British Museum," press release, June 2013, www.britishmuseum.org/about_us/news_and_press/press_releases/2013/pompeii_live.aspx.
11 British Museum, "Pompeii Live from the British Museum," press release.
12 Roberta Smith, "Leonardo's London Blockbuster: The Movie," review of *Leonardo Live*, *New York Times*, February 15, 2012, www.nytimes.com/2012/02/16/arts/design/leonardo-live-puts-london-exhibition-on-screen.html.
13 See, for example, Michael Renov, "Art, Documentary as Art," in *The Documentary Film Book*, ed. Brian Winston (London: BFI, 2013), 345–52.
14 In contrast to, say, the use of film and moving image *in* museums that Alison Griffiths discusses in terms of interactivity and immersion in her book *Shivers Down Your Spine: Cinema, Museums and the Immersive View* (New York: Columbia University Press, 2008).
15 See for example Barker, *Live to Your Local Cinema*; Tuck and Abrahams, *Understanding the Impact*; Janice Wardle, "'Outside Broadcast': Looking Backwards and Forwards, Live Theatre in the Cinema – NT Live and RSC Live," *Adaptation* 7, no. 2 (2014): 134–53; and Paul Heyer, "Live from the Met: Digital Broadcast Cinema, Medium Theory, and Opera for the Masses," *Canadian Journal of Communication* 33, no. 4 (2008): 591–604.
16 See Benjamin Doty, "Exhibitions in the Dark: Event Cinema's Promise for Museums and Galleries," *Museological Review* 20 (2016): 18–26; and Lorna Cruickshanks, "Pompeii Live: Performing Objects," *Museum & Society* 14, no. 3 (2017): 446–55.
17 Barker, *Live to Your Local Cinema*, 71.
18 Charles Gant, "The Numbers: David Bowie is Happening Now," *Sight & Sound* 23, no. 10 (2013): 17.
19 For a detailed description of the exhibition, see Ewa Czapiewska, "Life and Death in Pompeii and Herculaneum, Exhibition At the British Museum, 28 March–29 September 2013," *Papers from the Institute of Archaeology* 24, no. 1 (2014): 1–4.
20 Czapiewska, "Life and Death," 2.
21 This temporal emphasis reflected the British Museum's desire to avoid the broadcast being an exhibition tour and that the timeline of the eruption and its aftermath was "more compelling storytelling". Hannah Boulton (British Museum Press Office), email to author, August 2, 2018.
22 Cruickshanks, "Pompeii Live," 449.
23 Tony Bennett, "Civic Seeing: Museums and the Organization of Vision," in *Companion to Museum Studies*, ed. Sharon Macdonald (Chichester: Wiley, 2006), 276.
24 Bill Hillier and Kali Tzortzi, "Space Syntax: The Language of Museum Space," in *Companion to Museum Studies*, ed. Macdonald, 282.
25 Kali Tzortzi, "Movement in Museums: Mediating Between Museum Intent and Visitor Experience," *Museum Management and Curatorship* 29, no. 4 (2014): 347.
26 Sharon Macdonald, "Architecture, Space, Media: Introduction to Part III," in *Companion to Museum Studies*, ed. Macdonald, 221.

27 Jonathan Jones, "Vikings at the British Museum: Great Ship but Where's the Story?" review of *Vikings: Life and Legend, The Guardian*, March 4, 2014, www.theguardian.com/artanddesign/2014/mar/04/vikings-british-museum-ship-story.
28 Mark Hudson, "Vikings, British Museum, review: Like watching 'The Killing' in Stansted Airport," review of *Vikings: Life and Legend, The Telegraph*, March 4, 2014, www.telegraph.co.uk/culture/art/art-reviews/10673076/Vikings-British-Museum-review-Like-watching-The-Killing-in-Stansted-Airport.html.
29 Philip Auslander, *Liveness: Performance in a Mediatized Culture*, 2nd ed. (London: Routledge, 2008), 63.
30 Phil Grabsky, phone interview with author, October 2, 2018. Subsequent details and quotes about the distribution of the films are derived from this interview.
31 Doty, "Exhibitions in the Dark," 21.
32 Patrick von Sychowski, "How the British Museum's 'Viking's Live' is Set to Storm Event Cinema – An Interview with More2Screen," *CelluloidJunkie*, March 6, 2014, https://celluloidjunkie.com/2014/03/06/vikings-set-storm-event-cinema/.
33 Cruickshanks, "Pompeii Live: Performing Objects," 452.
34 Wendy Mitchell, "CineEurope Day 3: Paramount Sequels, Pompeii Live Success," *Screen Daily*, June 26, 2013, www.screendaily.com/news/distribution/cineeurope-day-3-paramount-sequels-pompeii-live-success/5057785.article.
35 Von Sychowski, "How the British Museum's."
36 One tweet from the British Museum's Head of Digital Media and Publishing Tim Plyming (@timplyming) on June 22, 2013, claimed that the screening was "no 2 highest ranking film in UK" after Warner Brothers' Superman reboot blockbuster *Man of Steel* on June 18.
37 Judith Flanders, "Pompeii Live from the British Museum, Review," review of *Pompeii Live, The Telegraph*, June 19, 2013, www.telegraph.co.uk/history/pompeii/10127808/Pompeii-Live-from-the-British-Museum-review.html.
38 Mark Hudson, "Leonardo Live with Mariella Frostrup and Tim Marlow, Review," *The Telegraph* online, November 9, 2011, www.telegraph.co.uk/culture/art/leonardo-da-vinci/8878510/Leonardo-Live-with-Mariella-Frostrup-and-Tim-Marlow-review.html.
39 Martin Barker suggests "democratisation" is a key characteristic of event cinema, or "livecasting" as he calls it in *Live to Your Local Cinema*, 73–80.
40 Additionally, the Exhibition on Screen films are available on DVD and via some streaming services, such as Kanopy.
41 Boulton, email to author.

10
MUSEUM MOVIES, DOCUMENTARY SPACE, AND THE TRANSMEDIAL

Asbjørn Grønstad

In John Berger's landmark book *Ways of Seeing* (1972), the author suggests that when a film remediates a painting, it functions as raw material for the "argument" that the director is making. The artwork, Berger claims, "lends authority" to the film, aiding the spectator in discerning the filmmaker's objective.[1] But is the filmed painting still the same object that we can observe and contemplate within the confines of the museum? What becomes of the painting's autonomy once the art is captured on film? Last but not least, what *new* ways of seeing might emerge from the reframing of art by the filmic apparatus? In this chapter, I want to explore the ways in which particular cinematic practices contribute to a re-articulation of the meaning of the work of art. Central to this analysis is the notion of a *transmedial* gaze, a concept that, as I will argue below, is useful for making sense of the particular kind of aesthetic remediation that occurs when images refract other visual objects. Questions pertaining to such scopic ecologies have acquired a new urgency with the more or less concurrent appearance of several films deeply invested in probing the experiential space of the art museum: *The Great Museum* (Johannes Holzhausen, 2014), *The New Rijksmuseum* (Oeke Hoogendijk, 2014), and *National Gallery* (Frederick Wiseman, 2014). These works may also be considered in the context of thematically connected art films such as Aleksandr Sokurov's *Russian Ark* (2002), shot inside the Hermitage Museum in St. Petersburg, Tsai Ming-liang's *Visage* (2009), filmed inside the Louvre, and Jem Cohen's *Museum Hours* (2012), in part set, like Holzhausen's documentary, in the Kunsthistorisches Museum in Vienna. While the background for this flourishing of "museum movies" is not my primary focus here, one could speculate that among its possible explanations are the ongoing commodification of art institutions, the globalization of the art world, and the heightened sense of media interest in cultural institutions funded through public means. When Ruben Östlund's *The Square* – an hilariously satirical send-up of the art world – won the Palme d'Or in 2017, it was possibly a symbolic affirmation of the growing visibility of the museum film.

Right from the birth of cinema, its affiliation with art has been palpable. The work of the Lumière Brothers, for instance, was considered a new phase of impressionism.[2] Later, the rise of the *film d'art* movement (championed by the United Nations Educational, Scientific and Cultural Organization and the Féderation internationale des Archives du Film) and the so-called "Golden Age" of the art documentary in the 1940s and 1950s further fortified cinema's relationship with the art sphere, as did the creation by Iris Barry of a film library inside the Museum of Modern Art in the mid-1930s. The 1950s in particular signal a fertile period for this relationship, with the release of Alain Resnais's *Gauguin* (1950), *Guernica* (1951), and *Statues Also Die* (co-directed with Chris Marker, 1953), as well as pivotal feature films with key scenes set in a gallery, such as Roberto Rossellini's *Voyage to Italy* (1954) and Alfred Hitchcock's *Vertigo* (1958). Furthermore, in the medium of television, Kenneth Clark's influential *Civilisation* aired on BBC2 in the spring of 1969. In films such as those of Rossellini and Hitchcock, Steven Jacobs notes, the space of the museum is rendered "uncanny," but at the same time that space also encourages a "contemplative gaze" (xi), which I take to denote a gaze steeped in thoughtfulness and momentarily unconcerned with external action. In Jacobs's view, the museums in *Voyage to Italy* and *Vertigo*, while linked to death, become symbols of "cinematic self-reflection" (xi).

The three films that I discuss below – *National Gallery*, *The Great Museum*, and *Museum Hours* – all in their own ways rejuvenate this contemplative gaze. For example, one of the effects of Wiseman's unwavering emphasis on the gallery as a holistic universe unto its own is that the discrete artworks never eclipse the museum itself as the chief topic of the film. Despite the camera's propensity for animating the pictures (one critic suggests that the film allows us to see the paintings "as if for the first time, naked and unobstructed"),[3] Wiseman's vision is ecological rather than works-centered. The subject of his film is not paintings, much less one particular painting, but rather the institution itself, the myriad relations that exist between the gallery and its collections, between the individual works, and between the world of the institution and the medium of documentary film. In order to make sense of this multilayered visual environment, I want to suggest, it may be useful to consider the conceptual triad of the transvisual, the transmedial, and the transaesthetic. Another related question that I would also like to bring up concerns the affinity of films like *National Gallery*, *The Great Museum*, *Visage*, *Russian Ark*, and others with the notion of *cinéma d'exposition*, or "exhibition cinema," as discussed by Jean-Christophe Royoux.[4] The phenomenon that Royoux identifies is the augmented presence of cinematic works inside the spaces of the gallery, for example, in the form of multi-screen works, installation projects, and serial projections. One consequence of this interaction, Erika Balsom notes, is an ongoing transformation of the domains of both art and cinema.[5] While there is evidently a fundamental difference between exhibiting filmic/cinematic works in the gallery on the one hand, and turning the world of the gallery into a given film's subject matter on the other, the two phenomena still seem aesthetically related and an argument could be made that they manifest different aspects of the broader concept of *gallery cinema*.

Heterovisuality

One theoretical term that connects these different instantiations (the transvisual, the transmedial, and the transaesthetic) is *heterovisuality*, the interspersing of different visual media in the same work or arena. There are several different concepts available, sometimes used interchangeably, to describe heterovisual processes, and elsewhere I attempted to delineate their specificity.[6] The aforementioned conceptual triad of transvisuality, transmediality, and transaesthetics could, for instance, be seen as attached to their respective disciplinary locations – visual culture studies, (new) media studies, and philosophical aesthetics. But film as an object belongs to all of these discursive realms at once, privileging none. Although the transvisual appears to be close to the ways in which I have described a film such as *National Gallery* above, I would claim that we need to mobilize the other two concepts to obtain a more precise awareness of what is going on when a film encases a different visual medium. In an article about Ming-liang's *Visage*, I discuss transvisuality in terms of the interrelated notions of remediation and intertextuality.[7] In this reading, inspired by Gilles Deleuze's notion of *figure*,[8] the transvisual is a phenomenon or practice capable of transforming the appearance of an already existing visual object. One example would be Wong Kar-wai's refiguration of Edward Hopper's *Nighthawks* (1942) in his 2007 feature film *My Blueberry Nights* (2007). Importantly, the transvisual incites an interest in what I have called "the material density of the screen," an amplification of the opacity of the image (198). This is profusely demonstrated in *Visage*, the occasionally impenetrable film that the Louvre commissioned Ming-liang to make as part of their "Louvre Invites Filmmakers Program." Before shooting commenced, the director examined the paintings in the Louvre for three years, and the ensuing film is ostensibly about a Taiwanese filmmaker working on an adaptation of the Salome myth inside the museum. In the process, he endures many setbacks, such as the death of his mother, a volatile producer, challenging work conditions (filming inside a sewer and in a snowstorm), and a missing animal, to name a few. Deployed throughout are numerous frames or screen-like configurations that negotiate the boundary between transparency and opacity – windows, mirrors, monitors, gates, aquariums, plastic curtains, ventilator shafts, and faces covered in snow or by bandages. Unlike "regular" visuality, the transvisual foregrounds the optically opaque as well as "the image as a matrix rather than an object, constantly evolving and mutating, easily alterable and always resisting the figurational stasis so essential to the mimetic" (197).

Moving on to transmediality, over the last decade and a half much has been made of the culture of convergence that new digital media help generate, a technological environment where formerly discrete media co-exist on the same platform. Convergence in this shallow sense may be contrasted with the wholly different and deep sense of convergence produced by processes of transmediality, in which the medium-specific registers of distinct media blend together to create a new and impure aesthetic ensemble that cannot be reduced to any singular medium. When a sign migrates from one medium (painting) to another (film), it changes both phenomenologically and ontologically. But, since the transmedial prompts a convergence of gazes, the object also in turn shapes the new medium of which it has formed a part. Moreover, the "new" medium, as I have argued elsewhere, "gets modified not only by the content of the object, but also by the spectral vestiges of the medium that is no longer there."[9] Transmediality thus involves the possibility that a medium might exert an influence on another medium obliquely, or from a distance, since an image is never just an autonomous object or representation; it always contains a communicative surplus, and this surplus is its medium-specific qualities.[10] The presence of, say, Holbein's *The Ambassadors* (1533) in a given film conveys not only the content of the painting but also, albeit indirectly, a shade of its mediality. A film immersed in the world of paintings becomes in a way somewhat "painterly," just as a novel with photographs becomes somewhat "photographic."

If transmediality designates features of the medium that mark not only the object but also its remediated life, the transaesthetic denotes experience or content that exceeds the medium-specific. The concept could be taken to mean narrative matter that remains constant across different medial manifestations (like the skeletal structure of a particular narrative), but it could also denote the transference of a certain sensibility, attitude, or mode from, say, a film to a piece of music or from a painting to a novel. For example, *Upstream Color* (Shane Carruth, 2013) is by no means an adaptation or transposition of Henry David Thoreau's *Walden* (1854), yet the experimental science fiction film manages to convey part of the sensibility of that text through means that are specifically cinematic.[11]

National Gallery

Wiseman's *National Gallery* is a wide-ranging examination of the internal life of the London gallery that is also subtly attuned to that distinctive environment's rich minutiae. The film's sensitivity to the relay of gazes eminently captures the complexities of a transmedial mode of looking. As viewers, we are observing museumgoers looking at paintings that are themselves embroiled in acts of looking. Wiseman's dense processual imbrication of scenes and images cumulatively achieves a depiction of the museum that lays bare its tangled interrelationships of art, labor, patronage, and capital. The framing of the visual world of the gallery by the film camera, furthermore, adds an additional layer of mediation to this image ecology and also foregrounds the act of looking as a social practice. The camera's transmedial look serves to unveil the hidden affinities between images and their social, historical, and technological relations. How Wiseman's film organizes this ecology of gazes interacting inside the museum is something that I will return to below.

Few artists in any medium have examined the inner life of human institutions more meticulously and persistently than Wiseman. From his controversial first film *Titicut Follies* (1967) to his recent work *Ex Libris: New York Public Library* (2017), the filmmaker has tirelessly documented an extensive array of social establishments – hospitals, schools, law enforcement, the military, the vivisection industry, the ballet, the university, the courts, and many more. While Wiseman attempted to shoot a film about the Metropolitan Museum of Art in the early 1990s, a project that came to nothing when the museum required compensation, it was only when the National Gallery welcomed him to film with few constraints that his museum film materialized. Taking three months to shoot, *National Gallery* exhibits the same non-narrative approach that has become a hallmark of Wiseman's filmography. The eschewal of staged scenes, the absence of an explanatory voiceover and the scarcity of research undertaken before the cameras roll promote complexity, ambiguity, and openness – qualities that align Wiseman's projects with conventional modernist values, as well as with those of post-war art cinema. But the director's deceptively modest agenda to see "what was going on in particular kinds of social settings" still inspires a more intellectually ambitious objective, in that the completed film could be construed as a theoretically informed response to the events witnessed on screen.[12] Whether the space observed is a police department, a university, or a museum, Wiseman's camera seems particularly preoccupied with capturing the tacit value systems undergirding the institution in question. In *National Gallery*, the crew's access not only to the artworks themselves, but also to the museum's basement, restoration processes, and fundraising activities, enables a multifaceted description, one that is sensitive both to textual aesthetics and historical context. J.M.W. Turner's oil painting *Fighting Temeraire* (1839), for instance, alludes to the gallery's less palatable history of militarism and conquest. The eponymous gunship of Turner's painting participated in the Battle of Trafalgar in 1805, abetting Nelson's victory, and the gallery's foundation in 1824, clearly nationalistic in purpose, was in fact partly about honoring military triumphs.[13] Its first holdings, including works such as Titian's *Venus and Adonis* (1554) and Hogarth's *Marriage à la Mode* (1745), were purchased from the collection of the banker, connoisseur, and Caribbean plantation owner John Julius Angerstein, lending a colonial dimension to the museum's origin.

Wiseman's observational approach is particularly apt for the subject matter of this film, as it is consistent with the main activity going on in the institution itself. *National Gallery* features an abundance of artworks, and the director's framing often underscores the gaze of the characters. Many of the shots of paintings are also cropped, honing in on a particular section of the work and keeping not only the rest of it, but also the frame, the plaque, and the wall, off-screen. Reaction shots showing the visitors engrossed in observation are frequent and, peculiarly, in quite a few cases these reaction shots are neither preceded nor succeeded by the object scrutinized. Sometimes the spectators are even framed in ways that recall those in the paintings. One could thus argue that Wiseman's project is not just about cinema looking at art, and in the process generating a transmedial effect, but also about capturing subjects absorbed in their encounters with the artworks. It is as if Wiseman highlights the act of looking itself, an undertaking reminiscent of the German artist Thomas Struth's *Museum Photographs* (1989–90). But, bar a few exceptions, even Struth included the art object inside the frame for the most part.

But a striking aspect of a film so intently focused on practices of looking is the considerable amount of time it dedicates to talking about the art (Figure 10.1). At one point or another we are treated to talks or discussions about, for instance, Camille Pissarro's *Boulevard Montmartre at Night* (1897), Peter Paul Rubens's *Samson and Delilah* (1609–10), Holbein's *The Ambassadors* (1533), Titian's "Poesie" paintings (1550s), Michelangelo's *The Entombment* (1500–01), Nicolas Poussain's *The Triumph of Pan* (1636), as well as works by Leonardo, Velázquez, Van Gogh, and others. The various lectures serve a dramaturgical function in that they inscribe relatively lengthy blocks of narrative speech in intervals between sequences that either show a montage of paintings or let us eavesdrop on meetings concerning budgets, institutional profile, or the needs of the audience.

Inevitably, a set of prevailing themes emerge from the talks, themes that likely disclose some of the inherent values of the institution. It is likely that Wiseman shot several more of these lectures, but the ones he left in the finished film give us an indication of their relative significance within the context of his work. Among the issues brought up are the exhibition history of certain paintings, the human figure, the intention of the artist, the balance between realism and abstraction, the role images play in capturing and preserving a fragment of ephemeral reality, the danger of images, the question of ambiguity and interpretation, the narrative skillfulness of painters, the colonial history of the museum, the fact that art can be about anything (a point remarkably reminiscent of Jacques Rancière's justification for the separateness of art),[14] the current relevance of a given painting, and, finally, interart poetics. The ample consideration of the latter topic throughout Wiseman's film adds to its transmedial nature. Transmediality as a process occurs whenever the film camera grazes upon the paintings in the gallery, but it also materializes in the accentuation of painting's relation to the other arts. Showing the paintings through the camera lens

FIGURE 10.1 *National Gallery*
(Frederick Wiseman, 2014)

might also be a way of fostering an awareness of the mediated nature of the works themselves. As deeply canonized artifacts, the images and objects in the museum assume an existential givenness that might obscure their status as mediations. The film camera as a technology of representation enframes the art objects in a way that reminds us not only of the mediality of the cinematic apparatus but also, through textual contiguity, of that of painting and sculpture. The transmedial moments thus work to distance the viewer from the potentially overwhelming immediacy of the artworks. At one point, a museum guide encourages the audience "to view paintings or narrative paintings as early films" and as forms of entertainment. In a discussion of Titian's large-scale mythological "Poesie" paintings, the lecturer draws attention to the lyrical quality of the works and their relation to the Roman poet Ovid's *Metamorphosis*. Ovid, the painter's favorite poet according to the guide, used words in a visual way. Pondering Jean-Antoine Watteau's *The Scale of Love* (1715–8), a group of interlocutors debate the likelihood of the artist knowing an instrument and of the sheet music in the image representing real, playable notes. The most substantial reflection on the transmedial that we are privy to, however, is the then museum director Nicholas Penny's argument about Nicolas Poussain's *The Triumph of Pan* (1636) in terms of the contest between the different arts: how the artist attempts to incorporate something sculptural into the painting and how painting could do things that the art of sculpture could not. Near the end of the film there is also a scene showing the poet Jo Shapcott reading her own "Callisto's Song" as a gesture toward Titian's *Diana and Callisto* (1556–9). Wiseman even includes a dance performance taking place in front of two paintings, juxtaposing the movement of the ballet with the stasis of the paintings. Finally, a close-up montage of severe faces and gazes from various paintings punctuates the film, as if to celebrate the sovereignty of the pure act of looking itself.

The Great Museum

In addition to encompassing all these ideas and topics, *National Gallery* is a film of relentless background murmur, a film of extras, and a film unafraid to be submerged in beauty. While obviously comparable, Johannes Holzhausen's *The Great Museum* is quite different, although it is not difficult to see how one could be tricked by superficial correspondences into thinking their projects are basically the same. One critic, for example, claims that the two films utilize "strikingly similar tactics," evidenced in artistic choices such as the elision of voiceover narration and talking heads, and the willingness to flaunt the "quietness" and the "quotidian" tasks that define the space and rhythm of the museum.[15] But Wiseman's omission of such staples of documentary cinema have long since become too prevalent to be meaningfully used as indicators of aesthetic semblance. *National Gallery* is also considerably less quiet than *The Great Museum*; it contains more environmental noise and the numerous snippets from the art historical talks are in a louder register than the more subdued conversations in Holzhausen's film. The *Slant* critic's impression that both films essentially concern themselves with the prosaic day-to-day operations of the institution is moreover imprecise at best. This is true of *The Great Museum*, but *National Gallery* is just as, if not more, invested in the meaning of the canonical artworks as it is in the practical routines of running the museum.

Although Wiseman's film is keenly interested in what is happening behind the scenes, in business meetings, and in various strategies to cultivate the museum's public identity, these passages should be considered in relation to the thematically and narratively central position occupied throughout by the art itself. Where *National Gallery* captures the wider ecology of the institution, from board meetings to the audience's sustained engagement with the paintings, *The Great Museum* mostly observes the practices, preparations, and procedures going on backstage. In a certain sense Holzhausen's film portrays the museum as a workplace, whereas Wiseman portrays it as a place to visit for education and entertainment. Holzhausen's interest is the last stages of a long restoration of the Kunstkammer (the Habsburg art collection) and the imperial treasury and the *process* leading up to an exhibition. Wiseman's interest lies more with the finished *product*, and its cultural significance and interpretive possibilities. The two films also differ with respect to the kinds of media receiving the most attention, representational painting in *National Gallery* and material objects such as small statues, jewelry, and miniature ships in *The Great Museum*. This is not to say that paintings are not part of the story in Holzhausen's film, but they take up less filmic space and are often enveloped in Bubble Wrap when they are in fact shown – they are thus framed more as precious objects than as pictures.

Another way of framing the disparity between the two films would be to suggest that in *National Gallery* the art works themselves act as the main protagonist, while in *The Great Museum* the gallery is assigned this function. For Holzhausen possibly more so than for Wiseman, the museum is a concrete building as much as an institution in the more abstract sense. The copious shots of paintings in *National Gallery* threaten to occlude the specificity of the museum's spaces. This is less of an issue in *The Great Museum*, which rarely lets us forget about the building's opulent architecture and interiors. In a style that calls to mind the aesthetic of other Austrian documentarians, like Nikolaus Geyrhalter and Michael Glawogger, the film features several symmetrical extreme long shots.[16] In the film's opening shots, for instance, the bright red carpets exert a stronger pull on the viewer than the painting in the process of being moved. Later in the film, there are a few high-angle shots that show the lush splendor of a space filled with prominent patrons awaiting a grand opening. Then there are the frequent scenes depicting diverse forms of manual labor taking place within the quarters of the museum, chores which all in one way or the other involve material upkeep, whether of the art or of the building itself. Floors are cleaned, statues dusted, wallpaper removed, walls painted, carpets swept, paintings inspected for insects, floors demolished, and weeds pulled out. Rather than showing curators talking about the works, Holzhausen seems to prefer situations in which conservationists and touch-up artists are busy working on objects, whether statues, figurines, uniforms, swords, miniature ships, or a stuffed polar bear (Figure 10.2). Hands rather than eyes appear to be the locus of action in this particular ecosystem. This imbues the film with a powerful sense of texture and tactility.

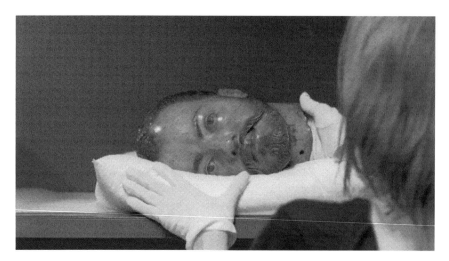

FIGURE 10.2 *The Great Museum*
(Johannes Holzhausen, 2014)

That *The Great Museum* is a film more centered on the life of material objects than on visual representation is also borne out by its showcasing of a set of particularly cherished possessions. In terms of the attention lavished upon these items within the structure of the film, they take on a saliency the equivalent of which would be the discussions of Pissarro or Poussain in *National Gallery*. The first is a magnificent textile, an imperial military uniform, donated to the museum by a prominent local family. In the film, the entrustment of the outfit is emphasized more than the object itself, with the elderly owner shown in conversation with museum representatives. When the president comes to visit in a different scene, he is shown the royal crown, on which the film lingers for a while. Toward the end, there is a lengthy sequence from a press conference, at which the facsimile version of the Vienna Coronation Gospel is unveiled. The museum director explains that only the cover of the original is on display at the Secular Treasury, as the manuscript itself cannot be exposed to light on a daily basis. With the production of a facsimile edition with 333 copies (each purchasable for 30,000 euros), the entire book has thus been made publicly accessible, albeit to an elite audience.

It is the museum itself (and its historically resonant objects, such as those detailed above) that seems to be the greatest source of pride for its custodians. In the few scenes where (unwrapped) paintings do appear, there is scarcely a mention of their history and meaning. "What if we hang *Mars and Venus* on the left instead of the *Filetto*?" is about as far as the art historical deliberation goes. In several scenes Holzhausen also emphasizes the intimate relation between the artworks and the ceiling fresco, which, according to one of the executives, uniquely displays some of the figures that are also part of the collections. But if the institution in *The Great Museum* comes across as a tad more introverted than that of Wiseman's film, the former also features moments that are explicitly critical of the museum. In a rather tense and slightly uncomfortable segment, one of the guards complains that after many years of service she still has not been introduced to the museum's management. This not so subtle indictment of the hierarchical structure of the institution is supplemented by a monologue by (presumably) one of the curators, who is openly skeptical about the enduring legacy of the Habsburgs. The fact is, he says,

> that the aesthetic imperial legacy is under our aegis and we manage and present it. The question is, how do we approach it? Are we doing it, aesthetically speaking, as faithful servants of this imperial house? Or are we doing it as self-assured individuals in the here and now? I find it all quite dominant, very immediate, and a position one can all too easily retreat to.

In reply to this, his interlocutor briefly states that "that's the marketing." Even more so than its British counterpart, the museum in Holzhausen's film seems intensely concerned about the legacy and the branding of the institution. At the same time, the segments dealing with this could also be read as a critique of the museum's questionable preoccupation with cultural capital and imperialist nostalgia.

Whether the cinematized objects are classical paintings, as in *National Gallery*, or uniforms, jewelry, or the museum building, as in *The Great Museum*, Wiseman's and Holzhausen's films are both transmedial works that filter a discrete visual world through the material and formal *dispositif* of documentary film. By this process the sites and images are transformed into something else. Inserted into a new narrative, they become part of a different discourse. If we go back to Berger's remark that the artworks provide substance to the filmmaker's "argument" or "objective," what exactly are these arguments and objectives, and how do they influence the way we approach the art objects? For one thing, the films would appear to refute the old but recalcitrant position that paintings are autonomous artifacts. Both *National Gallery* and *The Great Museum* argue instead that the artworks form relational nodes in an extensive ecology contingent upon a complex network of institutional, economic, cultural, and critical circumstances. Secondly, the films show that the language of cinema can offer a singular way of experiencing the museum, rejuvenating our act of looking through completely altering our access to the artworks. In the museum, we are guided by the trajectory and internal relations that the curators have chosen for us. A film, on the other hand, is at liberty to reconfigure the contents of the museum space through aesthetic affordances such as montage, sequentiality, cropping of images, various sound and musical effects, and voiceover narration. This might seem obvious, but at the same time it is easy to underestimate the crucial perceptual and phenomenological differences between watching a painting "live" in a gallery and watching the same painting in mediated form as a sign integrated into a chain of other signs.

Museum Hours

A third "argument" that the museum films could be found to convey involves the permeable boundary between art and life. With their emphasis on everything from material upkeep to marketing strategies for making the collections speak to contemporary concerns, Wiseman's and Holzhausen's films expose the rather common misapprehension that the sanctified artworks exist in their own rarefied sphere, divorced from the everyday lives of their audience. In Jem Cohen's essayistic *Museum Hours*, the third and last film I will consider here, there is no such boundary between art and lived experience. Cohen, who has directed music videos for R.E.M. songs such as "Talk About the Passion," "Country Feedback," and "Nightswimming," seamlessly interweaves the world of painting and the world of human emotion. Also set in the Kunsthistorisches Museum in Vienna, *Museum Hours* applies the musings of a museum guard, provided in a calm voiceover, as a bridge between the world of the paintings and the lives of the protagonists. While *Museum Hours* is technically a feature film, its style – like other art films shot in museums such as *Visage* and *Russian Ark* – is close to a documentary aesthetic.[17] The transmedial straddles the genres of both documentary and fiction, so we may ask if the distinction matters when it comes to our filmic experience of real institutional spaces, and if so, how.

Unlike Holzhausen's film, *Museum Hours* actually dedicates a fair amount of screen time to showing the paintings in the gallery. Johann (Bobby Sommer), the guard, freely shares his thoughts about the art. One day he meets Anne, a jetlagged and mildly disoriented middle-aged woman from Montreal (played by the singer Margaret O'Hara), who is in town to visit her hospitalized cousin. New to Vienna and on meager funds, Anne takes to spending much of her time in the Kunsthistorisches Museum, where she befriends Johann, an affable and soft-spoken gay man who had managed punk bands in a previous career. As he points out, "I had my share of loud, so now I have my share of quiet." Exhibiting an unusual sensitivity to the particularity of spaces, Cohen's film skillfully sutures the world of the artworks and the lived experience of the people who look at them. Sometimes the director cuts from a fragment of a painting showing birds in a tree to an image of birds and trees outside, as well as from a close-up of Johann's hands to a section of a painting with hands. Johann firmly believes that there is always something new to discover in a painting, even after six years of working as a guard. As an example he mentions that he just noted a small detail in a Bruegel painting, a frying pan jutting out from someone's head, that he had never seen before. This sharp attention to aesthetic minutiae – and to its potential to reinvigorate our gaze – pervades the entire film (Figures 10.3 and 10.4). In a prolonged talk on several of Bruegel's paintings, *The Tower of Babel* (1563) and *The Conversion of St. Paul* (1567) among them, the guide (Ela Piplits) stresses the multiple points of attention in his paintings and that the works might be about something else, or more, than their titles let on. Comparing his painting to documentaries, the guide talks about Bruegel's interest in everyday scenes and in landscapes (as a subject, not just background), getting into

FIGURE 10.3 *Museum Hours*
(Jem Cohen, 2013)

FIGURE 10.4 *Museum Hours*
(Jem Cohen, 2013)

a quarrel with a narrow-minded visitor who fails to discern that paintings could contain more than the ostensible theme would suggest. But Cohen's awareness of the importance of looking hard and finding something of value in the most inauspicious, nondescript places extends beyond the artworks themselves.

Besides being a gallery film and maybe a distant relative of Abbas Kiarostami's *Certified Copy* (2010) and Richard Linklater's *Before* series (1995, 2004, 2013), *Museum Hours* also embodies some of the characteristics of the city symphony. Interspersed among the digitally shot medley of paintings and the unhurried conversation scenes are a vast number of 16mm shots of Vienna: streets, buildings, passersby, waiters, snooker games, toddlers stumbling about, playgrounds, posters and bulletins, metro stops, shops, skateboarders, tree trunks, traffic, train stations, street signs, footprints on the ground, and pigeons. Again and again Cohen cuts to these unexceptional spaces in an insistent rhythm that makes us attend to what we are otherwise prone to overlook, both in paintings and in the street. There is a descriptive quality to this poetics, as if Cohen's camera wants to say "here is this particular building, there is that particular street corner." In this regard, the film's form recalls some of the ideas of the American poet Mark Doty, who both in his literary and non-fiction work promoted the art of description and infused it with an almost ethical significance. "[T]he more we can name what we're seeing," Doty writes, "the less likely we are to destroy it."[18] The abundance of descriptive shots in *Museum Hours* seem to perform the visual equivalent of such a process of naming. But there is also a moving scene early in the film in which Anne asks Johann to describe some of the paintings in the museum to her cousin, who is in a coma, in the faint hope that his friendly and patient voice might trigger something. So Johann talks about Rembrandt's dark self-portraits, Cohen cutting away to the paintings, and then about Giuseppe Arcimboldo's *Summer* (1563), during which Johann's pose mimics that of the "summer man" in the painting.

Museum Hours is in part about Johann's rediscovery of a city that had become too familiar to be noticed properly. It is also, as one critic has suggested, about the possibility of finding beauty not only in canonical works of art but "in every corner and crevice of life, from the debris on wet streets to the careful gait of an old woman caught outside in bad winter weather."[19] The same critic goes on to claim that looking at the fragments of art, as well as of the world around us, entails the kind of "practiced contemplation" cultivated in *Museum Hours*. This might be the foremost contribution of what I like to call transmedial practices of looking – the capacity of cinema as a medium to re-present to us already existing images and make us discover in them something that we had not seen before. In this, there is no difference between art cinema and documentary, as they both enact, as André Bazin famously noted, a "transference of reality" from the object to the image.[20]

Notes

1 John Berger, *Ways of Seeing* (London: BBC and Penguin Books, 1972), 26.
2 See Steven Jacobs, "Introduction," in *Framing Pictures: Film and the Visual Arts* (Edinburgh: Edinburgh University Press, 2011), ix.
3 Ryan Gilbey, "A View Unbroken," *New Statesman*, January 9, 2015, 48.
4 Jean-Christophe Royoux, "Remaking Cinema," in *Cinema, Cinema: Contemporary Art and the Cinematic Experience*, ed. Jaap Guldemond (Rotterdam: Nai, 1999), 21. For a similar idea, see Raymond Bellour, "Of An Other Cinema," in *Art and the Moving Image: A Critical Reader*, ed. Tanya Leighton (London: Tate Publishing/Afterall Books, 2008), 406–22. See also Michael Rush, *Video Art* (London: Thames and Hudson, 2003), 117–8; Catherine Elwes, *Video Art: A Guided Tour* (London: I.B. Tauris, 2005), 170; Michael Newman, "Moving Image in the Gallery since 1990," in *Film and Video Art*, ed. Stuart

Comer (London: Tate Publishing, 2009), 88; and Catherine Fowler, "Remembering Cinema 'Elsewhere': From Retrospection to Introspection in the Gallery Film," *Cinema Journal* 51, no. 2 (2012): 26–45.
5 Erika Balsom, "A Cinema in the Gallery, a Cinema in Ruins," *Screen* 50, no. 4 (2009): 411.
6 See Asbjørn Grønstad, "Enfolded by Cinema: The Transvisual Gaze in Tsai Ming-liang's *Visage*," in *Transvisuality: The Cultural Dimension of Visuality, Volume 2: Visual Organizations*, eds. Tore Kristensen, Anders Michelsen & Frauke Wiegand (Liverpool: Liverpool University Press, 2015), 193.
7 Grønstad, "Enfolded by Cinema," 192.
8 Gilles Deleuze, *Cinema 1: The Movement-Image*, trans. Hugh Tomlinson and Barbara Habberjam (London: Athlone Press, 1986), 178.
9 Asbjørn Grønstad, "Refigurations of Walden: Notes on Contagious Mediation," in *Literature in Contemporary Media Culture: Technology – Subjectivity – Aesthetics*, eds. Sarah J. Paulson and Anders Skare Malvik (Amsterdam: John Benjamins, 2016), 208.
10 See also Asbjørn Grønstad, "Is There a Transmedial Dispositif? Aesthetic Epistemes and the Question of Disciplinarity," *The Nordic Journal of Aesthetics* 23, no. 42 (2012): 34.
11 See Grønstad, "Refigurations of Walden," 208.
12 Donald E. McWilliams, "Frederick Wiseman," *Film Quarterly* 24, no. 1 (1970): 17.
13 See Jonathan Conlin, *The Nation's Mantelpiece: A History of the National Gallery* (London: Pallas Athene, 2006).
14 In *Aisthesis*, Jacques Rancière notes that the aesthetic sphere, unlike other social domains, is defined by the fact that "anything whatsoever can belong to it." See Jacques Rancière, *Aisthesis: Scenes From the Aesthetic Regime of Art*, trans. Zakir Paul (London: Verso, 2013), x.
15 Clayton Dillard, "*The Great Museum*," *Slant Magazine*, April 19, 2015, www.slantmagazine.com/film/review/the-great-museum.
16 I owe this observation to Roger Hallas.
17 This has also been noted by some of the reviewers. For instance, see Tim Grierson, "Review of *Museum Hours*," *Paste Magazine*, August 6, 2013, www.pastemagazine.com/articles/2013/08/museum-hours.html.
18 Mark Doty, *The Art of Description: World Into Word* (Minneapolis: Graywolf Press, 2010), 108.
19 Tina Hassannia, "Review of *Museum Hours*," *Slant Magazine*, December 22, 2013, www.slantmagazine.com/dvd/review/museum-hours.
20 André Bazin, "The Ontology of the Photographic Image," trans. Hugh Gray, *Film Quarterly* 13, no. 4 (1960): 8.

11
"SEEING TOO MUCH IS SEEING NOTHING"

The place of fashion within the documentary frame

Matthew J. Fee

While fashion has played a key role in fiction film, from "It Girl" Clara Bow and classical Hollywood's *The Women* (George Cukor, 1939) to more contemporary offerings, such as *The Devil Wears Prada* (David Frankel, 2006) and *Personal Shopper* (Olivier Assayas, 2016), its presence has likewise proliferated across a wide range of nonfiction media. Alongside its television incarnations (e.g., *Project Runway*, *Live from the Red Carpet*) and its ubiquity across digital and social media platforms (Instagram and fashion blogs), documentary cinema has also increasingly turned its attention to things sartorial. To be sure, cinema's nonfiction focus on fashion, while more prevalent in recent decades, is neither new nor restricted to the documentary feature form. "Fashion films" that stage the dynamic interaction between fashion and film extend from the birth of cinema to the present day, taking on forms such as early-twentieth-century commercials (including some supposedly created by Georges Méliès); newsreels and "cinemagazines"; designer-sponsored films produced to substitute for – or complement – runway shows; promotional films directed by notable filmmakers, such as Martin Scorsese, Baz Luhrmann, Kenneth Anger, and David Lynch; and behind-the-scenes documentaries exploring the work of specific couturiers as well as national fashion traditions and industries.[1] Indeed, it is this latter branch of the fashion film's diverse "pantheon" (to use Marketa Uhlirova's phrase) that I examine in this chapter, as it has particularly flourished in recent decades. And while some of these examples interrogate fashion's contentious status as art, all of these films document how various cultural institutions place fashion within different contexts, compelling us to consider how such aesthetic objects are remediated into consumable images.

Like other arts documentaries, fashion's presence in documentary features has predominantly focused on the individual creativity of particular fashion designers, such as *Unzipped* (Douglas Keeve, 1995) and its account of the development and launch of Isaac Mizrahi's 1994 collection; *Valentino: The Last Emperor* (Matt

Tyrnauer, 2008), which covers the designer's retirement and final collection; and *Dior and I* (Frédéric Tcheng, 2014), which chronicles Raf Simons's first collection as the creative director for Christian Dior. In the same way, two of the latest documentaries, *McQueen* (Ian Bonhôte and Peter Ettedgui, 2018) and *Westwood: Punk, Icon, Activist* (Lorna Tucker, 2018), profile and celebrate these individual designers as synonymous with the development of contemporary British fashion. Although differing in not simply their central characters but also their cinematic style and temperament – making use of aesthetic devices ranging from static talking heads to hyper-kinetic digital effects, with tones spanning the effervescent and the elegiac – all of these documentaries figure the fashion designer as the resilient creative force and genius, bearing out Stella Bruzzi and Pamela Church Gibson's assertion that "Fashion has developed its own grand narrative around the centralization of the individual couturier."[2]

Another collection of fashion documentaries similarly maintains a focus upon individual talent. In these films, though, it is not the designers but rather the people who engage with fashion from the "sidelines," but with these sidelines nevertheless situating us in the front rows of fashion shows: fashion photographer Bill Cunningham in *Bill Cunningham: New York* (Richard Press, 2010); columnist and former *Vogue* editor-in-chief Diana Vreeland in *Diana Vreeland: The Eye Has to Travel* (Lisa Immordino Vreeland, Frédéric Tcheng, and Bent-Jorgen Perlmutt, 2011); designer and fashion icon Iris Apfel in *Iris* (Albert Maysles, 2014); and fashion editor André Leon Talley in *The Gospel According to André* (Kate Novack, 2017). But in the midst of this boom in nonfiction media with an eye to fashion, there is one further group of documentaries that deserve particular critical attention. Fashion is an essential element to these feature-length nonfiction narratives as well, with a variety of singular personalities likewise dominating their observations. However, these documentaries concern themselves more so with fashion located in the context of cultural institutions such as the magazine, the department store, and the art museum. In the earlier mentioned works that document specific and singular designers, photographers, personalities, and editors, fashion most frequently functions as a means of relaying the individual's vision, creativity, resilience, passion, and talent. This chapter, however, moves away from fashion as mere conduit of creative expression. Instead, it examines fashion's central role, the place of fashion, if you will, in documentaries concerned with the cultural institutions that promote fashion as image, commodity, and art: *The September Issue* (R.J. Cutler, 2009); *Scatter My Ashes at Bergdorf's* (Matthew Miele, 2013); and *The First Monday in May* (Andrew Rossi, 2016).[3] As a result, all three films powerfully document how these institutions transform fashion from haptic objects into more abstract, multiple, and dynamic occasions for optical engagement. Given its simultaneous aesthetic and narrative foregrounding of the very question of fashion's status as art, particular attention will be dedicated to Rossi's *The First Monday in May*.

Each of these three films contains certain scenes that we have come to expect from fashion documentaries (e.g., runway models strutting the catwalk, cameras flashing at celebrity sightings, and a host of designers making appearances).

These films all similarly rely on the standard documentary trope of the talking-head interview. They also repeatedly use expressive cinematography to provide mannequin-draping garments with both movement and tactility through, for example, sweeping camera movements and tracking shots through spaces, as well as tilts and pans along close-ups of the garments that display their stitching, fabric textures, beadwork, etc. Moreover, fashion documentaries commonly achieve momentum through structuring their narratives according to a looming deadline, with the development, production, completion, and launch of a designer's collection via its grand runway reveal propelling these films towards their narrative conclusions. In the documentaries by Cutler, Miele, and Rossi, though, it is not a runway show that supplies the culmination of the film's creative trajectory. With *The September Issue*, *Scatter My Ashes at Bergdorf's*, and *The First Monday in May*, the narratives progress forward, respectively, in the five months anticipating the publication of *Vogue*'s September issue in 2007; the seven weeks leading up to the unveiling of Bergdorf Goodman's 2011 Christmas window display "Carnival of the Animals"; and the eight months prior to the launch of the Met's 2015 Costume Institute exhibition, *China: Through the Looking Glass* (and its attendant annual gala, held on the first Monday in May).

This shift in motivating deadline alerts us to another more notable and shared alteration across these documentaries concerned with how institutions "place" fashion. Significantly, they lack any of the conventional creation scenes that habitually transpire in fashion films, specifically scenes of designers researching, becoming inspired, sketching, selecting fabrics, producing garments, fitting models, organizing runway shows, troubleshooting last-minute calamities, negotiating backstage drama, and reading next-day reviews. On the rare occasions when these documentaries include such scenes, they serve as opportunities to channel the unique and laudable qualities of their respective institutions, rather than, per se, an individual designer's creativity and vision.[4] Missing from these films is thus coverage of the production processes of the garments themselves, with fashion marketing, consumption, and promotion of finished products occupying a much more prominent role. One of the most telling instances of this prioritization of consumption over production occurs in *Scatter My Ashes at Bergdorf's*. In the film, there is one instance when someone explicitly references the actual chain of clothing production, noting:

> This whole chain of events, from the farmer that is shearing wool off the lamb, sending it to the factory to be woven into thread, sending it to the mills to make these beautiful Merino wool double-faced fabrics that end up in a Ralph Rucci Chado jacket that sells for $10,000, is an incredible line of employment and commerce.

Indicative of a documentary that highlights the buying and selling of fashion over its creative labor, we learn about this production process not from a designer, or even someone working in an atelier, factory, or mill, but rather from the department store's director of personal shopping. In lieu of a focus on fashion's design processes,

The September Issue, *Scatter My Ashes at Bergdorf's*, and *The First Monday in May* are more concerned with what happens *after* the creative and production processes conclude, chronicling instead the behind-the-scenes processes of these garments' eventual placement in spaces of display, respectively, within the pages of *Vogue* magazine's legendary September issue; on the shop-floors and in the windows of New York City high-end department store Bergdorf Goodman; and in the galleries of the Met.

Rather than concentrating on a singular designer or other creative professional (as is the case in most fashion documentaries), each of these films divides its attention across a variety of characters and the combination of their creative efforts to place fashion in a magazine, department store, or art museum. For example, in *The September Issue* we follow the magazine's creative director, Grace Coddington, and its editor-at-large, André Leon Talley, while *Scatter My Ashes at Bergdorf's* introduces us to the store's senior director for visual presentation, David Hoey, and its fashion director, Linda Fargo. In *The First Monday in May*, the range of characters varies even more, and includes Met staff Andrew Bolton, Thomas Campbell, Harold Koda, and Maxwell Hearn, as well as film directors Baz Luhrmann and Wong Kar-wai. Given the popularity of *The Devil Wears Prada* as both novel and film, though, it may come as no surprise that one character achieves prominence across all three documentaries: *Vogue* editor and Met Museum trustee Anna Wintour.[5]

This chapter will now focus on Rossi's *The First Monday in May*, not merely for its high profile amongst fashion documentaries (it opened the 2016 Tribeca Film Festival), but also because, more importantly, it locates ongoing debates around fashion's status as art front-and-center narratively and aesthetically in relation to the largest art museum in the United States. Moreover, through its account of both the exhibition and its accompanying annual benefit gala, the documentary comprehensively examines fashion's placement across artistic, publishing, celebrity, and commercial contexts. Rossi had previously directed *Page One: Inside the New York Times* (2011) and *Ivory Tower* (2014), documentaries that investigated the institutions of journalism and higher education. Rossi saw his turn to the Met in *The First Monday in May* as a continuation of his ongoing exploration of "celebrated institutions." In fact, Rossi claimed that his documentary could actually be understood to investigate two "institutions": the Met and the Anna Wintour "complex" and "mythology." Rossi has even gone so far as to describe *The First Monday in May* as an unofficial sequel to *The September Issue*.[6]

Rossi's comment about the film's dual institutional focus is not merely a clever remark about Wintour, but proves rather instructive for analyzing the documentary itself, as the film alternates between two lines of action. The first line involves the Met's Costume Institute and its fashion exhibitions. The Institute sponsors one to two exhibitions each year by drawing on its "collection of more than thirty-three thousand costumes and accessories represent[ing] five continents and seven centuries of fashionable dress and accessories for men, women, and children, from the fifteenth century to the present," as well as through partnering with other museums around the world.[7] While some of the exhibitions have been monographic in nature (e.g., *The World of Balenciaga*; *Yves Saint Laurent: 25 Years of Design*; *The House of Chanel*; and *Alexander McQueen: Savage Beauty*), other exhibitions have taken a more thematic approach (e.g., *Man and the Horse*; *Superheroes: Fashion and Fantasy*), including some that explored fashion through specific national and historical contexts (e.g., *The Glory of Russian Costume*; *The Eighteenth-Century Woman*; and *AngloMania: Transgression and Tradition in British Fashion*).

The First Monday in May documents the development, production, and opening of the 2015 exhibition *China: Through the Looking Glass*. A collaboration between the Met's Costume Institute and its Department of Asian Art, the exhibition sought to "vividly [reveal] how some of the most creative minds in the world of Western fashion design have been inspired by Chinese imagery and aesthetics."[8] Curator Andrew Bolton described the exhibition as a "two-way conversation," one in which cinema frequently mediates between Western fashion and the "collective fantasy" of its Chinese inspiration.[9] Exhibition reviews often questioned whether Bolton's "fantasy" trafficked in appropriation, Orientalism, and superficialities, rather than inspiration. And while one review argued that the exhibition "is not meant to be a critical assessment of the fashion industry's non-fiction, politically correct relationship with China's culture, history, or its people" as it "underscores the complicated nature of cultural representation," many others expressed disappointment that the exhibition's vast scope failed to provide the nuance, depth, context, or examination of cultural implications necessary to even begin to address such risks.[10] Nevertheless *China: Through the Looking Glass* proved incredibly popular with museum audiences, until recently holding its status as the most popular fashion exhibition in the history of the Costume Institute, while it remains one of the Met's top ten most popular exhibitions.[11]

The second line of action in *The First Monday in May* revolves around the Costume Institute's annual benefit that accompanies the spring exhibition, which is held at the Met on the first Monday in May, one of only four days in the year when the museum is closed.[12] First held as a "midnight supper" in 1948 – two years after the Museum of Costume Art merged with the Met, consequently establishing the Costume Institute – the annual event serves as the Institute's primary fundraising event. Since 1995, with the exception of two years, it has been co-chaired and organized by Wintour.[13] Nicknamed "the Party of the Year," and now popularly known as "the Met Gala," the event has also been labelled the "Oscars of the East Coast" and "the Super Bowl of charity events" in recognition of its heightened profile and expansive celebrity guest list that includes film stars, musicians, athletes, and politicians.[14]

As the opening of *China: Through the Looking Glass* approaches, the documentary alternates between preparations for the exhibition and the gala. On the one hand, we follow discussions and the set-up around the exhibition involving the director of the Met Museum, Thomas Campbell; curators Harold Koda and Andrew Bolton; the director of Asian Art, Maxwell (Mike) Hearn; and the exhibit's artistic director, Wong Kar-wai. They engage with logistical questions around lighting schemes and the flow of visitors, as well as larger questions around the relation between the artworks and the fashions, fears of turning the Met into "Disneyland," and concerns around Orientalism, racism, and critical responses to the show. Indeed, at times Bolton seems quite enamored of the possibilities of controversy, insisting at one point that "the show should be controversial and provocative." Bolton goes so far as to propose the placement of Mao-inspired fashions in the Met's Buddhist art gallery, as yet another example of "a lot to see" as "the material is so rich" in the exhibition – a proposal that inspires a skeptical Wong to retort, "But try not to make the show too busy. Because seeing too much is seeing nothing." On the other hand, we follow Wintour and her staff, and the gala's creative consultant, Baz Luhrmann, as they compile invitation lists, map out seating charts, determine color schemes for place settings, negotiate salary for featured performer Rihanna, express dissatisfaction with *Vogue*'s new offices, and assist Wintour's daughter in trying on her gown for the gala (indeed, this is oddly the only instance in a film about fashion in which we witness someone trying on clothing).

The documentary's fundamental structural and narrative contrast between the art exhibition and its celebrity gala – between the worlds of art and entertainment – becomes explicit in a central preoccupation of the film: the debate around whether fashion's relation to commerce precludes its consideration as art, and hence whether it is appropriate to display fashion in a museum as venerated as the Met. *China: Through the Looking Glass* gives significant concrete expression to this aesthetic and ideological question surrounding fashion's status as art by incorporating the fashions into the Costume Institute's basement galleries *and* existing galleries on the second floor of the museum that showcase Chinese art and artifacts from the Asian Art department; this debate thus becomes physically embodied in the gallery space of the Met itself. It is this integrated placement of the various clothing and accessories in the Asian art galleries that causes the greatest unease for Hearn, inciting him to voice concern that the Chinese art will become "wallpaper" and a "stage prop," with the "imposition of the design so powerful that it overshadows the intellectual content," risking that these ancient works become "misinterpret[ed]" or "demean[ed]" by their pairing with the fashions.

But Hearn is not the only person in the documentary to comment upon this possibly contentious relationship between art and fashion. After a slow-motion sequence of red-carpet arrivals at the Met Gala, *The First Monday in May* opens with Wintour lauding fashion's ability to "create a dream, create a fantasy," before she immediately segues into admitting, "But there might be some questions about whether fashion belongs in a museum like the Met." Campbell, Bolton, and Koda will all subsequently answer this question affirmatively throughout the film, with Campbell framing the uncertainty as the result of an antiquated distinction between "painting, architecture, and sculpture" versus the "decorative arts"; Bolton describing those questions as outmodedly based in a "nineteenth-century idea of what art is"; and Koda somewhat exasperatingly explaining the "perennial debate about whether or not fashion can ever be art." Quite paradoxically – yet in a manner of equal frustration – designers Jean Paul Gaultier and Karl Lagerfeld will emphatically *deny* such an equivalency between fashion and art, as an astonished

Gaultier counters that his clothes do not belong in a museum and a vexed Lagerfeld invokes Coco Chanel's self-definition as a dressmaker to provide the final word.

This question posed throughout *The First Monday in May* as to whether fashion may accurately be considered art has dominated considerations of fashion's place in museums for quite some time. While there are of course nuances that challenge a simplistic affirmation or denial, deliberation on the issue may broadly be understood across two competing approaches, each focusing upon particular dimensions to fashion – between those who argue that fashion's complex creative dimensions speak to its status as art and those who argue fashion's commercial and momentary nature prohibits its consideration as such. As Valerie Steele summarizes regarding the latter view,

> fashion has tended to be dismissed as superficial, ephemeral, and material. By contrast, art has been valorized as significant form, eternally beautiful, and spiritual in nature. [...] art is generally perceived as *transcending* its commodity status – in contrast to fashion, which seems to wallow in its commercial nature.[15]

The surge in museum-based fashion exhibitions over the past few decades has stimulated questions about "the suitability and hierarchical place of fashion in museum settings" ever more frequently and emphatically.[16] This proliferation of fashion exhibitions draws from the very same cultural interest and commercial opportunity that is driving the simultaneous boom in fashion documentaries.[17] As Steele points out, although numerous museums have amassed and subsequently displayed notable dress collections – with Boston's Museum of Fine Arts and London's Victoria and Albert Museum doing so since the nineteenth century – questions nevertheless persist throughout history around fashion's museum "worthiness." And while "confusion as to whether fashion is art has almost always existed," a critical discourse on fashion's status as art may be traced at least to the mid-twentieth century, specifically to art historian Remy G. Saisselin's examination of the connections between poetry and fashion via Baudelaire and Dior.[18]

A range of factors alongside the sheer growth of fashion exhibitions brought fashion's relation to art increasingly to the fore in the decades leading up to Rossi's documentary. The debate reached a fever pitch in the 1980s, in particular surrounding the Costume Institute's decision to feature a living designer for the first time in its exhibition *Yves Saint Laurent: 25 Years of Design* (1983). Prior to the Saint Laurent exhibition, "conventional exhibitions at museums were primarily reserved for artworks or historic costumes, rather than for current fashions," for fear that exhibiting the work of living designers would displace artistic value and integrity with commercial self-promotion.[19] The Saint Laurent exhibition's curator was Diana Vreeland, and her work from 1972 through the early 1980s as a special consultant on the Met's Costume Institute exhibitions similarly, and significantly, provoked conversations around fashion as art, with Vreeland creating "atmospheric and sometimes ahistorical fashion exhibitions that have polarized opinion ever

"Seeing too much is seeing nothing" **181**

since but very much put fashion on the curatorial map."[20] Finally, when designers along with corporate sponsorship and donations have appeared to interfere with certain museum exhibitions (e.g., Giorgio Armani's $15 million donation to the Guggenheim in advance of its 2000 exhibition on the designer's work, Karl Lagerfeld's influence over a failed 1999 exhibition, or Chanel Incorporated's funding of the Met's 2005 Chanel retrospective), it is not difficult to understand the skepticism that has often greeted locating fashion as museum-worthy art.[21]

While the talking heads of *The First Monday in May* might dispute whether fashion can be considered art, the documentary's aesthetic patterns rhetorically answer this question affirmatively throughout the film. For example, when we move into the backstage of the Met at the start of the film, the sign "yield to art in transit" heralds an immediately subsequent cut to the transport of garments to the Costume Institute. The documentary then continues to place fashion as Met-worthy art by lauding the curatorial scope of its collection, with a superimposed intertitle announcing, "The Met's Costume Institute houses the largest collection of fashion in the world." Shots of various items of clothing are carefully captioned (e.g. "Jacobean Bodice c. 1616"; "18th century pannier"), thus framing them as museum objects with extensive archival and aesthetic histories, which counters any dismissal of their importance because of the supposedly ephemeral nature of fashion. And finally, *The First Monday in May* includes numerous sequences that demonstrate the exceptional preservation efforts taken with its fashion holdings (Figure 11.1).

It is not simply with edits, captions, and expository sequences, however, through which the film forges a cinematic equivalency between art and fashion. As noted earlier, there are a number of aesthetic patterns shared across the fashion documentary genre. In Rossi's film, these stylistic elements do not merely document both the Met's art collection and its Costume Institute holdings; on closer

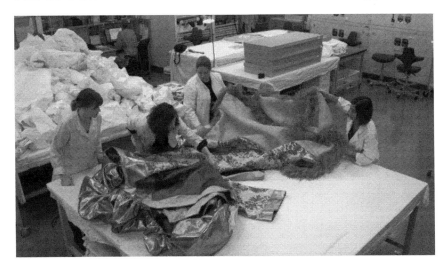

FIGURE 11.1 *The First Monday in May*
(Andrew Rossi, 2016)

182 Matthew J. Fee

inspection, its *mise-en-scène* and cinematography also generate aesthetic parallels, as the documentary both chronicles *and* connects the Met's more traditional "art" holdings (e.g., painting and sculpture) with its Costume Institute acquisitions. For example, elegantly flowing camera movements around gallery corners reveal the museum's traditional as well as decorative arts contents. Close-ups emphasize the textures of artworks both painterly and sartorial (Figures 11.2 and 11.3). Low-angle shots accentuate the magnitude of what is on display. And slow tracks into balanced compositions of both architectural temples and fashion vitrines both

FIGURE 11.2 *The First Monday in May*
(Andrew Rossi, 2016)

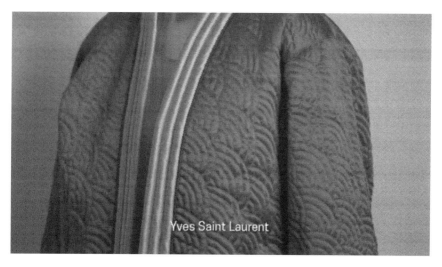

FIGURE 11.3 *The First Monday in May*
(Andrew Rossi, 2016)

center and please the eye, while we repeatedly witness curators put final adjusting touches on both artifact and raiment.

Regardless of whether we perceive fashion's placement in a museum as an evolution or as a violation of our understanding of art, its positioning in a documentary encourages a series of additional, provocative reconsiderations of what exactly happens to fashion and our experience of it when it becomes mediated by the image – particularly the moving image. In other words, Rossi's documentary directs our attention to yet another tension besides exhibition and gala, or art and entertainment. That is, museum exhibitions themselves, and doubly a documentary that chronicles fashion's placement in such an exhibition, tellingly underscore the tension between fashion as image and fashion as object. In the midst of late-twentieth-century technological changes – particularly developments in digital media – fashion's status as image and/or object became essential to comprehending the public's experience of it:

> [T]he role of the image in fashion shifted. No longer mere representation, the image frequently became the commodity itself ... new media and increased fashion coverage made previously elite fashion accessible to a mass audience, but only as image, never as object.[22]

As Fiona Anderson similarly claims when advocating for a museological practice that allows for the study of garments as both objects and images, the latter more accurately speaks to "the wider public's daily experience of high-end designer fashion, which is most usually through images rather than the garments themselves."[23]

The First Monday in May critically acknowledges this engagement with fashion as photographed image on two occasions: first, when Bolton maps out the exhibition contents for Wintour in an early planning meeting; and second, through a sequence that depicts the production of the exhibition catalog. We must remember, though, that while fashion's placement in a museum ostensibly involves its three-dimensional staging (often accompanied, as these preceding scenes reveal, by two-dimensional renderings in exhibition storyboards and catalogs), it fundamentally exists in the museum space as something to be looked at – experienced more so as an image than as an object, with museum audiences prohibited from touching the fashion on display. Regardless of whether we consider it art, fashion's placement in a museum accentuates its "to-be-looked-at-ness," as opposed to its being worn. To be sure, fashion is not alone in this regard, as the placement of objects within a museum underscores their status as aesthetic objects of visual contemplation. Consider, though, how aspects of fashion display push this process further than with other objects, such as the prioritizing of frontal display, which can downplay the three-dimensionality of the garment. Museum fashion's loss of embodiment as it is transformed into pure spectacle becomes even more apparent through the photographs and video footage that often accompany exhibitions. Fashion's original dynamic purpose as an object worn on a live body – rather than as a static display draped on a faceless mannequin – is paradoxically recalled for the museum-goer through such two-dimensional images. *The First Monday in May* stresses this dynamic of visual contemplation on numerous instances throughout the film, with its multiple shots of persons – particularly Bolton – looking. In fact, the only people we witness carefully touching the fabrics are the museum staff with their gloved hands, thus communicating fashion's importance as preserved art.[24]

In foregrounding fashion's visuality (i.e., its status as image), documentary film consequently emphasizes those same qualities to which the museum-goer's experience of fashion are restricted. *The First Monday in May* is not alone in this regard, however, as this limited and singularly visual perspective on fashion likewise dominates the other institutionally-focused documentaries discussed at the start of this chapter. To be sure, the prioritization of engaging with fashion as image may not be as surprising in *The September Issue*, given its concentration on fashion placed in such a heavily illustrated magazine as *Vogue*. In fact, some of the most prominent editorial spreads, whose production the documentary chronicles, actually accentuate fashion's more spectacular dimensions – not simply "color blocking," but also attempts to visually render "texture." It is rather remarkable, though, that in *Scatter My Ashes at Bergdorf's*, an account of a luxury department store for which fashion's status as an object to be touched and worn lies at the core of its consumerist mission, the documentary's narrative trajectory ultimately spotlights fashion's status as something to be seen – as a disembodied image. With dresses captioned to indicate their respective designers, viewed by rapt mass audiences behind glass, and animated through tracking camera movements, the film's concluding sequence of the store's grand unveiling of its celebrated window display thus places fashion in a manner decidedly similar to that of the other Fifth Avenue denizen documented in *The First Monday in May*.

Nevertheless, we must remember that there is often a crucial difference between how fashion is experienced by those who observe fashion within these documentaries' profilmic stories (via a magazine spread, store window, or museum exhibition), and those who view fashion through the documentary film genre that chronicles these institutions. Specifically, while both scenarios involve fashion mediated by or as an image, fashion's placement in the documentary creates a *moving* image from a stationary one.[25] Marketa Uhlirova argues that in twenty-first-century fashion advertising, moving images have supplied "an enticing alternative ... with a different kind of sensorial and experiential complexity," with fashion films "re-present[ing] clothing as a living organism."[26] Movement may be accomplished in two ways: through the direct audio-visual capture of garments in movement, or through the use of *mise-en-scène* and cinematography to imbue static garments with dynamic movement. The expressive use of these latter cinematic devices compensates for the lack of a tactile experience of clothing, as well as for the absence of sensory experiences attendant to encountering garments in a department store.[27] This shift from static to moving images arguably alters our experience of fashion, supplanting a "position of consumption" with a "position of spectatorship";[28] for Gary Needham, however, this transformation is better understood as a synthesis of the two positions, consequently producing "hybrid modes of engagement in which old and new media, and activity and passivity, productively merge."[29]

"Seeing too much is seeing nothing" 185

While the aforementioned studies examine moving images in promotional fashion films, we must also be sure to include documentary as part of these discussions; for in the wider developments within digital media, the fashion industry has increasingly incorporated moving images across a wide range of both formats and platforms.[30] Including documentary film in this conversation may, in fact, allow us to explore the "immanent political charge" that the genre supposedly possesses because of "its attention to the production processes" involved in "fabricating and disseminating fashion."[31] Based on these specific criteria, the political potential of *The First Monday in May* as a fashion documentary is questionable, especially taking into account, as discussed earlier, the dearth of actual scenes of fashion production. Yet, if we consider the multiplicity of viewing positions embodied in contemporary fashion imaging practices (magazine, store window, exhibition) in tandem with the nonfiction films that animate these images while they simultaneously document our encounter with them, we cannot deny the impact that such diverse and dynamic visual relations offer in featuring "ubiquitous questions of how to see, how to evaluate, how to display, and how to experience fashion on screen."[32] And while these questions are posed specifically in conjunction with fashion films, I would argue that their engagement with and mediation of fashion as both image and object proves instructive to our consideration of other audio-visual documentation of the visual arts, helping us to appreciate "tension(s) in which the screen is in a creative tussle with the culture it appears to represent."[33]

This "creative tussle" is perhaps best observed at the conclusion of *The First Monday in May*. Its final scenes concentrate on extended sequences of red-carpet arrivals, with Justin Bieber singing and posing, and designers and celebrities, such as Michael Kors, Jean Paul Gaultier, Kate Hudson, and Alicia Keys, acting as docents who escort us through the exhibition. We may witness museum-goers queuing to

FIGURE 11.4 *The First Monday in May*
(Andrew Rossi, 2016)

experience fashion as art within the galleries of the Met Museum and its Costume Institute – as an intertitle informs us that "More than 800,000 people visited *China: Through the Looking Glass*" – but the closing credits harken back more so to Rossi's declaring his film as a possible *September Issue* sequel. Right at the end of the film, we focus on the production of the *Vogue* tie-in publication for the celebrity benefit, with the film's final image presenting the magazine cover of Rihanna on the red carpet (Figure 11.4).

The documentary concludes with fashion's placement in the art museum ultimately re-placed by its location in a fashion magazine, with fashion thus emphasized as image on multiple levels, its place fixed to be looked at – in exhibition, in magazine, and in documentary. With this closing preponderance of image placements and spectator engagements – and recalling Wong's earlier caveat – fashion documentaries such as *The First Monday in May* push us to confront both what and how exactly we are seeing, leaving us to determine whether in seeing so much, we are, in fact, really seeing nothing.

Notes

1 Marketa Uhlirova, "100 Years of the Fashion Film: Frameworks and Histories," *Fashion Theory: The Journal of Dress, Body and Culture* 17, no. 2 (2013): 137–57.
2 Stella Bruzzi and Pamela Church Gibson, "Introduction," in *Fashion Cultures: Theories, Explorations, and Analysis*, eds. Stella Bruzzi and Pamela Church Gibson (London and New York: Routledge, 2000), 2.
3 These are not the first documentaries to examine fashion in relation to larger institutional contexts. For example, Frederick Wiseman's *Model* (1981) and *The Store* (1984) are two earlier examples that consider fashion's place in the social contexts of modelling and retail through documenting, respectively, the Zoli Agency and overall New York City modelling scene, and a Dallas-based Neiman Marcus department store. For more on these earlier works, see Alex Joseph, "Second Looks: Two Films about Fashion by Frederick Wiseman," *Fashion Theory: The Journal of Dress, Body and Culture* 20, no. 1 (2016): 103–16.
4 For example, *The September Issue* frames Thakoon Panichgul as evidence of the ability of *Vogue* – and Anna Wintour in particular – to discover and nurture new talent; *Scatter My Ashes at Bergdorf's* introduces us to Ally Hilfiger and her collection, only to document its failure to secure a place at Bergdorf Goodman, due to the highly discerning taste of the department store and its fashion director, Linda Fargo; and *The First Monday in May* includes Chinese fashion designer Guo Pei within a sequence immediately following debates around appropriation and stereotyping, as a means for the Met and its Costume Institute to correctively demonstrate its supposedly more respectful engagement with Chinese culture.
5 Although Wintour appears in only one sequence in *Scatter My Ashes at Bergdorf's*, the explicit description that Fargo "wields power in a different way than Anna Wintour does … she's incredibly approachable and charming" ensures that Wintour remains a significant presence, if only paradoxically by her absence and in comparison to the documentary's ongoing focus on Fargo's friendliness and humor.
6 "Interview with Director Andrew Rossi," *The First Monday in May*, DVD. Directed by Andrew Rossi. New York: Magnolia Pictures, 2016.
7 "The Costume Institute," the Metropolitan Museum of Art, accessed May 28, 2019, www.metmuseum.org/about-the-met/curatorial-departments/the-costume-institute.

8 Maxwell Hearn, "A Dialogue between East and West," in *China: Through the Looking Glass* (New Haven and London: Yale University Press, 2015), 13.
9 Andrew Bolton, "Toward an Aesthetic of Surfaces," in *China: Through the Looking Glass*, 20.
10 Robin Givhan, "The Fantasy of China: Why the New Met Exhibition is a Big, Beautiful Lie," review of *China: Through the Looking Glass*, *Washington Post*, May 5, 2015, www.washingtonpost.com/news/arts-and-entertainment/wp/2015/05/05/the-fantasy-of-china-why-the-new-met-exhibition-is-a-big-beautiful-lie/. See also, for example: Holland Cotter, "Review: In 'China: Through the Looking Glass,' Eastern Culture Meets Western Fashion," review of *China: Through the Looking Glass*, *New York Times*, May 7, 2015, www.nytimes.com/2015/05/08/arts/design/review-in-china-through-the-looking-glass-eastern-culture-meets-western-fashion.html; Amanda Holpuch, "Met's China: Through the Looking Glass Show Presents a Fantasy of the Far East," review of *China: Through the Looking Glass*, *The Guardian*, August 8, 2015, www.theguardian.com/fashion/2015/aug/19/china-through-the-looking-glass-show-breaks-metropolitan-museum-record; and Véronique Hyland, "The Met's China Show is Beautiful, But Elusive," review of *China: Through the Looking Glass*, *The Cut*, May 4, 2015, www.thecut.com/2015/05/mets-china-show-is-beautiful-but-elusive.html.
11 *China: Through the Looking Glass* attracted 815,992 visitors, superseded only recently by the 1.65 million museum-goers who visited 2018's *Heavenly Bodies: Fashion and the Catholic Imagination*. "1,659,647 Visitors to Costume Institute's *Heavenly Bodies* Show at Met Fifth Avenue and Met Cloisters Make It the Most Visited Exhibition in The Met's History," Metropolitan Museum of Art press release, October 11, 2018, www.metmuseum.org/press/news/2018/heavenly-bodies-most-visited-exhibition.
12 The other three days are Thanksgiving Day, Christmas Day, and New Year's Day.
13 "The Costume Institute," the Metropolitan Museum of Art, accessed May 28, 2019, www.metmuseum.org/about-the-met/curatorial-departments/the-costume-institute.
14 The "Oscars of the East Coast" nickname is mentioned in Vanessa Friedman, "What Is the Met Gala, and Who Gets to Go?" *New York Times*, May 3, 2018, www.nytimes.com/2018/05/03/fashion/what-is-the-met-gala-and-who-gets-to-go.html; André Leon Talley calls it "the Super Bowl of charity events" in *The First Monday in May*.
15 Valerie Steele, "Fashion," in *Fashion and Art*, eds. Adam Geczy and Vicki Karaminas (London and New York: Berg Publishers, 2012), 13–14, author's emphasis.
16 Alexandra Palmer, "Reviewing Fashion Exhibitions," *Fashion Theory: The Journal of Dress, Body and Culture* 12, no. 1 (2008): 123. See also, Sung Bok Kim, "Is Fashion Art?" *Fashion Theory: The Journal of Dress, Body and Culture* 2, no. 1 (1998): 51–71; Sanda Miller, "Fashion as Art; is Fashion Art?" *Fashion Theory: The Journal of Dress, Body and Culture* 11, no. 1 (2007): 25–40; and N.J. Stevenson, "The Fashion Retrospective," *Fashion Theory: The Journal of Dress, Body and Culture* 12, no. 2 (2008): 219–35. Alexandra Palmer has also provocatively noted that clothing exhibitions are often derided in museum contexts as being under-researched and thus less intellectually rigorous; however, the need to frequently rotate the objects of such exhibitions due to the deleterious consequences of lighting, fabric weight, etc., does not permit the depth of research that is able to be afforded to more permanent – or at least longer-term and thus more accessible – museum objects. Alexandra Palmer, "Untouchable: Creating Desire and Knowledge in Museum Costume and Textile Exhibitions," *Fashion Theory: The Journal of Dress, Body and Culture* 12, no. 1 (2008): 31–63.
17 As Bruzzi and Church Gibson claim regarding the place of fashion in the twenty-first century: "The well-publicized, heavily sponsored fashion exhibition has arguably become a permanent fixture of this new landscape. [...] And leading designers, who now see

their own work displayed in museums and galleries, are sufficiently well known, in our fashion-literate new millennium, to merit the making of documentary films depicting their careers." Stella Bruzzi and Pamela Church Gibson, "Introduction: The Changed Fashion Landscape of the New Millennium," in *Fashion Cultures Revisited: Theories, Explanations and Analysis*, eds. Stella Bruzzi and Pamela Church Gibson, (London and New York: Routledge, 2013), 6–7.
18 Kim, "Is Fashion Art?" 53.
19 Kim, 52.
20 Peter McNeil, "'Why Don't You' – Think for Yourself? *Diana Vreeland after Diana Vreeland*," *Fashion Theory: The Journal of Dress, Body and Culture* 18, no. 4 (2014): 420. Harold Koda provides specific tales of such theatricality in the documentary *Diana Vreeland: The Eye Has to Travel* (2011) when he shares how Vreeland would paint mannequins and walls as well as pump fragrances into the galleries. "What this did for the critics," notes Koda, "was evoke Bloomingdales." See also Deborah Silverman's *Selling Culture*, for an argument that understands Vreeland's Costume Institute exhibitions as indices of 1980s cultural concerns with an aristocratic sense of wealth and consumerism. Deborah Silverman, *Selling Culture: Bloomingdale's, Diana Vreeland, and the New Aristocracy of Taste in Reagan's America* (New York: Pantheon Books, 1986).
21 Valerie Steele, "Museum Quality: The Rise of the Fashion Exhibition," *Fashion Theory: The Journal of Dress, Body and Culture* 12, no. 1 (2008): 7–30.
22 Caroline Evans, "Yesterday's Emblems and Tomorrow's Commodities: The Return of the Repressed in Fashion Imagery Today," in *Fashion Cultures*, 97.
23 Fiona Anderson, "Museums as Fashion Media," in *Fashion Cultures*, 376.
24 Of course, as a curator Bolton can look *and* touch, but noteworthy is the dominance of his viewing and reacting to the fashions.
25 This is not to say that the institutions documented in these films do not make use of moving images – and here I am thinking of short videos incorporated into websites, stores, and galleries.
26 Marketa Uhlirova, "The Fashion Film Effect," in *Fashion Media: Past and Present*, eds. Djurdja Baerlett, Shaun Cole, and Agnès Rocamora (London: Bloomsbury, 2013), 118.
27 Gary Needham, "The Digital Fashion Film," in *Fashion Cultures Revisited*, 103–11.
28 Needham paraphrasing fashion historian Nathalie Khan, 106.
29 Needham, 106.
30 Nick Rees-Roberts, "Backstage with Loïc Prigent: Documenting Process from Gaultier to Chanel," *Film, Fashion & Consumption* 5, no. 2 (2016): 149–64.
31 Adam Syzmanski, "*Bill Cunningham New York* and the Political Potentiality of the Fashion Documentary," *Film, Fashion & Consumption* 1, no. 3 (2012): 290.
32 Needham, "The Digital Fashion Film," 106.
33 Needham, 106.

PART V
Art worlds and film worlds

12
CHALLENGING THE HIERARCHIES OF PHOTOGRAPHIC HISTORY

Trisha Ziff, interviewed by Roger Hallas

Over the past decade, Mexico City-based curator and filmmaker Trisha Ziff has forged a unique pathway in visual arts documentary. Well established as a renowned and award-winning photographic educator and curator, she began to make documentary films about photography in the late 2000s. In a field where the professional divisions between art curation and arts documentary production remain fairly rigid, she has managed to develop a critical practice which moves creatively between the curation of exhibitions and books and the production of documentary films. While each of her four feature films about photography approach the matter of framing the medium in different ways, they all share the pursuit of challenging the hierarchies of photographic history. *Chevolution* (2008) delves into the history of an iconic twentieth-century image, the *Guerrillero Heroico*, Alberto Korda's fabled 1960 portrait of Che Guevara, by exploring the ironies, contradictions, and paradoxes in its prolific global circulation and appropriation as it careened between radical inspiration and naked commerce. In *The Mexican Suitcase* (2011), Ziff situates the rediscovered trove of over 4,500 Spanish Civil War negatives by Robert Capa, Gerdo Taro, and David "Chim" Seymour in relation to the Republican exile to Mexico, which opened its doors to provide safe haven to tens of thousands of Spanish refugees after the war. *The Man Who Saw Too Much* (2015) examines the ethics of looking at death through a portrait of the Mexican photojournalist Enrique Metinides, sometimes dubbed "the Mexican Weegee," who has spent his life documenting injury and death for the tabloid press. *Witkin & Witkin* (2017) expands Ziff's elaboration of the artist documentary in two directions by creating a dual portrait of Jerome and Joel-Peter Witkin, identical twins who have each forged successful careers in different visual media – Jerome in figurative painting and Joel-Peter in art photography. In the following interview (based on conversations in 2016 and 2018), Ziff discusses her work through the interaction between curation and documentary filmmaking, the aesthetics of framing photography in film, and her relationship to funders, subjects, and audiences.

How did you come to photographic curation and how do you see your turn to making documentaries in relation to your early career in photographic education?

I went to art school at Goldsmiths to study sculpture in the 1970s. I was the only woman student in my year and found the traditional way of creating work to be compromising. In my last year I moved into a more conceptual part of the school, known as the "back fields," where there were women teaching, including Mary Kelly and Rita Donagh. In the photography department I also worked with interesting artists who were women, such as Jo Spence and the Hackney Flashers. I became fascinated with documenting. Early on I found ways of using photography in different contexts where I found myself, but I was never a photographer. I was much more concerned with how the medium functions in terms of storytelling. When I graduated Goldsmiths it was the beginning of the community arts movement. In my first job I worked with children and the elderly in a housing estate in South London. From there I moved to Camerawork, which was quite established by that point in the East End. After about a year and a half working and teaching in the community darkroom, I moved to Ireland to set up Camerawork Derry with the support of activist Mary Nelis, who had two sons in prison on the blanket protest.[1] At that time I was politically active around the British occupation of Ireland, especially in anti-imperialist feminist solidarity work with the women in Armagh Prison. The workshop was established to put cameras in the hands of young people in Derry so their narrative wasn't dependent on the journalists who came from the outside to tell their stories. They could tell their own stories, empowering both their narrative and their voice in the community. I got funding, set up a darkroom, and produced exhibitions. Participating in Camerawork impacted what those young people have done throughout their lives. I originally went to Derry for a year, but ended up staying five. Faction Films in London produced a documentary, *Picturing Derry* (David Fox and Sylvia Stevens, 1985), about the workshop, its approach to photography, and the ways in which photography had been used in different contexts to represent Derry (it was broadcast on Channel Four in its experimental television strand, *The Eleventh Hour*).

When I finally returned to England, I became the director of Network Photographers, working with professional photojournalists. I collaborated with photographers Mike Abrahams and Laurie Sparham on *Still War: Photographs from the North of Ireland* (1990), a photobook that was really grounded in my experience in Ireland. Even though I have never studied photography and never described myself as a photographer, I have always worked with photography in different guises, using photography to tell the stories I wanted to tell. My subsequent curatorial work in photography continues that fundamental concern with storytelling. In the workshops, I saw myself as more of a motivator to teach people to tell their own stories and to validate people who thought their stories weren't important in a bigger picture. I suppose that was empowering for young people who had a history of not being validated because they came from nationalist communities, they didn't have a formal education, or they were women. My own curatorial work has been about validating marginalized or neglected stories that I myself wanted to tell, using photography as a medium, or using the photograph, as an excuse to tell the stories that really interested me. In other words, my curatorial work and documentary films have been consistently grounded in challenging hierarchies of photographic value and history.

What were the particular challenges of moving from curation to documentary filmmaking with your feature film Chevolution?

When I embarked on making *Chevolution*, I would never have described myself as somebody who was going to work in film. The project was an exhibition and a book.[2] The film grew out of the reality of both, but there was never an intention that there would be a film when I first developed that project. I didn't see myself in any way as a filmmaker – I was a curator. The project was inspired by a conversation I had with Darrel Couturier, a Los Angeles gallerist who represented Alberto Korda. Shortly after Korda died, I asked Darrel, "I wonder what it was like to be remembered for a single image?" Korda had taken thousands of images, but it is the Che image by which he is remembered. I approached the project almost like a game: how long could I sustain my audience's interest looking at a single image? In an exhibition, you take your audience through a three-dimensional space to tell your story; in this particular exhibition, they were essentially looking at hybrid repetitions of the same image. That was the challenge – to construct a narrative out of that reiteration.

I first presented the project as a slide show at Les Rencontres d'Arles, when Martin Parr curated the festival in 2004. The subsequent exhibition ended up being this kind of superhit. Opening at the California Museum of Photography in Riverside, it went to the International Center of Photography [ICP], the Victoria and Albert Museum [V&A] and other museums in Spain, Turkey, Mexico, and the Netherlands. Two friends of mine who were Hollywood producers saw the Riverside show and told me it would make a great documentary. Since I didn't know how to go about that, they took me to their agent at CAA. Ultimately, Netflix commissioned the film through its early production company Red Envelope Entertainment. So, there I was, having never having made a film, with a budget, making a film for an American corporation on the image of Che Guevara (with all the contradictions around America's relationship to Cuba).

It was complicated and I chose to collaborate with Sylvia Stevens, a UK-based documentarian with a lot of experience and with whom I had previously worked together on *Picturing Derry* and *Oaxacalifornia* (1994). She would direct and I would produce. Netflix were critical of the first cut. They found it too academic and wanted something more populist for a young American audience. They wanted "T-shirt Che," and Sylvia's film was too thoughtful, appealing to an older audience. So, after several cuts she withdrew and I was left to deliver the film. I brought on board a young Mexican editor, Luis Lopez. We got a revised budget and had to shoot more material to meet the vision of Netflix. The film changed as we added more interviews, including celebrities like Gael García Bernal and Antonio Banderas, and digital morphing graphics produced by Luis, which visualized the proliferation and transformation of the image as it circulated through different cultural contexts (Figure 12.1). In the end, *Chevolution* was a hybrid of both visions. On reflection, as Netflix has grown into a major production powerhouse, I can now better understand what happened with *Chevolution*; Netflix are all the time concerned with their demographics, generating product to suit their algorithm over the vision of the filmmakers.

The film faced similar challenges as the exhibition had – how to translate a single image into a compelling narrative – but the organization had to be temporal rather than spatial. My inspiration was Gary Hustwit's documentary *Helvetica* (2007). I loved that film. There's a real discipline in taking a single idea or object and exploring it in great detail from all perspectives. It took a sixtieth of a second for Korda to make that image of Che and my film spends ninety minutes telling the narrative of that fraction of a second. There is a sort of *Rashomon* quality to it. I know it is dirty word today, but I first learned to think for myself through a Marxist perspective. Everything for me is about material context, pulling something apart and looking at it from so many different perspectives. It is how I see and understand the world. Art historian David Kunzle and the Center for Political Graphics supported me with my film. In 1997 David had curated a show at UCLA on the iconography of Che, which was very much grounded in art history, the world of the poster makers, and Cuban culture.[3] I took my project much more into the contemporary world of commerce. Moreover, I curated that show using eBay. Rather, I didn't curate it, I shopped it. I used eBay as my source for many of the exhibits. The way we see and the way we consume have changed fundamentally. What you do curatorially then reflects that contemporary reality.

FIGURE 12.1 *Chevolution*
(Trisha Ziff, 2008)

Ultimately, the film had a lot of problems because it went through so many different versions. In a way, it is a corporate film, another commodity, just like the Che T-shirt. It was a challenging experience overall but I don't regret it because I learned how to be a filmmaker in the process.

Unlike Chevolution, *where you were transforming your own exhibition and book into a film, your documentary about the Mexican Suitcase was developed separately from the exhibition and book. You were directly involved in the recovery of the Mexican Suitcase for the ICP, but your documentary differs substantially in focus from Cynthia Young's curatorial approach in the ICP's exhibition.*[4] *Your film seems as carefully attuned to the complex history of these photographic objects as it is to the images that they contain and to the photographers who produced them. What led you to take this approach to one of the most celebrated rediscoveries in recent photographic history?*

I always say that I recovered the Mexican Suitcase (Figure 12.2), I didn't discover it. The knowledge of its existence went back a long time in letters to Jerald Green, a Spanish professor at Queens College, and to Cornell Capa at the ICP, from Ben Tarver, an American filmmaker in Mexico City, who had possession of these boxes of negatives from the Spanish Civil War, allegedly by Robert Capa. In 2007 I dropped in to the ICP while I was in New York to see the chief curator, Brian Wallis, who was a friend. During our chat, he asked if I would help them see what they could find out about these negatives since I was in based in Mexico City. It was as casual as that. If I hadn't popped in to see him, who knows if the photographs would have ever been recovered or not. Back home, I found someone who knew who Ben Tarver was and I called him. It took me about three months before I pinned him down to meet with me. Tarver had contacted the ICP because he knew he had something of value and he was surprised that no one followed it

FIGURE 12.2 *The Mexican Suitcase*
(Trisha Ziff, 2011)

up properly. It made no sense. Why was that the case? I have my theory, but it is purely my own speculation. I think the ICP didn't follow it up because they were essentially interested in one thing, Cornell's obsession with his brother's iconic photograph, *The Fallen Soldier*. Was the image there to prove its authenticity? It was a potential Pandora's box given the discourse around that image which perhaps created ambivalence for the ICP. Was it going to fuel this debate further or was it going to solve it? Perhaps better not to know. I could be completely wrong, but that is my analysis of why Tarver's letter was not followed up. The sadness in all of it is that during this procrastination, Capa's friend and darkroom assistant Tchiki Weiss died in Mexico City. Because those boxes were originally in his possession, we lost all this information with Tchiki's passing.

It is a miracle of circumstance that I found Tarver and that he hadn't sold the negatives. Then, during the six months of shooting the film, he had a massive stroke. He is somewhat of a tragic figure, but his generosity is important to be acknowledged. The return of the photographs became the subject of debate. For some, the negatives were spoils of war, they should not have been in Mexico, and the return to their owners was imperative. For others, they were the patrimony of Mexico and should not be returned to the ICP. I went to see the Mexican Minister of Culture and told him that I intended to take the negatives out of Mexico and return them to the estates of the families of the photographers Capa, Seymour, and Taro. He supported my decision, although I was highly criticized in Mexico for doing that. I included Mexican photographer Pedro Meyer in the film to articulate that opposing point of view. I was seen as something like a bounty hunter by some in Mexico. But if you support authors' rights, it was the correct thing to do ethically. It was also the right thing to do legally. I will always defend my decision to return the negatives to the estates. We live in a digital age where everyone can get access to the images today, so it does not matter as much if they're in a fridge in New York or Mexico City. In fact, it is better that they're in New York because the cultural infrastructure in Mexico is more fragile in terms of funding for archives. Furthermore, by returning the negatives to where the majority of the material from the three photographers is archived, we were able to find out information which would never have been recovered otherwise.

Did the ICP handle all those things well? I have my misgivings! Part of the deal I made with ICP was that when I returned the negatives, the story of their recovery would break in the Mexican press simultaneous to its reporting in the US. But the ICP leaked the story ahead of time to the *New York Times* and never informed us in Mexico. I found out accidentally when I received a call out of the blue from a journalist from the *Times* asking for a comment. The ICP also consistently chose not to honor Mexico and its role in this narrative. Moreover, if you look at the book and wall text in the exhibition on the Mexican Suitcase at the ICP, you could be forgiven for thinking that a stork had somehow magically returned the negatives to the ICP! The focus was on validating Capa and discovering which images were his and which weren't (i.e. Gerda's or Chim's). Nowhere did they tell the narrative of why the suitcase ended up in Mexico. In my opinion, it was a revisionist version of the events, because it was precisely Mexico's relationship to the Republic in Spain that saved those negatives. Lázaro Cárdenas's socialist-leaning government in Mexico saved the lives of many Republican refugees fleeing Spain while the United States refused them entry. The boxes that constitute "the Mexican Suitcase" ironically become a metaphor of exile. For the ICP to omit this story both obscures the history of American foreign policy at that time and diminishes Mexico's role in giving safe passage and asylum to Spanish Republicans, who otherwise would have perished on the beaches of Argelès-sur-Mer in France or in Nazi extermination camps. I pushed for changes to the exhibition but the focus was on the photographs – as if a photograph exists without a context. For me, it is the context that is the most interesting thing about these negatives.

Tarver's original contract with the ICP granted him the film rights to use the 4,500 images from the Mexican Suitcase, but he had a time limit of two years to make his film. As time passed, I knew that the ICP were eager to sell the rights to the BBC if his contract lapsed, so I convinced him to transfer them to me, otherwise he'd lose them and nobody was going to tell what I considered a very important version of this story. Within six months I had secured the funding. Tarver came on board as a paid researcher and associate producer. What I hoped to do in the film was to remove a sense of the hierarchy of photographic history through a critique of the photojournalist as the purveyor of history. I liked the idea of taking Capa off his pedestal by diminishing the image of the heroic photojournalist and giving equal power to the other photographers. People in Spain were upset that I didn't focus more on Capa's story, but for me the film was really about how we look at these photographs today, especially given the long history of silence in Spain during the years of Franco's rule. As soon as you put images in a frame, stick them on a wall in a museum, and make people line up to buy an expensive ticket and file past them, you are creating a hierarchical version of how we see and understand the past. The work undertaken by curators Cynthia Young and Kristen Lubben for the exhibition catalog was nevertheless extraordinary: locating precisely where the photographs were taken and identifying many of the people in the images so that the journeys of the photographers during their trips to the front and covering the war could be fully understood.

When I saw the *Mexican Suitcase* exhibition at the Museu Nacional d'Art de Catalunya in Barcelona, there was an additional exhibition of local photographers on the top floor of the museum; it was the first time that anyone in Catalonia had seen an exhibition of snapshots of people's lives in relation to the Spanish Civil War. The space was empty compared to the big show downstairs, but the visitors upstairs were looking for photographs of relatives, people they knew, and streets they could recognize. I distinctly remember someone weeping in the space as they recognized someone from their past. For me, this small exhibition demonstrated the power of the family album. My film was an attempt to give context to the images

198 Trisha Ziff

and to challenge that hierarchy of value by not prioritizing Capa's photojournalism over other types of photography, such as these snapshots and images by anonymous photographers, which I also included in the film. To me, a snapshot has equal interest and importance to a photograph that we consider art or photojournalism. I am interested in giving equal space to what might be termed "high and low" photography. This connects back to the ethos of my earlier projects, such as *Hidden Truths*, the project I created about Bloody Sunday in Derry, in which I brought together British army photographs, the evidential photographs, the aerial photographs, the local newspaper photographs, the work of photojournalists (such as Gilles Peress), the mass card portrait, and the family album.[5] We can only understand "truth" to emerge from the coming together of all these different visions.

The sequence in the film about the concentration camps in Argelès illustrates this well. Capa went into those camps on behalf of the French government to illustrate an article on how well the French were treating the Spanish refugees. It was propaganda. If you look at the images from the Mexican Suitcase that I didn't include in the film, there are lots of pictures of chefs in kitchens cutting meat, as well as the temporary housing they built. This was all to show the "good life" in the camps on the beaches. But there was another story, the story told to me by the old men who were camp survivors, the story of the suicides and of the people who preferred to return to Spain even though they knew they would inevitably be shot by Francoists. In a Mexican archive I found these other photographs that aren't by Capa. We don't even know who took them. They told a very different, and harsh, story of people burrowing under the sand to keep warm. For me it was important both to refuse the limitation of only including images from the Mexican Suitcase and to contextualize the images taken by Capa with the memories of those who experienced the camps. I think they are all evidence. They are true and not true. Just because it is Capa doesn't make it any more significant than if it is an unknown or lesser known photographer.

When I showed the film at the Sofia International Film Festival in Bulgaria in 2016 after not having seen it in a while, two things happened. First, screening *The Mexican Suitcase* in the current context of the refugee crisis in Europe revealed to me how the film has such a vitality and life in our current historical moment. And second, this woman stood up during the Q&A after the screening. She told the story of her parents and how there had been a radical brigade from Bulgaria, which had been lost from Bulgarian history under Soviet occupation. Her parents had met in Spain; her mother was a nurse and her father a soldier. She gave me this tiny little picture of her parents so that I would have something of theirs from Spain. One recovered history begets another. In fact, at least once a week for two years after the film's release, I would get a letter thanking me for making the film from somebody who was related to or knew one of the refugees on those boats to Mexico.

Your third documentary on photography, The Man Who Saw Too Much, *turned attention to a single photographer, Enrique Metinides, with whom you had collaborated extensively on a 2012 retrospective exhibition and book,* 101 Tragedies of Enrique Metinides.[6] *How did you approach the task of framing a single photographer's images within film and why did you choose to parallel his career in the late twentieth century with contemporary photojournalists shooting the ongoing crisis of violence in Mexico?*

In a way, Metinides's photographs were much easier to work with because he thinks in a cinematic way. He draws his way of seeing from cinema, particularly melodrama and crime films. Enrique got given an iPad and his grandson put a lot of his photographs on it. So he learned how to swipe: image, image, image. You see that a little bit in the film because it is an interesting new way of moving through images. But it is another thing to be directly on the receiving end of this, sitting in his bedroom as he is commenting, "Look, murder, murder, murder!" You end up feeling like you've been assaulted. I said to Enrique, "Enough! I can't see any more photographs." You can't see after a while, but he wouldn't stop. I was actually screaming, "I can't see another one of these pictures." He has no comprehension of the impact of his images on others because he is so used to looking at them. While making the film, I was always conscious of their impact on my audience. Once in the film Metinides turns to the camera and says, "Terrible image. Enough?" And then he kind of smiles as though he is enjoying it. I do think that the film has a relationship to pornography, certainly to voyeurism. Another moment in the film during the exhibition at Aperture in New York, I decided to film the audience in the gallery looking at the photographs and their reactions sometimes reveal fascination and at other times horror – for me they represented another layer of looking (Figure 12.3). In Metinides's photographs he would often include the onlookers at the scene of an accident; I then played with it and took it to a new level with the audience's reaction to the photographs in the gallery. Similarly, the

FIGURE 12.3 *The Man Who Saw Too Much*
(Trisha Ziff, 2015)

cinema audience also becomes the next layer of onlookers. In Capa you have this photographer who goes out to take pictures in this moral way as the documenter of atrocity and war so that the rest of the world would know. Metinides's motives are curiosity, obsession, and selling newspapers. He cared less about the bigger story. He even says at the end of the film, "Better not to know." His commitment is not to information or truth but to his own fascination with what is in front of him.

On the other hand, my understanding of the younger press photographers changed as I followed them covering the violence of Mexico today. At first, I thought of them as camera-carrying vultures. They hear about a murder and can't wait to make their pictures – it seemed so grotesque. I spent night after night hanging out with them in an old police station, waiting for the phone call and then zoom, off we would go in search of an image. Yet, I ended up thinking that these photographers are amazing! They bear witness to something that the government wants to be invisible to us. And whether it is used in the sensational tabloid press or not, what they create is a document of what happens night after night in a country which would rather remain blinkered to the reality. I ended up having immense respect for them. Their repetitive images may be published in a sensationalist context, but they prevent us from forgetting. That is critical because we live in a culture of silence and invisibility in Mexico. Through populism and sensationalism, this information, this truth, manages to get through; it is what is not censored, which is a contradiction. Paper a museum wall with all of these images and it is going to tell you a great deal about contemporary Mexico.

I loved that these photographers take care of each other – they watch each other's backs. That is why I added in a postscript interview after the credits in my film, where the photographers talk about the recent murder of their colleague Rubén Espinosa. Rubén's murder in 2015 brought home to the middle-class Mexican Left the danger to us all. It was so brutal that his colleague, who arrived at the scene to photograph, could not even recognize his body. What happens when the photographer takes the call and photographs his own murder? He is the witness to his own death. You can't look at Metinides's work now without making reference to the photographs which are made today, which fill the tabloids, the yellow press. What are they telling us? How has the violence changed? How do we look at sensational photography? In Mexico Metinides is the father of this genre of press photography.

Metinides was a difficult subject to interview. He goes into performance mode, telling the same stories over and over again. It is his way to keep control. It is only when he is left out in the cold that something real happens because Metinides depends on an audience to manipulate. When he is in control, he just repeats himself. When he is vulnerable, you actually get glimpses of his truth. So, on the very last day that we filmed, we borrowed this big space to construct a black box and then I found an uncomfortable wooden chair for him to sit on. I told the crew to avoid eye contact with him and to wear all black so that they would disappear into the background as much as possible. It was important that he was not relaxed, not at ease. The only person to make eye contact would be me. In essence it was like a simulated interrogation scene. It was hard for me to see it through, precisely because he is an elderly man now. At the end I had no more questions to ask him, so I just looked at him. He stared back at me, folded and unfolded his arms, and said, "Do you have another question?" I just shrugged my shoulders and said no. But the camera kept rolling; unsure of how to respond, he began to get annoyed. He rolled his eyes and looked around the room and then just stared at me. He became vulnerable, almost tearful, as if something was going to break. At that moment he revealed that everything he'd seen had hurt him. I saw an old man trying not to weep trying to hold it all together. I believe it is the moment that redeems him, and we see the toll of everything he has witnessed in his life, no different from a war photographer suffering from a version of PTSD.

Your most recent art documentary and exhibition, Witkin & Witkin, *incorporates a strong comparative dimension through its exploration of a photographer and a painter. Has the addition of a new medium (painting) to the mix changed the dynamics of your integrative curation and filmmaking?*

With *Witkin & Witkin*, I thought about the exhibition and the book in the context of the film because by then I was a filmmaker.[7] The book became a script for the film. I invited different people to write a chapter for the book. All the women you see in the film wrote chapters. I thus got to know my characters before I filmed them because they had first participated in the book. For instance, Sarah Jane, the twins' older sister, wrote a chapter; later, when we filmed her, I knew exactly what questions to ask. Aside from Joel and Jerome, I purposely chose to interview only women characters. I had in my head this image of the two male artists surrounded by women, their "enablers," who are invisible in the final work of art. I wanted to give the women who made it possible for them to make their work the visibility they deserved. The book helped me define that strategy as well as structure the film. The exhibition was always an exhibition, but I also knew that I wanted to film its process for the documentary.

Since *Witkin & Witkin* is built around these characters and their stories, there aren't that many images of Jerome and Joel's work in the film. Jerome's paintings are very illustrative. What I appreciate about Jerome's pictures is that they take you into a history of the world. It is a random history, but they take you into reality, whether it is the Nazi concentration camps, the Syrian boy on the beach in Greece, or the destruction of Aleppo. I selected works in which the world impacted the way in which Jerome painted. I chose paintings to illustrate his stories, not really to present and analyze his art. With Joel, it is almost the other way around. His work has influenced other artists, filmmakers, and designers, such as Mark Romanek and Alexander McQueen, which I wanted to show. You also don't see that much of Joel's work in the film. The focus is much more about the process, how he constructs his images (Figure 12.4). I focused on two specific shoots, partly because his work is difficult to put on film, but also the fact that the process is inherently fascinating. That process interested me more than the final image. Although his work is meticulously staged and highly constructed, it is also about the decisive

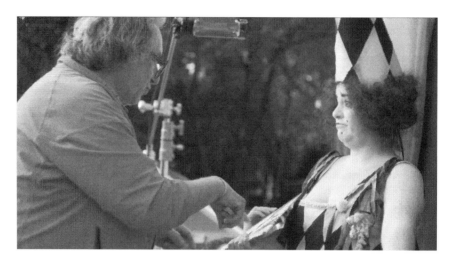

FIGURE 12.4 *Witkin & Witkin*
(Trisha Ziff, 2017)

moment of photography. I learned that by observing him. He doesn't take that many photos and he knows immediately when he has got what he needs. In the end, *Witkin & Witkin* is much more about the relationship between the twins than about their art. I was worried about that, that either one of them might say, "this isn't a film about our art." However, neither of them ever said that to me.

Considering your approach to filming photography more broadly, do you take a purist approach to maintain the stillness of photography or does the reframing of photography through film require an engagement with dynamism?

It is not just a matter of stillness and motion, but also format. Format becomes an issue and a problem to solve. Many of Joel's images are square, so they don't fit in the film frame. A lot of Capa's images are horizontal, whereas Chim used the portrait format much more. Capa's photographs are much more cinematic. His work lends itself to the cinematic frame. Very few Witkin photographs do that. With Joel, I literally went into the frame. I didn't do that with Capa because I could move across his images on a contact sheet. You'd see the whole thing. I took liberties with Joel's work, reframing and cropping them. I had quite a few discussions during production and some people were horrified that I would do that. I talked to Joel about it and I think he understood. He certainly never considered it a problem; he is very generous in that way. It also impacted the presentation of Jerome's painting. But I think in most cases of Jerome's work, I showed the whole frame. For me, there are no rules. I just make sure that I am conveying what I am trying to say in a way that doesn't disrespect the artist, in a way in which the artist is going to feel comfortable. Jerome and Joel have never said to me that I undermined their work by doing what I did with their images. Likewise, the only thing Metinides said was that I didn't put enough of his photographs in the film, but he never complained about how I did it.

I think the rhythm of a film matters. The relationship to music matters. But it is complicated because you're making a film about things that were essentially created to be looked at in their stillness. You have to find different solutions. You have to remember that by the time I am editing the film, I've seen each image hundreds of times and for the person watching the film, it may be the first time they're seeing it. That is something I have to remind myself of, not only about images but content in general. I ask for feedback from others, but I don't really show it to others until I get to final cut. I would never lock a picture until showing it to a lot of people first and getting back notes. Also, when you see a photograph on a screen huge, like the cinema screen, you see things you never saw before. When you're editing, you're editing on a small screen and then boom, on the big screen you can see so much more. So, I always make sure I see the final cut on a large screen, before locking picture because it inevitably reveals errors and information that I've missed.

My understanding of how you present a still image in the context of film has developed over time and with experience. I had originally planned to collaborate with another director on the Witkin project, but we ended up disagreeing about fundamental issues. He argued that one has to remain true to the photograph and see the entire image on the screen in a static format without any camera movement. I totally disagree with this kind of purism. You're telling your narrative through the moving image; to stop on a framed still inevitably takes you outside the narrative. I think a film has to take you to a different place visually. It has to give its audience something beyond the photograph to validate it being inside a film. Otherwise, just buy a book or go to an exhibition. I think that is something I continue to struggle with in terms of making films about photography. It is hard thing to do. You are not putting the image in a frame and thinking of it as a single image.

There has been a boom in photography documentaries over the last two decades. How do you see your own work in relation to this boom?

A lot of the recent documentaries are monographs about individual photographers. I hope my films aren't that. Maybe they use the format. You think it is about Metinides, but it is really about voyeurism. You think it is about Joel-Peter and Jerome Witkin, but actually it is about two brothers, about commitment to a vision, about getting old and dysfunction. *Chevolution* is not about Che or Korda but about an iconic image and its endless appropriation. Maybe other photographic documentaries do this too, but many of them really stick to being portraits of the artist. I have never really been interested in just telling the story of a photographer. It is through the photographer that I can tell other stories. In some ways, I am now moving into unknown territory because I am known as someone who makes films about photography and right now I want to tell other stories, challenge myself, and do something different.

Notes

1. With the withdrawal of Political Status in 1976, Republican political prisoners refused to be criminalized by wearing prison uniforms. Kieran Nugent, the first blanket protester, famously said, "You'll have to nail it to my back," and was thrown a blanket by the authorities, and thus the blanket protest began.
2. Trisha Ziff, *Che Guevera: Revolutionary Icon* (New York: Harry Abrams, 2006).
3. See David Kunzle, *Che Guevara: Icon, Myth and Message* (Los Angeles: UCLA Fowler Museum of Cultural History, 1997).
4. Cynthia Young, ed. *The Mexican Suitcase: The Rediscovered Spanish Civil War Negatives of Capa, Chim and Taro* (New York and Göttingen: International Center of Photography/ Steidl, 2010).
5. Trisha Ziff, *Hidden Truths: Bloody Sunday, 1972* (Santa Monica: Smart Art Press, 1998).
6. Trisha Ziff, ed. *101 Tragedies of Enrique Metinides* (New York: Aperture, 2012).
7. Trisha Ziff, ed. *Witkin & Witkin: Joel-Peter Witkin, A Photographer; Jerome Witkin, A Painter* (Mexico City: Trilce Ediciones, 2018).

13

ON THE HISTORY (AND FUTURE) OF ART DOCUMENTARIES AND THE FILM PROGRAM AT THE NATIONAL GALLERY OF ART

Margaret Parsons, interviewed by Marsha Gordon

Margaret Parsons, who has a BA in Fine Arts and Sociology from Boston University and an MA in History, Museum Studies, and Folk Culture from the State University of New York, began working at the National Gallery of Art in Washington, DC, in January 1978. She started her over-forty-year career at the Gallery as part of the in-house media production team in the making of art documentaries for television and schools, such as a series of art shorts produced in the 1970s and 1980s known as *Awareness* and the hour-long documentary *A Place To Be: The Construction of the East Building of the National Gallery of Art 1968–1978* (Charles Guggenheim, 1978). Today, film production at the Gallery is handled quite differently, and largely designed to accompany special exhibitions.

Almost from the time it opened to the public in 1941, the National Gallery supported the notion that motion pictures and other audio-visuals had the potential to reach a larger audience wanting to know more about art. By the early 1960s with the arrival of J. Carter Brown, first as assistant to the director and then as director of the National Gallery, the museum developed a mission to raise the consciousness of the American public and provide better art education through film. According to Parsons, Brown believed that American schools, in general, were not taking the lead in providing aesthetic awareness for young students, and he felt that the Gallery could, to some degree, take on this role through a more active film production unit. A few of those early films – for instance, *The American Vision* (J. Carter Brown, 1966), *Femme/Woman: A Tapestry by Joan Miró* (Robert Pierce, 1979) and *Mobile by Alexander Calder* (Robert Pierce, 1979) – now reside in the National Gallery of Art archive. Brown also urged the use of supplementary means – audio lectures, slide programs, films, and live performances – to enhance the visitor experience within the museum.

When the Gallery's East Building opened in the summer of 1978, Parsons began to see a potential for the new theater and its large projection room with dual 35mm and 16mm projectors. Parsons put together the first series of films for the National Gallery of Art in the spring of 1979 (Figure 13.1). Prior to this time, there were

FIGURE 13.1 Poster for the first *Films on Art* program at the National Gallery of Art, Washington, DC, 1979.

Courtesy of the National Gallery of Art.

only occasional screenings, not an integrated ongoing program. The spring 1979 program consisted entirely of art films like *Henri Matisse Paper Cut-Outs* (Shelby Newhouse, 1978) and *Noguchi: A Sculptor's World* (Arnold Eagle, 1972). As the series evolved, Parsons began to imagine a more coherent program of screenings that went beyond films on art to include filmmaker retrospectives and thematic cycles. She started this more diverse and inclusive film programming, which continues to the present day, in 1981.

This chapter is the result of a series of interviews conducted via email between Marsha Gordon and Margaret Parsons, which transpired over the course of 2018. This content has been edited into essay form.

The art documentary

With regard to the origins of my interest in the art documentary and how it has evolved over time, I recall watching in a college theater somewhere in the Boston area in the 1960s a feature film entitled *The Titan: Story of Michelangelo* (Robert Flaherty, Richard Lyford and Curt Oertel, 1950). It was black and white, very dramatic, and included impressive footage that I think had been partly compiled from archival material, but also some newer footage. Robert Flaherty had been involved in the production.[1] The film was awesome. I had never seen, before that, a long feature film devoted to an artist. Of course, in the 1950s and 1960s, commercial television and especially National Educational Television would frequently have programming devoted to art. It was not uncommon, and I saw a lot of art footage on TV. But *The Titan* was so theatrical and excessive, and I'm sure it screened in 35mm.

The next time I was seriously thinking about art films was when I started working on them. I did research for the National Gallery's productions and assisted in various ways: conducting interviews with art historians, chasing after artists, such as Alexander Calder who would arrive at the museum to install a work, assisting cinematographers in any way that I could, and making sure our production schedules proceeded apace. At the same time, I was discovering such places as the Canadian Centre for Films on Art and its esteemed director Dorothy Macpherson. Today, I think that the Centre's collection has been subsumed into a larger national archive, so the Centre itself no longer exists. Then, there was the Museum of Modern Art (MoMA) and its Department of Film, and personalities such as Bill Sloan who, in the 1970s, was at the New York Public Library (and later at MoMA). It was Bill, and also Margareta Akermark at MoMA, who made me realize that the so-called film on art is not only a special genre of movie making, but also an outlet for scholarship and research. Macpherson, a British citizen who arrived in Canada in the 1940s, met John Grierson and worked for the National Film Board of Canada (NFB) before joining the National Gallery of Canada, where she established the Canadian Centre for Films on Art. She would carefully examine filmographic and bibliographic information, write annotations and compile them for publication.

Her catalogs were famous, especially her source book *Films on Art*, which served as an invaluable resource for curators and programmers for over two decades.[2]

By the mid 1980s, I was regularly attending the annual art film festival in Montreal, the International Festival of Films on Art. At that time, there were several big international festivals devoted to the genre. During that period, I also met Nadine Covert, who for many years headed the Educational Film Library Association and organized its American Film Festival in New York, a prominent annual showcase and competition for documentaries. By the mid 1980s, Nadine was helming the Getty's Program for Art on Film, a joint undertaking of the J. Paul Getty Trust and the Metropolitan Museum of Art. She asked me to become one of the project's panelists and to join their editorial board, where I got to know many filmmakers and art historians who were seriously interested in experimenting with new techniques and approaches for making films by and about artists. That was a productive and rewarding time, and an experience that really expanded my own thinking about the form.

Most of my critical thinking about art documentaries is now done while viewing new films online, at festivals, or in commercial theaters. It is difficult to precisely define what constitutes a successful, thought-provoking or appealing work for me. One of the more effective art films of recent years was *Beuys* by Andres Veiel (2017). Yet, reviews in *Variety* and other trade publications were generally unkind to the film and the filmmaker, criticizing him, in a sense, for not being more conventional in his approach to the subject. So, once again it seems that beauty remains in the eye of the beholder. I will discuss Veiel's film in more detail later in the interview.

Finding an audience

Public television, museums, universities and commercial cinemas have all undoubtedly played key roles in shaping the history of the art documentary. To this list, it is important to add the film festival, another cultural institution that has influenced the history and form of the genre. All of these institutions have similar objectives related to their own potential and effectiveness. Stated simply, with respect to the topic of art and artists, they all want and need to find a way to present art-related cinema in a way that educates or enlightens their respective audiences while somehow enhancing their own status as cultural institutions.

The very term "art documentary" brings to mind a huge and fluid genre that encompasses practices as diverse as those of, say, Michael Blackwood, Hans Namuth, Perry Miller Adato, Thomas Riedelsheimer, Ai Weiwei, Henri-Georges Clouzot and major commissioning producers like the BBC and ZDF. Institutional convention and practice are related organically to distribution or, to put it more bluntly, how these art films manage to get seen at all.

Aside from any aesthetic or artistic aims, the goal of the independent filmmaker is to have the work seen as widely as possible – in different situations, many times. But unlike the commercial film industry, which strives for widespread distribution to a maximum number of people, the distribution of the art documentary is less pervasive and less predictable. Without question, art museums, specialized festivals, television and schools have always been sought out by distributors as the principal sites for exhibition of the art documentary. Now, of course, art films and art series are consumed online to a large degree, even older productions. Prominent art historians who have written and narrated notable art historical series, such as Brian Sewell, Wendy Beckett, Mary Beard, Simon Schama, Robert Hughes and Kenneth Clark, can and do still have a huge following on YouTube. It's too early to fully assess just how the internet is shaping institutional viewing habits.

Today there are at least two prominent film festivals devoted exclusively to the art documentary: the International Festival of Films on Art in Montreal and the Artecinema International Festival of Films on Contemporary Art in Naples. Both have become important gatherings for filmmakers, programmers, producers, distributors and many other influential consumers of art, as well as the public. At these festivals, ideas are absorbed and exchanged, deals are made, new possibilities for exhibition open up and new filmmakers are exhibited, influencing the overall aesthetic (and marketable) development of the practice. An annual event since 1981, the Montreal festival is now the oldest festival of its kind in the world, where the programming spans all historical periods and all art forms (i.e. the performing arts as well as the visual arts). Established in 1996, Artecinema is smaller and more specialized than the Montreal festival, and includes a carefully selected program of films on contemporary visual artists, architects, and photographers. As articulated in its 2018 press release, the festival "offers the public an invaluable opportunity to comprehend the poetics of these artists, to observe them at work in their studios, and as an illustration of the evolution of various languages of contemporary art."[3] These festivals also allow the general public in these cities to see art documentaries in a theatrical setting, which they might not otherwise be able to do.

There were sincere attempts in the 1970s and 1980s to codify the art documentary and, at the same time, to shape this form in new, even experimental, ways. The aforementioned Program for Art on Film was one of the most notable of these projects. Program manager Nadine Covert remembers that this collaboration was conceived by Karl Katz and Wendy Stein at the Metropolitan Museum of Art's Office of Film and TV.[4] They pitched the joint project to the J. Paul Getty Trust, which funded it from 1984 until their priorities changed in 1994, as they were then involved in building the new Getty Museum and looking to support more West Coast projects. The Program's principal activities were the Art on Screen Database and the Production Lab.[5] For the database, Covert and her colleagues collected data on about 26,000 films on art from all over the world. Covert notes that,

> during its brief ten years of existence, the database was a unique and valuable resource for filmmakers and scholars. But it hasn't been updated for the past 20+ years, so that limits its value. It was a project ahead of its time, before online access and computer research became ubiquitous.

The Production Lab produced a dozen short films which were collaborations between filmmakers and art historians focused on pre-nineteenth-century art, which had not received as much attention in art documentaries as later periods. The goal was to encourage innovative productions that would experiment with novel film techniques and still have a strong art history component. The resulting productions were assembled into a boxed set of videos, and later DVDs, that were distributed by Katz's company, MUSE Film and Television, until his death in 2017, when the company closed. Since there was no archival film footage from which to draw, making films about pre-nineteenth-century art was thus a greater challenge. Each project was a collaboration between an art historian or subject expert and an established filmmaker. In each case, the historian was told that he or she would have equal say with the filmmaker about the content and approach. Each film would be relatively short, and the art itself, rather than an artist biography, would dominate.

Perhaps the most famous film to come from the Production Lab was a collaboration between painter David Hockney and filmmaker Philip Haas, *A Day on the Grand Canal with the Emperor of China (or Surface Is Illusion But So Is Depth)* (1998), on the topic of Chinese scroll painting, one of Hockney's passions. This film is still in distribution and has recently received a 2K restoration funded by its distributor Milestone Films. The Lab productions hold up well, and the subjects are timeless. But whoever takes over the distribution will have to promote them again, if they are to find new audiences.[6] One of the more interesting experimental aspects of the Production Lab was to encourage art historians to work with offbeat or avant-garde filmmakers to achieve a less didactic approach. For example, the surrealist animators Timothy and Stephen Quay (also known as the Brothers Quay) were brought in to direct *De Artificiali Perspectiva or Anamorphosis* (1991) with the art historian Roger Cardinal. In that film, a puppet figure demonstrates the principles of anamorphosis as a painting technique (Figure 13.2). For *Painted Earth: The Art of the Mimbres Indians* (1989), avant-gardist Anita Thacher joined forces with art historian J.J. Brody and commercial cinematographers who specialized in techniques for "diving" into a pottery bowl, for example, to engage in visual play with the bowl's designs. Japanese video artist Takahiko Iimura was commissioned with architect Arata Isozaki to make *Ma: Space/Time in the Garden of Ryoan-ji* (1989), a forty-six-minute film about the celebrated early-sixteenth-century garden in the Zen temple of Ryoan-ji in Kyoto and the classical Japanese principles of *ma*, which govern its design.

My colleague in the film department at the National Gallery, Joanna Raczynska, is a documentary filmmaker who has worked in various ways with documentation of the arts, especially for online publications. Raczynska believes that the current state of media art and documentary film funding, in general, greatly influences the formation and support of various documentary production practices. She cites the NFB and their decades-long relationship with the legendary Alanis Obomsawin, who joined that organization in an administrative capacity in the 1960s before she was encouraged internally within the NFB to make her own films with their support. Raczynska observes that other funding agencies like the Ford Foundation,

FIGURE 13.2 *De Artificiali Perspectiva or Anamorphosis*
(the Brothers Quay and Roger Cardinal, 1991)

the Sundance Institute, the Independent Television Service and American Documentary (producers of the *POV* series for PBS) support works for broadcast, theatrical release and the festival circuit where the documentary in general has a stronger presence than ever. She notes that,

> Perhaps the increase in distribution possibilities with streaming and podcasting makes the art documentary, as well as the art of documentary, much more accessible than ever before. The form of delivery also influences the format of the work, where interactive and serial documentaries have taken center stage over single-channel theatrical films.[7]

Raczynska also believes that filmmakers who make non-fiction works where art practice or the artists themselves are the subjects tend to ask more of their audiences than those documentaries that are primarily informational:

> These makers' intentions are more philosophical than didactic, often engaged in blurring distinctions between the age-old terms of documentary, non-fiction, experimental, biographical or autobiographical work. I am thinking specifically of the film *Breaking the Frame* (2012) about performance artist and avant-garde filmmaker Carolee Schneemann; the filmmaker, Marielle Nitoslawska, who teaches documentary film production at Concordia

University, has often stated that she had a hard time getting festivals to show this film because it was not 'documentary enough' for the documentary film festivals, nor 'experimental enough' for the experimental film festivals.

While there are more film festivals operating now, Raczynska observes that they tend to dismiss certain genres and privilege commercially "hot" products over risk-taking works that might require multiple viewings and more from their audiences than simple reception.

Film on art

There can be an awkward relationship between filmmaking as a form of expression versus filmmaking that is more focused on didactic and pedagogic objectives. In the past, that was typically the case for art documentaries – a problematic relationship between these two sorts of practice, film-as-art and film-on-art. With the possible exception of the MoMA, many art museums, at least in North America, generally preferred to retain filmmaking for teaching or outreach purposes, even engaging in in-house production of moving-image media to support exhibitions and collections. Complicating this view was the definition of what an artist's work-on-film really entailed.

In general, compared to artist cinema, documentaries were often viewed as more industrial or mechanized – reproducible, pragmatic and not the work of an artist, so to speak. But, with a deeper view of the situation today, I think it is difficult to make these same judgments now. There is no reason why a documentary about an artist could not also be called an artistic film. There are many examples that could qualify as both. Plus, lower-budget documentaries (many artist documentaries fall into that category) tend to be a serious artisanal vision of one or perhaps two people. Within museum practice, the line of demarcation between film-as-art and film-on-art has eased up a bit in recent years. For one thing, now that most art museums are collecting and exhibiting moving-image media in their galleries, the overall standards and criteria have been shifting. It has become acceptable to experiment with production techniques in general, and with films about artists in particular. The worthier art documentaries are, in my view, also film-as-art. Currently there are also dynamic new production technologies that can cut cross traditional genres, things like immersive sound or even hybrid fiction/non-fiction filmmaking. There is no reason why these more experimental techniques have to be limited to narrative or art cinema only.

The National Gallery's current and historical role in using film for art education, and how that might compare to other major art museums, is another matter. My colleague Leo Kasun, the education resources and former production specialist at the Gallery, has recently been delving into the history of the Gallery's relationship with film and art education. According to Leo, the Gallery's annual report for 1942 (the museum opened in 1941) listed 8mm film strips showing 300 paintings and sculptures in the collection, apparently produced with the help of a US Army film crew. These film strips (silent, no voiceover) were the earliest of the Gallery's Extension Programs, a name that continued to be used for outreach projects to schools and other groups through the 1970s and early 1980s. These early, silent introductory films to the Gallery's collections continued to be produced through the 1940s, and data concerning usage started to be gathered by the early 1950s for reporting to Congress in the annual request for the federal budget. Along with film strips, high-quality framed reproductions of paintings, huge folded exhibition posters and LP records with narrative commentary were also distributed in packages sent out through the mail. Eventually, 2" x 2" color slides were added to this mix.

By 1961, the museum was making higher-budget 16mm films with sound tracks. The first on record was called *Art in the Western World* (not to be confused with the 1989 British television series of the same title). Compared to other art museums with similar outreach programs during this period, the National Gallery appears to have been the only American museum engaged in full-time film production and making it available to a national audience, in keeping with the Gallery's mission "to serve the United States of America in a national role."[8] The Metropolitan Museum of Art was doing similar work, but only for an audience in the New York City area. Plus, the Gallery's programs were free of charge, whereas other museums would generally charge for this kind of outreach service. Two slightly later landmarks for the Gallery's education mission were the exhibition and distribution of the BBC's fourteen-part, blue-chip series *Civilisation* with Kenneth Clark and J. Carter Brown's film *Treasures of King Tut* in 1975, a film funded by the IBM corporation.[9] Both screened at the National Gallery in 35mm, these films were made available in 16mm prints to schools, universities, civic groups and museums across the country through the Extension Service.[10] Many prints were used, worn, and replaced for decades.

From 1973 to 1981, the Gallery partnered with the local PBS affiliate WETA to produce sixteen different *Awareness films*, a series of short monographic films on 16mm that focused on individual artists. The series was wildly popular with the public, not only through the Extension Service, but also on public television itself, which used the films as short five- or six-minute fillers between longer shows. Not all of the 16mm Extension Service films were ultimately digitized, but many of them were, and digitized versions of many older films are still in circulation today.

Today, the Gallery has a full-time, in-house production staff, primarily to produce thirty-minute films to accompany major exhibitions. These works are shown in high-resolution formats in small theaters within exhibition spaces and then circulated through Educational Resources (the former Extension Service). One of the main concerns, in terms of distribution, is keeping up with technological changes; for example, streaming new material to TV affiliates in the fifty US states and even internationally. The current audience through television is estimated to be thirty million viewers per year, primarily in the Northeast, as well as twenty cities in California via local cable stations. The Gallery still publishes a full-color catalogue of extension programs, *National Gallery of Art: Online and Free Loan Resources*, and approximately 13,000 of these catalogues were distributed in 2018 through the National Art Education Association. Another 6,000 catalogues were shipped to correctional facility administrators, and the staff has begun mailing a similar number to assisted care and retirement homes. One recent development is that by the end of 2018, programs will more than likely be available only through download, rather than through the distribution of DVDs.

Within the documentary film world, the independent status of the film-on-art as a small, but useful, category is well established. Perhaps a straightforward way to demonstrate this is through a reference to historiography, or the generally accepted belief about the origins of the term "film-on-art" itself as Dorothy Macpherson outlined them in 1977:

> It was in the late 1930s that the film genre known today as the film-on-art achieved a status which earned it the right to independent recognition. Until then it had been swallowed up in the broad mass of documentary, the term invented by John Grierson to cover the creative treatment of actuality. [...] In 1951 in Florence, Carlos Ragghianti produced his *Répertoire général international* which listed and described more than a thousand titles. UNESCO [the United Nations Educational, Scientific and Cultural Organization], too, published three consecutive listings, 1949, 1951, 1953, covering most of the filmmaking countries in its international membership. The unique actuality of the film-on-art had become apparent. The films made from 1939 on were vastly different from the picture postcard sequences of scenery and famous buildings for which the name was at first used.[11]

The basic tenets of this assumption about the genre's origin remain unchallenged, and today the film-on-art persists as a minor but prestigious subset of documentary filmmaking. In documentary festivals and competitions, of course, the film about art competes against other kinds of content, and in the end the merits of technique, rather than subject matter, determine the film or films with the highest status.

However, the so-called art world – that is, art institutions and the discipline of art history itself – presents a more nuanced, but equally inflexible, view of the status of the film-on-art. And that status is considerably lower overall than in the film world. The art world tends to be much more structured in its judgements about the significance of the physical object and awards status to anyone directly associated with the object. Stated another way, the closer to the physical object or the "unique work of art," the higher the status.[12] The actual study, curation, analysis or conservation of a painting, drawing, sculpture, print or photograph has, and will continue to have, higher rank in any institution of art than any recording on film of that artwork or the filmic documentation of its making. Any true "expert" can exist only in direct juxtaposition to the artifact itself. This sort of reverence for closeness to the object could be viewed as a fetish, but it discreetly and insistently determines position or status in the art world. Film, by its physical nature alone, is already in the realm of reproduction and thus lower in the pecking order. According to this logic, education and filmmaking are important, but they are not art nor art historical scholarship.

One interesting shift in this thinking is that now certain kinds of moving-image works, including some with hybrid documentary elements, are being collected by art museums that wish to accumulate more technology-based and time-based media works. These accessioned art works are subject to obsolescence of various kinds, losses, faulty installation and other forms of damage. Thus, the field of time-based media art conservation was created to identify and treat the inevitable damage. To this degree, one might say that moving-image works (including documentary) are gathering new prestige in the art world, but only time will tell how this new category of object effects the status of film and the art documentary.

Film as art

Aside from the very visible shifts in the technology of filmmaking itself (e.g. digital cameras, stabilization tools, higher resolutions, better editing software and so forth), the most perceptible shift that I have noticed in recent years with respect to the "film on art" documentary could be stated like this: film-on-art is aiming to become film-as-art. That may sound glib, but the shift is fairly evident in the tension between presenting clear and concrete information (didactic content) versus a foregrounding of formal stylistic elements. This is part of a greater emphasis on film style within documentary film in general. To name just a few recent art documentaries that fit into this vein – Marielle Nitoslawska's *Breaking the Frame* [2014], *Immortality for All: A Film Trilogy on Russian Cosmism* (Anton Vidokle's 2017 study of Soviet art and architecture) or even Agnes Varda's collaborative hybrid with the French artist JR, *Faces Places* (*Visages Villages*, 2017) – one immediately recognizes how the art documentary is now intentionally closer to what was once categorically known as experimental.

That is not to suggest that didactic content is no longer a principal feature of art documentaries. Many classics of the genre, such as Emile de Antonio's *Painters Painting* (1973), or Perry Miller Adato's *Georgia O'Keeffe* (1977), relied more heavily on conventional techniques, but will remain unparalleled in the history of art. Rather, more often now than before, key factual information or content is simply revealed less palpably, or merely alluded to within the formal elements of the work. This approach has certain logical advantages for the filmmaker, since facts once expressed explicitly in voiceover, subtitles, or intertitles can sometimes be questionable or misleading. But the main advantage of a more formalist approach is that, on the whole, documentaries have become more aesthetically pleasing to watch. For example, composing longer takes (going beyond what was once considered a standard editing pace for the genre) can result in a more visually beautiful work. Carefully arranging a long take for film is not unlike creating a painted canvas; in both instances, the elements of color, framing, lighting and design have to be considered and composed. Look at the opening long track, for example, of Jennifer Baichwal's *Manufactured Landscapes* (2006), a feature documentary on Canadian landscape photographer Edward Burtynsky. This shot, lasting several minutes and tracking the entire length of a huge factory floor in China, was nothing short of dazzling, both visually and emotionally. Like many sequences in the film, the cinematography appropriately echoed the design and the narrative of Burtynsky's own photography. Baichwal has suggested in interview that "if this film were didactic it would imply an easy answer," alluding to the fact that Burtynsky's photographs deal with manmade environmental catastrophes.[13]

The question of intermediality in the practice of art documentary has so many facets, not the least of which might be a discussion of film versus digital capture. 35mm film stock could once capture faint and delicate details lacking in video capture, thus making the recording of expressive media like graphic arts more authentic, which raises the question of whether or not earlier films should still be viewed in their original film formats. That is a question that continues to vex the film community. But aside from the aesthetic issues related to lens technology, lighting, editing and even sound technology, I prefer to view the challenges of intermediality as related to filmmaker definitions; that is, what a filmmaker proposes for any particular project, rather than what he or she considers to be a priori issues within an artistic medium itself.

Another way of articulating this is to examine the challenges that arise within a particular filmmaker's objectives. Let's consider several cases. German filmmaker Heinz Emigholz specializes in recording architecture on film by defining and delineating the formal structure of whatever building he is filming. As a result, his films, such as *Schindler's Houses* (2007), *Loos Ornamental* (2008), or *Parabeton: Pier Luigi Nervi and Roman Concrete* (2012) (Figure 13.3), are fixated on precise framing and shots of specific architectural details arranged in a predetermined order. Emigholz's camera is usually slightly canted during filming, thus allowing him to include more information within the frame, a trait that he realizes is idiosyncratic, but which he feels suits his purposes of recording a building in space and time. He usually avoids filming people within the buildings and also eschews narration, relying instead on ambient sound to fill his soundtracks. He also uses available natural light, thus capturing a building at a precise moment in time. All of these techniques reinforce the notion that what is being recorded is a sort of memory of the history of the building. Emigholz's editing then presents his sequence of shots as discrete pieces of a building (both exterior and interior) for the viewer to recombine mentally into a whole without explicit directorial intervention, therefore allowing the viewer to form his or her own sense of the architect's universe. He states, "I never believed that foreground should be reserved for action and actors and background for architecture and landscape," and "you have to enter a certain mode of meditation to grasp the films."[14] His filmed spaces, often those of prominent modernist architects and theorists such as Adolf Loos and Rudolph Schindler, emanate a sort of tension or ambiguity, thus emphasizing a break with classical norms.

Another example is *Beuys*, Andres Veiel's documentary about the provocative and nearly unclassifiable postwar German artist Joseph Beuys whose highly influential artwork included painting, sculpture, drawing and, most notably, performance and happenings. Beuys frequently used non-traditional materials, some of which were organic (such as animal fat or honey) and manufactured articles (like felt and gold

FIGURE 13.3 *Parabeton: Pier Luigi Nervi and Roman Concrete* (Heinz Emigholz, 2012). Courtesy of Grasshopper Film

leaf). Beuys' references were extremely broad, yet also highly personal. He often expressed the notion that art and life were inseparable, such that "everyone is an artist."[15] Veiel spent years on research for the film by studying huge amounts of extant archival footage of Beuys' performances and installations. The result is a brilliant compilation of found and archival footage, combined with some carefully edited onscreen interviews. Veiel could only have defined his aesthetic challenge – how best to capture the late artist Joseph Beuys and his many-faceted, multi-media creations – after spending years in protracted research and culling a huge volume of footage from which to work and edit. The filmmaker's vision in this case was also affected by his years in theater. But no a priori assessment of how to best capture the constantly shifting experiences of this unclassifiable artist existed for the filmmaker, and his challenges arose from observation and empirical evidence.

Trisha Ziff's *Witkin & Witkin* (2018) about the seventy-nine-year-old identical twin artists Joel-Peter and Jerome Witkin, both well-known and respected American artists, is another case in point. Joel-Peter, a photographer, creates staged tableaux that are frequently disquieting and provocative; his photographs explore uncomfortable themes such as sex, disability, and death, and present people who live on the margins of society. His work resides in major museum collections around the world. Twin brother Jerome Witkin, on the other hand, is a figurative painter, a distinguished artist and also an admired teacher (he was until recently a professor in Syracuse University's School of Art). Joel-Peter calls himself a "visual adventurer" and has never had an interest in teaching. But the work of these estranged twins shares certain concerns that at first might be hard to perceive, for instance, morality and the human condition. As children, the twins were very close and connected. As adults, they have lived far apart and have rarely communicated. However, several years ago they began exhibiting their work together in major exhibitions, a transformational moment in the lives of both artists. The film reveals several interesting and uncanny details, one of which is related to American artist Edward Hopper. Joel-Peter and Jerome were both inspired to create a work based on Hopper's *New York Movie* (1939), a well-known painting of an usherette in a movie theater. Jerome's painting and Joel-Peter's photograph shared some motifs in common, but neither had any clue that the other was working from this particular source of inspiration.

The point here is that filmmaker Ziff was treating these two media, photography and painting, as means to an end. The end was finding commonality, cohesion, and yet also complexity in the work of two twins who did not share similar artistic aspirations. Yet, Ziff reveals that a distinctive psychological harmony existed. She stated in an interview,

> What fascinated me was how different they are; the contradictions, identical yet different; in their personalities, their way of working, even where they live, one in the snow of Syracuse, the other in the desert of New Mexico. Everything about them is different, and yet their work has profound overlaps and similarities in the roots. The norm is closeness of twins, not the separation. I have immense respect for their work, but also their stories, their lives, the hurdles, the losses, their survival.[16]

Thus, Ziff's challenge was to delve below the surface of the specific media, painting and photography, to find and represent threads of their mutual identity.

Finally, it's interesting to note here that the most universal and malleable expressions (arguably) of the transmedial occur in collaborations between filmmakers and photographers. An illustration is *Manufactured Landscapes* mentioned above. Filmmaker Jennifer Baichwal and photographer Edward Burtynsky's alliance succeeded in unifying their objectives – Burtynsky's to continue his artistic representations of contemporary landscape, and Baichwal's to record human manipulation of the environment. Another illustration was the active partnership that developed between photographer-artist JR and filmmaker Agnes Varda in *Visages Villages* (*Faces Places*, 2017), a film that tracked their photographic sojourn through rural France.

Looking to the future

Current circumstances of production and funding are different in various parts of the world; moreover, many documentary films are international co-productions. For example, the latest film on Christo, *Walking on Water* (Andrey Paounov, 2018), documents *The Floating Piers*, a project on Lake Iseo in Northern Italy designed by Christo and his late wife, Jeanne-Claude. This film is an American and Italian co-production featuring an American-based Bulgarian artist (Christo), a Bulgarian writer and director (Paounov), and a fully international crew.

It seems that the United States and Europe have different funding paradigms for supporting cultural filmmaking. Europeans in general believe that public funding of the culture and the arts is a birthright, while in the US either private endowment or the commercial sector are expected to be the main facilitators for culture. For Americans, public funding is deemed to be reserved for other areas, such as education. The American film industry, a commercial juggernaut largely producing feature narratives, is not really concerned with documentary production, unlike many smaller (especially European) countries, where there is not such a large feature-film industry, but where independent producers of documentaries can and do set the tone for the national cinema. Thus, good documentaries or documentary hybrids are entered in international festivals. Europeans also engage in de-centralized and regional funding of filmmaking to a large extent, so that funds can come in close to home.

There are many specialized funds based in Europe, such as the Hubert Bals Fund in the Netherlands, which was set up by the International Film Festival Rotterdam to provide grants to talented filmmakers from Africa, Asia, Latin America, the Middle East and parts of Eastern Europe, enabling emergent filmmakers from the Global South and underdeveloped national film industries to realize their projects. In the UK, there is an interesting situation with respect to the British Film Institute, one of the main supporters of new art documentaries, which uses and distributes funds from the National Lottery for film production, including art documentaries. Swiss Films, a national film promotion agency, notes that the number of documentaries produced in Switzerland is approximately double the number of fiction features, not including documentaries funded primarily by foreign sources.

Another reason why Europeans make many worthy art documentaries stems simply from their educational system and the continual presence and exposure to art and architecture, including public garden design, within local communities. Publicly funded galleries, theaters, concert halls, opera houses and performing arts centers are everywhere in towns and cities nationwide, offering cultural opportunities year-round. In the United States, such art is not available on a daily basis outside major urban areas. Thus, filming art and the making of art documentaries is not something that necessarily becomes an option for otherwise artistic young people in America. In Europe, it is a more natural professional pathway because the knowledge base and cultural institutions to support it are already there. In Europe, despite the recent era of austerity in many countries, art and arts funding are still understood to be essential for the pleasure and welfare of citizens. In the States, this topic of arts education and funding is still unresolved.

In my observations, the so-called art documentary will be around for the foreseeable future and beyond. Firstly, and most importantly, filmmakers are naturally drawn to other artists as raw material for their own work. This has always been the case and will continue to be the case. Secondly, the institutional need to educate audiences, and in so doing enhance the institution itself, will continue to drive the need for better or more appealing and relevant art film production.

Notes

1. Curt Oertel's German-Swiss co-production *Michelangelo: Life of a Titan* (*Michelangelo: Das Leben eines Titanen*, 1940) was re-edited by Robert Flaherty with an English voiceover commentary by Frederic Marsh, released as *The Titan: Story of Michelangelo* in 1950 and won the Academy Award for Best Documentary in 1951.
2. Dorothy Macpherson, *Films on Art* (New York: Watson-Guptill Publications, 1977).
3. "Artecinema 2018," Artecinema, accessed May 29, 2019, www.artecinema.org/artecinema-press.
4. The information that follows derives from an email from Nadine Covert to Margaret Parsons, 26 September 2018.
5. Most of the films documented in the Getty Research Art on Screen database were produced between 1970 and 1998, with selective coverage of productions from 1915 to 1969. Each of the roughly 26,000 citations includes a synopsis, credits, country, language, production date, format, and other filmographic data. The last addition to the database was made in 1998. The database includes productions from more than seventy countries. Subjects covered include fine arts (painting, sculpture, drawing), architecture, archaeology, photography, decorative arts, design, costume, crafts, folk arts and related topics such as aesthetics and creativity. Media formats covered include film, video, videodisc, multimedia and CD-ROM productions. The database is still accessible to the public through the Getty Research Institute website. "Art on Screen," Getty Research Institute, accessed March 16, 2019, www.getty.edu/research/tools/article_databases/art_on_screen/.
6. The website for MUSE currently indicates that Kino Lorber will take over the distribution of the company's films and its assets will be handed over to the non-profit organization Indie Collect, in order to facilitate the preservation and archiving of the films. "About Muse," Muse Film and Television, accessed March 16, 2019, www.musefilm.org/about-muse.
7. Email from Joanna Raczynska to Margret Parsons, 2 October 2018. All subsequent quotations from Raczynska derive from this communication.
8. "Mission Statement," National Gallery of Art, accessed March 16, 2019, www.nga.gov/about/mission-statement.html.
9. Thousands flocked to the North American premiere of the *Civilisation* series at the Gallery in 1969.
10. The national distribution of *Civilisation* was enabled through matching funding from the National Endowment for the Humanities and the Xerox Corporation.
11. Macpherson, *Films on Art*, 7.
12. Samuel J.M.M. Alberti, "Objects and the Museum," *Isis* 96, no. 4 (2005): 559–71.
13. "Q&A with *Manufactured Landscapes* filmmakers Jennifer Baichwal and Edward Burtynsky, Film Forum," *Film Forum Podcast*, accessed March 16, 2019, http://01f070d.netsolhost.com/mp3/ManufacturedJune202007.mp3.
14. Aaron Cutler, "Heinz Emigholz: Building in Time," *Sight & Sound*, web-exclusive interview, November 24, 2016, www.bfi.org.uk/news-opinion/sight-sound-magazine/interviews/heinz-emigholz-building-time.
15. See Joseph Beuys, *Every Man an Artist: Talks at Documenta 5*, ed. Clara Bodenmann-Ritter (Frankfurt: Ullstein 1972), 5–20.
16. "The AFI DOCS Interview: WITKIN + WITKIN Director Trisha Ziff," American Film Institute Online Newsletter, 10 May 2018, http://blog.afi.com/the-afi-docs-interview-witkin-witkin-director-trisha-ziff/.

INDEX

#MeToo movement 140
4851 (Ai, 2009) 83–4

A.I.R. Gallery 136
Abrahams, Mike 192
Abramović, Marina 6, 14, 99–111; cinematic documentation 103, 107, 108, 110; documentation of performance 99–111; and embodiment 104, 105–6; institutionalization of 99, 105; performance of 99–111; place in the work of 109–10; use of still photography 102, 105, 109, 110; violence in the work of 106
Acconci, Vito 104
Adato, Perry Miller 208
African American artists 3, 12, 136
agalmatophilia 29
Ai Qing 83
Ai Weiwei 82–93; and collaboration 82, 85, 86, 87–90; documentary filmmaking of 83–4, 87; embodied performance of 84–5; participatory nature of works 84; politics of 83–4; public perception 85
Ai Weiwei: Never Sorry (Klayman, 2012) 82, 86–93; authority in 86, 87–90; biographical logic of; funding of 86, 88; global icon in 91–3; artist filmmaking in 88–90; paratexts of 82, 86, 87, 90–3
Ai Weiwei: The Fake Case (Johnsen, 2013) 83, 93
Alékan, Henri 23
Alpers, Svetlana 15
Always on Sunday (Russell, 1965) 7
American Vision, The (Brown, 1966) 205
Anderson, Fiona 183
Andre, Carl 136, 138
Andrew, Penelope 131
Anelli, Marco 109–10
Anger, Kenneth 174
Anthropocene (Burtynsky, 2018) 9
Apfel, Iris 175
architecture 1, 3, 11, 12, 24, 28, 105, 167, 179, 215, 216, 219
Argott, Don 9
Arnheim, Rudolf 4, 23

art documentaries; art world and 214–15; audiences for 208–9; cinematography in 7, 31, 149, 152, 153, 154, 182, 184, 216; conceptualization of 10–17; and digital technologies 9; distribution of 1, 8, 23, 36, 38, 83, 92, 107, 110, 208–9, 211, 213, 214; experimentation in 2, 130, 212; festivals for 209; film-on-art and film-as-art 212, 214, 215; funding of 210–11; future of 218–19; history of 3–10; intermediality in 3, 10, 216; philosophical function of 211; television 2, 5, 6, 9, 35, 38, 46, 208, 213; subgenres of 5–7
art education 205, 212, 213
art history 2, 4, 6, 11, 13, 17, 34, 46, 100, 128, 129, 130, 134, 135, 136, 140, 194, 210, 214
Art in the Twenty-First Century (Art21) 9
Art of the Steal (Argott, 2009) 9
art museums 2, 4, 15–16, 160, 175, 186, 209, 212
Art Must Be Beautiful, Artist Must Be Beautiful (Abramović, 1975) 101
Art on Screen Database *see* Program for Art on Film
art world 15, 16, 17, 39, 46, 80, 82, 113, 114, 116, 118, 122, 123, 128, 129, 131–4, 136–8, 140, 160, 214, 215
Artecinema International Festival of Films on Contemporary Art 209
Arthuys, Phillippe 31
artistic reputation *see* artists; public image and reputation
artists; public image and reputation 6, 9, 34–7, 39–40, 43–7, 69, 76, 82–5, 90–3, 99, 105; *see also* global icons
Artists Must Live (Read, 1953) 41
Arts Council of Great Britain 7
As Is by Nick Cave (Falbaum, 2016) 108
Ash is Purest White (Jia, 2018) 69
Assayas, Olivier 174
Auslander, Philip 14, 101, 103, 104, 107, 110, 154
authorship 82, 83, 84, 86–7, 90; authors' rights 196

Index

automatism 13, 54, 57–61, 62; and cinema 59–60; and photography 59, 62; history of 58–9; in media theory 59; theories of 58–61

BBC (British Broadcasting Corporation) 5, 6, 35, 36, 38, 43, 46, 208, 213
Baca, Judith 136
Bacon, Francis 7, 70, 76–7
Baichwal, Jennifer 9, 215–16, 218
Balsom, Erika 161
Banksy 8
Barefoot Contessa, The (Mankiewicz, 1954) 30
Barker, Martin 148
Barry, Iris 1, 161
Barthes, Roland 62
Bauchau, Henry 31
Bazin, André 4, 10, 11, 23, 59, 62, 172
Beale, Simon Russell 152
Beard, Mary 147, 152, 154, 209
Bearden, Romare 12
Before series (Linklater, 1995-2013) 171
Beijing Bastards (Zhang, 1993) 75
Beisenbach, Klaus 105
Benjamin, Walter 6, 7, 59, 100
Bennett, Tony 15
Bergdoll, Barry 11
Berger, John 5–6, 8, 160, 169
Beuys (Veiel, 2017) 208, 216–17
Beuys, Joseph 104, 216–17
Bieber, Justin 185
Bill Cunningham: New York (Press, 2010) 175
Binge (Leeson, 1987) 135
Blackson, Robert 104–5
Blayton, Betty 12
bodies 25, 26, 30, 69, 70, 73, 76, 79, 80, 138, 149
Bolton, Andrew 177, 178–9, 183, 184
Bonhôte, Ian 175
Bow, Clara 174
branding 16, 80, 93, 154, 169
Braunberger, Pierre 4
Brazil 99, 109
Breaking the Frame (Nitoslawska, 2012) 211, 215
Breathing Machines (Hershman Leeson, 1966) 130
Brisley, Stuart 13
British Film Institute 7, 219
British Museum 16, 145, 146, 147, 151, 153, 154, 156, 157; *see also* individual exhibitions
Brody, J. J. 210
Brown, J. Carter 205, 213

Brown, Trisha 104
Brownstein, Carrie 129
Bruguera, Tania 134
Bruzzi, Stella 175
Burtynsky, Edward 9, 215

Cai Guo-Qiang 8, 74, 108
Cal Arts Conference 136, 139
camera lucida 55
Campbell, Thomas 177, 179
Canudo, Ricciotto 1
Capa, Robert 191, 195, 196, 197
Capa, Cornell 195, 196
Caravaggio (Jarman, 1986) 7
Cardinal, Roger 210
Carr, Cynthia 102
Cartier-Bresson, Henri 11
Certified Copy (Kiarostami, 2010) 172
Ceux de chez nous (Guity, 1915) 3
Channel Four (UK) 6, 7, 102, 192
Chen Kaige 75
Cheng, Meiling 85
Chevolution (Ziff, 2008) 3, 192, 193–5; distribution of 193–4; and Netflix 193–4; production of 193–4; status as commodity 195
Chicago, Judy 129, 133, 135, 137
China 13, 69–71, 75, 80, 85, 102, 178; contemporary art scene in 75; in work of Jia Zhangke 69–71, 80; mediated 69; nationalism and 69
China: Through the Looking Glass (exhibition) 16, 176, 178–9, 186; depiction in *First Monday in May* 178–9; Orientalism in 178, 179
Chinese Mayor, The (Zhou, 2015) 88
Christo and Jeanne-Claude 9, 14, 115–16, 120, 134, 218
Christo's Valley Curtain (Maysles and Maysles, 1974) 9
cine-portraits, *see* film portraits
cinéma d'exposition (exhibition cinema) 161
cinematic documentation *see* documentation
cinematography 7, 31, 56, 104, 149, 152, 153, 154, 176, 182, 185, 216
Circular Surface Planar Displacement Drawing (Heizer, 1970) 121
Civilisation; A Personal View by Kenneth Clark (1969) 5, 43, 161, 213
Clark, Kenneth 5, 43, 161, 209, 213
Clausen, Barbara 14
Clouzot, Henri-Georges 12, 23, 54, 208
Coddington, Grace 177
Cohen, Jem 16, 160, 170–2

Coleman, James 60, 61
collaboration 5, 9, 17, 24, 35, 38, 41, 47, 86, 90, 145, 178, 209, 210, 218
Collings, Matthew 5
Comité Internationale pour la Diffusion des Arts et des Lettres par le Cinéma (CIDALC) 23
Conceiving Ada (Hershman Leeson, 1987) 130
conceptualism 7, 60
Confessions of a Chameleon (Hershman Leeson, 1986) 135
consciousness-raising (CR) 15, 131, 137
contemplative gaze 161
Cork, Richard 45
Costello, Christine 156
Costume Institute *see* Metropolitan Museum of Art
Craig-Martin, Michael 149
Craigie, Jill 38
Cruickshanks, Lorna 152
Cukor, George 30, 174
Cunningham, Bill 175
curation 16, 105, 191, 192, 193, 201, 214
Cürlis, Hans 3
Current, The (Abramović, 2013) 109
Cut Piece: A Video Homage to Yoko Ono (Hershman Leeson, 1993) 135
Cutie and the Boxer (Heinzerling, 2013) 9
Cutler, R. J. 17, 175, 176

Dalle Vacche, Angela 2
Dauman, Anatole 4
David Bowie is Happening Now (2013) 148
David Hockney: Secret Knowledge (Wright, 2002) 55, 56, 57
Day on the Grand Canal with the Emperor of China, A (Haas, 1988) 11, 210
De Artificiali Perspectiva or Anamorphosis (Quay, 1991) 210, 211
de Thame, Rachel 147
decisive moment 11, 201–2
Deep Contact (Hershman Leeson, 1984) 130
Deleuze, Gilles 76
Delvaux, Paul 5, 23–4, 29–30; architecture in works of 26; desire in works of 26, 30; and Hollywood 24–5; stillness in works of 29, 30–1; and Surrealism 28–30; style of 27, 28; women in works of 26, 27, 30
Deus, João de 109
Devil Wears Prada, The (Frankel, 2006) 174, 177
Diana Vreeland: The Eye Has to Travel (Vreeland/Tcheng/Perlmutt, 2011) 175

digital technologies 9, 11, 60, 106, 110, 111, 162
Dinner Party, The (Chicago, 1974-79) 129
Dior and I (Tcheng, 2014) 8, 175
Disturbing the Peace (*Lao ma ti hua*, Ai, 2009)
Dix, Otto 3
Doane, Mary Ann 60
documentary studies 2, 17
documentation 9, 13–14, 15, 37, 43, 100–11, 113, 115, 185, 210; cinematic 103, 107, 108, 110, 111; documentary 43, 101, 103, 104, 107–8; film and 37, 111; performance 100–11; photographic 13, 14; theatrical 101, 103, 110
Documents 29
Donagh, Rita 192
Dong (Jia, 2006) 13, 68, 69, 71, 73–4, 76, 77, 78–80; bodies in 68, 73, 78–9; artistic practice in 79; structure of 78, 79
Doty, Benjamin 155
Doty, Mark 172
Double Negative (Heizer, 1969-70) 13, 121
Double Oval (Moore, 1966) 42
Dreams That Money Can Buy (Richter, 1948) 30
Dreyer, Carl Theodor 23
Duchamp, Marcel 1, 134, 135
Durgnat, Raymond 25

Eagle, Arnold 207
Eaux d'artifice (Anger, 1953) 30
Educational Film Library Association (EFLA) 208
Éluard, Paul 5, 25, 31
embodiment 30, 184; *see also* bodies
Emigholz, Heinz 216, 217
Emmer, Luciano 4, 10, 23
Ensor, James 24
essay films 2
event cinema 16, 145, 146, 148, 152, 154, 156
Ex Libris: New York Public Library (Wiseman, 2017) 163
exhibition documentaries 145–57; box-office success of 156; materiality in 151, 152; liveness in 148, 153–6; popular reception of 152, 153; remediation of museum experience 148, 149, 151, 153, 157; temporality and spatiality in 149, 151
Exhibition on Screen 16, 154, 156
Exit Through the Gift Shop (Banksy, 2010) 8
Export, Valie 104, 134

faces 36, 166
Fallen Star (art installation, Suh, 2012) 117–18

Fallen Star: Finding Home (film, Brunner-Sung and Stadler, 2016) 117–20, 121, 127; interview subjects in 118; site-specificity in 117–8; place in 117; collaboration in 118–20
Fargo, Linda 177
fashion documentaries 174–86; cultural institutions in 174–7; fashion designers in 174–5, 176, 185; movement and stillness in 176, 182, 184; politics of 185; consumption in 176, 184; tactility in 176, 184; remediation of fashion in 174
fashion films 174, 176, 184, 185
Fédération internationale des archives du film (FIAF) 23, 161
Fédération internationale du film sur l'art (FIFA) 23
Felleman, Susan 2, 25
feminist art movement 128, 129, 131, 132, 135–40
Femme/Woman: A Tapestry by Joan Miró (Pierce, 1979) 205
Festival of Britain 37, 39
film audiences 36, 69, 101, 103, 108, 110, 118, 133, 145–6, 156, 193, 199, 208
film distribution 1, 36, 38, 131, 208–9, 211, 213, 214
film festivals 130, 208, 209, 212
film funding 7, 75, 88, 210, 218–19
film portraits 6, 36–8, 47
films on art (*films sur art*) 4, 24, 35, 37, 207, 209
First Monday in May, The (Rossi, 2016) 16, 175, 176, 177–84, 185, 186; fashion cultures in 185–6; Anna Wintour in 177–9, 183; Metropolitan Museum of Art in 177–8, 179, 181; fashion as image or object in 174, 175, 181, 183–5; fashion as art 179–81; style of 181–2
First Person Plural (Hershman Leeson, 1984-96) 134
Five (Meltzen/Yudkoff, 1971) 12
Flaherty, Robert 23, 207
Fortnum, Rebecca 127
Foucault, Michel 71, 130, 136, 140
Fox, James 5
Franken, Don 118–20
Free, White, and 21 (Pindell, 1980) 137
Freud, Lucian 70, 76
Frostrup, Mariella 147

Gadamer, Hans-Georg 101
gallery cinema 162
Gant, Charles 148
Gao Ying 83
Gaslight (Cukor, 1944) 30
Gates, The (Maysles/Maysles, 2007) 9, 115, 116, 117, 120
Gauguin (Resnais, 1950) 5
Gaultier, Jean-Paul 179–80, 185
Georgia O'Keeffe (Adato, 1977) 215
Gerhard Richter Painting (Belz, 2011) 55, 74, 156
Geyrhalter, Nikolaus 167
Ghosh, Bishnupriya 86, 91–2
Ghost and Mrs. Muir, The (Mankiewicz, 1947) 30
Giannachi, Gabriella 130
Gibson, Pamela Church 175
Glawogger, Michael 167
Guernica (Resnais, 1950) 5, 161
global icons 13, 86, 91–2
Goldsmiths, University of London 192
Goldsworthy, Andy 9, 114
Golub (Blumenthal/Quinn, 1988) 55
Gospel According to André, The (Novack, 2017) 175
Govan, Michael 121–2, 123
Grabsky, Phil 154, 156–7
Graham, Martha 4
Graham-Dixon, Andrew 5
Graham Sutherland (Read, 1953) 41
Great Museum, The (Holzhausen, 2014) 161, 166–9; material objects in 168; gallery as protagonist in 167; branding in 169; museum practices in 167; tactility in 167
Great Wall of China: Lovers at the Brink, The (Grigor, 1988) 14, 99, 102
Greenblatt, Stephen 15
Grémillon, Jean 23
Grierson, John 1, 6, 35, 38, 42, 207, 214
Grigor, Murray 99
Grosz, George 3
Guerilla Girls 138
Guernica (Resnais, 1950) 5, 161
Guggenheim Museum (New York) 80, 99, 104, 181
Guitry, Sacha 3

Haacke, Hans 14
Haesaerts, Paul 12, 23, 24, 25, 38
Hackney Flashers 192
Hall, Donald 42
Han Sanming 72
Harlem Renaissance 7, 8
Harmon Foundation 3, 7
Hearn, Maxwell 177, 178, 179
Heidegger, Martin 72
Heinzerling, Zachery 9
Heizer, Michael 13, 14, 15, 121, 125

Helvetica (Hustwit, 2007) 194
Henri Matisse Paper Cut-Outs (Newhouse, 1978) 147, 207
Henry Moore (Read, 1951) 39–40
Henry Moore (Sweeney, 1946) 38
Henry Moore: A Study of His Life and Work (Read, 1965) 42
Henry Moore at Eighty (Read, 1978) 35, 37, 43, 45, 46
Henry Moore at Home: A Private View of a Personal Collection (Read, 1974) 35, 43
Henry Moore: One Yorkshireman Looks at His World (Read, 1967) 35, 37, 41, 42
Henry Moore: The Language of Sculpture (Read, 1974) 35, 37, 43–5
Henry Moore: Portrait of an Artist (Read, 1979) 46
Herzog, Werner 9
heterovisuality 162
Hockney, David 11, 55–6, 57, 210
Hoey, David 177
Holzhausen, Johannes 15, 16, 160, 166–7, 168, 169, 170, 216, 217
Hooligan Sparrow (Nanfu, 2016) 88
Hudson, Kate 185
Hudson, Mark 153
Huffington Post 9, 131
Hughes, Bettany 147, 151, 152
Hughes, Robert 5, 209
Human Flow (Ai, 2017) 82
Hung Huang 89
Hunt, Richard 12

Idylle à la Plage (*Idyll at the Beach*, Storck, 1931) 28
Iimura Takahiko 210
Image in the Snow (Maas, 1952) 30
Images d'Ostende (*Images of Ostend*, Storck, 1929) 28
Immortality for All: Trilogy on Russian Cosmism (Vidokle, 2017) 215
intermediality 3, 10, 17, 54, 55, 74, 79, 127, 148, 150, 156, 157, 216; definition 10; between film and exhibition 149, 150, 156, 157; between film and painting 10–11, 74, 79; between film and photography 194; between film and sculpture 127
International Art Film Federation (IAFF) 23
International Center of Photography (ICP) 193, 195–7
International Festival of Films on Art (Montreal) 102, 208, 209
International Institute of Films on Art (IIFA) 23

intertextuality 9, 162
Iris (Maysles, 2014) 175
Isozaki Arata 210
Ivory Tower (Rossi, 2014) 177

J. Paul Getty Trust 208, 209
Jackson Pollack (Namuth, 1951) 12, 38, 54
Jacobs, Steven 3–4, 115, 161
James, David E. 133
Janson, H.W. 31
Januszczak, Waldemar 5
Jenison, Tim 53, 54, 56, 61–2, 63, 64, 65; methods of 61–2, 63, 64; optical hypothesis of 53, 57
Jia Zhangke 13, 68, 69, 70, 76, 78; and China 69; and global capitalism 71; reception of films 69; relationship with Liu Xiaodong 76, 77–8
Jia Zhangke: A Guy from Fenyang (Salles, 2016) 76
John Piper (Read, 1954) 41
Johnsen, Andreas 83, 93
Jonas, Joan 104
Jones, Amelia 100
Jones, Caroline A. 12, 39
Jones, Jonathan 66, 153
JR 8, 215
Julien, Isaac 7

Kahn, Nathaniel 9
Kangxi Emperor's Southern Inspection Tour, The (1689) 11
Kara, Selmin 87
Kasun, Leo 213
Kelly, Mary 192
Kelly, Sean 100
Kentridge, William 60–1, 63
Keys, Alicia 185
Kiefer, Anselm 114
Klayman, Alison 83, 86, 87, 88, 89, 90, 93
Koda, Harold 177, 178, 179
Kollwitz, Käthe 3
Korda, Alberto 191, 193, 194, 203
Kors, Michael 185
Kracauer, Siegfried 4, 23, 35
Krauss, Rosalind 60–1, 63
Kulturfilme 3
Kunsthistorisches Museum (Vienna) 160, 170
Kurtz, Steve 134
Kwon, Miwon 14–15, 114, 116, 121
Kyrou, Ado 28

L. S. Lowry (Read, 1957) 41
La Belle et la bête (*The Beauty and the Beast*, Cocteau, 1946) 30

La Mort de Vénus (*The Death of Venus*, Storck, 1930) 28
L'Année dernière à Marienbad (*Last Year at Marienbad*, Resnais, 1961) 25
Labisse, Félix 24, 28
Lagerfeld, Karl 179–80
land art movement 114
Land Art (Schum, 1969) 113
Land of Enchantment: Southwest U.S.A. (Rodakiewicz,1948) 4
Last Train Home (*Guitu lieche*, Lixin, 2009) 88
Laura (Preminger, 1944) 30
Lawson, Alan 38
Le Bonheur d'être aimé (*The Happiness to Be Loved*, Storck, 1962) 28
Le Monde de Paul Delvaux (The World of Paul Delvaux, Storck 1946) 2, 4, 24–31; effect of paintings in 24, 26–8, 30, 31; cinematic logic of 27, 29; contributions to Surrealism 28–9; tactility of painting in 27; framing in 26
Le Mystère Picasso (*The Mystery of Picasso*, Clouzot, 1956) 12, 54, 55
Le Musée imaginaire (Malraux) 4
Leaning into the Wind (Riedelsheimer, 2017) 9
Leeson, Lynn Hershman 129–40; autobiographical work 132–4; exclusion by art world 131, 134; sexual politics of 132, 135, 137; recognition as feminist pioneer 128; transmedia storytelling and 130
Léger, Ferdinand 1
Leonardo Live (2011) 145, 146, 147, 149, 150, 151, 154, 156; cinematography in 149, 150; liveness of 154; pacing of 154; temporality and spatiality in 149, 151
Les Malheurs de la guerre (*The Troubles of War*, Storck, 1962) 28
Les Statues meurent aussi (*Statues Also Die*, Resnais/Marker, 1953) 5
Levitated Mass (Pray, 2013) 15, 120–6; artistic practice in 122; materiality in 121; interviews with subjects 121, 124–6; place in 121; public response to 122–6; status of art in 121–2, 124–6
Life and Work of a Great Sculptor: Henry Moore (Hall, 1966) 42
Lips of Thomas (Abramović, 1975/2005) 105, 106
Little Girls' Cheeks (*Hua lian ba'er*, Ai, 2009) 83, 84, 87, 88, 89, 90
Liu Xiaodong 13, 68, 70, 73, 74; embodiment in works of 70, 79; figurative painting 76; in *Dong* 73–4, 76–80; place in works of 73; reputation in China 76; style of 76–8; temporality in works of 78; use of color 76, 79
Liu Zheng 75
Live from the Red Carpet 174
liveness 13, 14, 38, 55, 148, 153–5, 156
Locatelli, Giorgio 147
Looking for Langston (Julien, 1989) 7–8
Loos Ornamental (Emigholz, 2008) 216
Lorna (Hershman Leeson, 1979-82) 130
Los Angeles County Museum of Art 121
Love is the Devil: Study for a Portrait of Francis Bacon (Maybury 1998) 7
Lovelace, Ada 130
Lovers: The Great Wall Walk, The (Abramović/Ulay, 1998), 102
Lowry, L.S. 35, 41
Lubben, Kristen 197
Luhrmann, Baz 174, 177, 179
Lumière Brothers 161
Lynch, David 174
Lynes, George Platt 7
Lynes, Krista 138

Ma: Space/Time in the Garden of Ryoan-ji (Iimura, 1989) 210
MacDonald, Kevin 8, 74, 108
MacGregor, Neil 151
MacKinnon, Catherine 131, 137
Macpherson, Dorothy 207, 214
Magritte, René 10
Magritte VR (2017) 10
Malraux, André 4
Man Who Saw Too Much, The (Ziff, 2015) 191, 198–201; viewer response in 199; violence in 199, 200; interviews in 200–1; photojournalists in 200; intermediality between cinema and photography in 199; relationship to pornography and voyeurism 199
Manet (2013) 156
Mangolte, Babette 14, 99, 104–6, 108
Manufactured Landscapes (Baichwal, 2006) 9, 215, 218
Mapplethorpe, Robert 7
Marina Abramović: The Artist is Present (exhibition, 2010) 103, 107
Marina Abramović: The Artist is Present (film, Akers, 2012) 99, 107, 108, 109, 111; distribution of 107, 108; artistic reputation and 107
Marlow, Tim 146, 149, 150
materiality 60, 69, 70, 71, 78, 137, 152
Matisse Live (2014) 145, 147–8, 149–50, 152, 154; pacing of 152; spatiality in 149–50

Maybury, John 7
Maysles, Albert 9, 115, 117
Maysles, David 9, 115
McEvilley, Thomas 102
McQueen (Bonhôte/Ettedgui, 2018) 175
medium 1, 3, 10, 59–61, 62, 148, 162–3; creation of new 163; digital technologies and 60; post-medium condition 1, 14, 60
Mendieta, Ana 138
Metinides, Enrique 191, 198, 199, 200–1, 203
Metropolitan Museum of Art 15, 164, 176, 177, 178, 179, 181, 186, 208, 209, 213; Costume Institute 176, 177, 178, 179, 180, 181, 182, 186; exhibitions of 176, 177–8, 180, 181
Mexico 195, 196, 197, 200
Mexican Suitcase, The (Ziff, 2011) 191, 195–8; authors' rights in 196; cultural patrimony in 196–7; Robert Capa in 198; status of photojournalist in 197, 198; recovery of "Mexican suitcase" 195–6; International Center of Photography in 195–7; refugees in 198
Micha, René 5, 24, 25, 31
Miele, Matthew 16, 175, 176
Millar, Iain 104
Miller, Jeffrey 136
mise-en-scène 7, 26, 73, 182, 184
Mission Impossible: Rogue Nation (McQuarie, 2015) 69
Mobile by Alexander Calder (Pierce, 1979) 205
Modigliani, Amedeo 10
Modigliani VR: The Ochre Studio (2017) 10
Moholy-Nagy, László 1
Monet, Claude 3
Monitor (1958-65) 7
Moore, Henry 2, 6, 34–47; canonicity of 43–6; collaboration with John Read 34–47; interest in landscape 41–2; performativity of 45, 46; perspective of 41; artistic practice of 39, 41–2; public perception of 39, 40, 41, 45–6
Mountains May Depart (Jia, 2016) 69
Muniz, Vic 8, 116–17, 120, 123
Mizrahi, Isaac 174
museum effect 15, 16
museum experience 153
Museu Nacional d'Art de Catalunya 197
Museum Hours (Cohen, 2012) 160, 161, 170–2; characteristics of city symphony in 171–2; emotion in 170; place in 172
Museum of Fine Arts (Boston) 180
Museum of Modern Art (MoMA) 1, 38, 99, 145, 161, 207; Film Library 1, 161

Music Lesson, The (Vermeer) 13, 53, 54, 57, 63, 65
My Architect (Kahn, 2003) 9
My Blueberry Nights (Wong, 2007) 162
Mystery of Picasso, The, see Le Mystère Picasso

Nairne, Sandy 7, 8
Namuth, Hans 12, 38, 39, 54, 208
National Educational Television 207
National Film Board of Canada 207
National Gallery (Wiseman, 2014) 15, 16, 161, 163–6, 167, 169; acts of looking in 164, 165; discussion of art in 165; social systems of art in 164, 167, 169; non-narrative structure of 164; transmedial look in 163, 165–6
National Gallery (London) 145, 147, 155
National Gallery of Art (Washington, DC) 17, 205–19; film and art education in 205, 212–13; film productions 213–14; partnership with public television 213; programming 205, 207, 213
National Gallery of Canada 207
National Portrait Gallery (London) 34
nationalism 69
Nauman, Bruce 104
Needham, Gary 184
Nelis, Mary 192
Netflix 108, 130, 193–4
Network Photographers 192
New Museum 139
New Rijksmuseum, The (Hoogendijk, 2014) 15, 160
Newhouse, Shelby 207
Nichols, Bill 117
Nietzsche, Friedrich 71
Nitoslawska, Marielle 211
Nixon, Richard 136
Nochlin, Linda 131
Noguchi: A Sculptor's World (Eagle, 1972) 207

Obomsawin, Alanis 210
O'Keefe, Georgia 4
Orientalism 77, 178, 179
Osnos, Evan 89
Out of Chaos (Craigie, 1944) 38
Over Your Cities Grass Will Grow (Fiennes, 2010) 114, 120, 127

Page One: Inside the New York Times (Rossi, 2011) 117
Painted Earth: The Art of the Mimbres Indians (Thatcher, 1989) 210
Painters Painting (De Antonio, 1972) 12, 55, 215

painting 10–11, 31, 39, 55, 59, 64, 65, 70, 79, 160, 163, 166, 169, 170, 201; and film 10–11, 31, 39, 55, 70, 160, 163, 201
Pandora and the Flying Dutchman (Lewin, 1950) 30
Pane, Gina 104
Panofsky, Erwin 11
Parabeton: Pier Luigi Nervi and Roman Concrete (Emigholz, 2012) 216, 217
Parsons, Margaret 205–19; biography of 205
Paul Delvaux ou les femmes défendues (*Paul Delvaux or the Forbidden Women*, Storck, 1970)
Penn and Teller 53, 57
Penny, Nicholas 147, 166
perception 11, 14, 15, 16, 31, 36, 57, 69, 73, 108, 121, 132, 135
performance 13–14, 37, 99–111, 137, 146, 200
performance art 3, 13, 14, 99–111, 137; documentation of 13, 14, 99–111; mediation of 100, 101; presence and absence in 100, 101, 106, 110; theorization of 101–2
Permeke, Constant 24
perspective 25–6, 28
Personal Shopper (Assayas, 2016) 174
Petrified Dog, The (Peterson, 1948) 30
Phelan, Peggy 100, 101, 104
phenomenology 15, 100–1, 114, 115–16, 117, 121, 127, 169
Photographer, The (Van Dyke, 1948) 4
photography 11, 14, 54, 58, 59, 60, 63, 191–2, 198, 202–3; relation to film 11, 14, 59, 60, 202–3; objectivity of 62; of art 218 status as art 54, 58, 59, 63
photojournalists 191, 192, 197, 198, 199
Picasso, Pablo 5, 37, 38, 39, 54–5
Pictures of Garbage (Muniz) 116, 120, 127
Picturing Derry (Fox/Stevens, 1985) 192, 193
Pindell, Howardena 135, 136
Piper, Adrian 135–6, 137
place 69, 71, 72, 73, 75, 110, 114, 151
Place To Be: The Construction of the East Building of the National Gallery of Art 1968-1978, A (Guggenheim, 1978) 205
Places of Power (Abramović, 2013-15) 109
Plastic China (*Suliao Wangguo*, Jiuliang, 2016) 88
Platform (Jia, 2000)
Pollock, Griselda 140
Pompeii Live (2013) 145, 146, 147, 151–2, 154, 156; temporality and spatiality in 151, 152; experts in 147, 151
pop art 1, 12

portrait films, *see* film portraits
Pour vos beaux yeux (*For Your Beautiful Eyes*, Storck 1929) 28
Power of Art (Schama, 2007) 7
Pray, Doug 15, 121, 123, 124
presence 13, 74, 100, 106, 114, 115, 147, 154
Program for Art on Film 208, 209; Art on Screen Database 209; Production Lab 209, 210
Project Runway 174
public image *see* artists; public image and reputation
public television, *see* television
punctum 62
Pygmalion myth 5, 29–30

Qiu Zhijie 75

Raczynska, Joanna 210
Rainer, Yvonne 104
Raven, Arlene 137
Ray, Man 1
Read, John 2, 5, 6, 34–47; collaboration with Henry Moore 34–47; film distribution and exhibition 36, 38, 40, 41, 47; politics of 45; style of 39, 42, 43
Rebecca (Hitchcock, 1940) 30
Reclining Figure: Festival (Moore) 38, 39
refugees 82, 191, 197, 198
Relation in Space (Abramović, 1976) 102
Relation Works (Abramović, 1976-79) 102, 103
remediation 10, 145, 148, 151, 153, 154, 160, 162
Remembrance (Nian, Ai, 2010) 84
Renoir: Revered and Reviled (2016) 156
Renov, Michael 1
Resnais, Alain 4, 5, 10, 23, 25, 27, 161
Riboud, Barbara Chase 12
Richardson, Michael 28
Riedelsheimer, Thomas 114, 115, 116, 208
Ringgold, Faith 129, 135, 136
Ritual in Transfigured Time (Deren, 1946) 30
Rivers and Tides: Andy Goldsworthy Working with Time (Riedelsheimer, 2001) 9, 114, 120, 127
Roberts, Paul 154
Rodin, Auguste 3
Rong Rong 75
Rosenthal, Rachel 132, 135
Rosler, Martha 136
Rossi, Andrew 16, 175, 176, 177, 180, 181, 182, 183, 185, 186
Royal Museums of Fine Arts (Belgium) 10

Royoux, Jean-Christophe 161
Rubens (Storck, 1948) 4, 24
Russell, Ken 5, 6–7
Russian Ark (Sokurov, 2002) 160, 161, 170
Ruttmann, Walter 1

Saisselin, Remy G. 180
Sankofa Film and Video Collective 7
San Francisco Museum of Modern Art 131
Sawney, Nitin 147
Scatter My Ashes at Bergdorf's (Miele, 2013) 175, 176, 177
Schaffende Hände (*Creative Hands*, Cürlis, 1923-6) 3
Schama, Simon 5, 7, 209
Schindler's Houses (Emigholz, 2007) 216
Schneemann, Carolee 211
Scorsese, Martin 174
Sculptor's Landscape, A (Read, 1958) 34, 37, 41, 42
sculpture 36, 39, 41, 115, 126, 152, 166; and film 36, 115, 166
SCUM Manifesto (Solanas) 135
Selisker, Scott 58
September Issue, The (Cutler, 2009), 16, 175–7, 184, 186
Serota, Nicholas 148
Seymour, David "Chim" 191, 202
Seven Easy Pieces (Mangolte, 2007) 99, 104–6
Shapcott, Jo 166
Shapiro, Miriam 135
Shaw, Fiona 147
Simons, Raf 175
Sims, Lowery Stokes 136
site-specific art 3, 14, 15, 113–127; definition 113–14; phenomenological 114, 116, 117, 121; social/institutional 114, 115, 116, 118, 121, 126; discursive 114, 116, 117, 118, 120, 124, 126, 127
Sixth Generation (Chinese film directors) 68, 74–5, 78; definition 78; politics of 75; style of 75, 78
Sky Arts 146
Sky Ladder: The Art of Cai Guo Qiang (MacDonald, 2016) 8, 74, 108
Smith, Chris 127
Smithson, Robert 13, 113
Snow, Peter 104, 147, 151
Solanas, Valerie 135
Song Dong 75
Song Yongping 75
Sorace, Christian 85, 86
Souris, André 5, 25
Space In Between: Marina Abramović in Brazil, The (del Fiol, 2016) 14, 99, 109

Sparham, Laurie 192
spatiality 11, 151
Spector, Nancy 105
Spence, Jo 192
Spilliaert, Léon 24
Spiral Jetty (Smithson, 1970) 13, 114
Square, The (Östlund, 2017) 160
Stadler, Valerie 117, 119, 120
Stanley Spencer (Read, 1956) 41
State of the Art (Nairne, 1987) 7, 8
Steele, Valerie 180
Stevens, Sylvia 192, 193
Still Life (Jia, 2006) 13, 68, 70–3, 74, 76, 78; global capital in 71; history in 71, 74, 79; labor in 70, 71, 76, 78; materiality in 70, 71; place in 71, 72, 73, 75, 76, 79; relationship to *Dong* 68, 71, 73, 74, 76, 80
Still War: Photographs from the North of Ireland (1990) 192
stillness 30, 31, 202, 203
Stock, Francine 148, 154
Storck, Henri 4, 10, 24–5, 26, 28, 31; relationship with Paul Delvaux 24, 25, 26, 27, 30, 31; space in the films of 26–7; stillness in the works of 30–1; Surrealism and 28–9
Strange Culture (Hershman Leeson, 2009) 134
Study in Perspective (Ai, 1995-2003) 90
Study of Negro Artists (1935) 3
subjugated knowledge 130, 137, 140
Suh, Do Ho 117–18; home and 118; site-specific art and 118–19
Sun Tunnels (Holt, 1978) 113
Sur les bords de la caméra (*At the Borders of the Camera*, Storck 1932) 28, 29
Surrealism 5, 10, 24, 25, 26, 28, 29–30, 31, 58; documentary and 28–30; in works of Henri Storck 28–9; in works of Paul Delvaux 28, 29–30
Syson, Luke 149, 150

Talley, André Leon 175, 177
Tania Libre (Hershman Leeson, 2017) 134
tactility 27, 167, 176, 184
Taro, Gerდa 191, 196
Tarver, Ben 195–7
Tate Modern 10, 16, 85, 145, 147, 148
Tcheng, Frédéric 8, 175
Teknolust (Hershman Lesson, 2002) 131
television 5, 34, 35, 36, 45, 104, 147, 207, 213; liveness 36, 38, 147; public television 2, 5, 9, 208, 213
temporality 11, 71, 78, 104, 138
Thacher, Anita 210

Three Gorges Dam 13, 68, 69, 74, 76, 78, 79, 80
Tim's Vermeer (Teller, 2013) 13, 53–66; artistic practice in 63–4; as artist portrait 53, 54; automatism in 54, 57, 62; elimination of accident 62; recreation of *The Music Lesson* 13, 54, 57, 63; status as possible hoax 57; time-lapse photography in 64–5
Times Up movement 140
Titan: Story of Michelangelo, The (Flaherty/Lyford/Oertel, 1950) 207
Titicut Follies (Wiseman, 1967) 163
Touch of Sin (Jia, 2015) 69
Touch of Venus (Seiter, 1948) 30
transaesthetic 161, 162, 163
transmediality 162–3, 165; convergence and 162–3; definition 162–3; transmedial gaze 16, 160, 163
transvisuality 162; intertextuality and 162; remediation and 162
Tsai Ming-liang 160, 162
Tucker, Maria 139
Tzortzi, Kali 153

Uhlirova, Marketa 184
Ulay 99, 102, 103, 106, 107
United Nations Educational, Scientific, and Cultural Organization (UNESCO) 23, 35, 161, 214
University of California, San Diego (UCSD) 117, 119, 120
Unknown Pleasures (Jia, 2002) 69
Unzipped (Keeve, 1995) 174
Upstream Color (Carruth, 2013) 163

Valentino: The Last Emperor (Tyrnauer, 2008) 174
Van Der Zee, James 7
Van Dyke, Willard S. 23
Van Gogh (Resnais, 1948) 5, 27
Varda, Agnès 8, 215, 218
Variétés 29
Veiel, Andres 208, 216
Vermeer, Johannes 13, 53, 54, 57, 58, 61, 64, 65
Vertigo (Hitchcock, 1958) 161
Vertov, Dziga 1
Victoria and Albert Museum 148, 180, 193
Vigo, Jean 1
Vikings Live (2014) 146, 147, 152, 153, 154, 156; reception of 153; audience engagement in 156; violence 68, 73, 76, 106, 199, 200
virtual reality technologies 9–10, 66

Visage (Tsai, 2009) 160, 161, 162, 170
Visages Villages (*Faces Places*, JR/Varda, 2017) 8, 215, 218
Visité à Picasso, Une (*Visit to Picasso*, Haesaerts, 1950) 12, 24, 38
Voyage to Italy (Rossellini, 1954) 161
voyeurism 26, 199, 203
Vreeland, Diana 175, 180

WACK!: Art and the Feminist Revolution (2007) 139
W.A.R.: Voices of a Movement (website) 128, 130
Walker, John A. 2
Walker, Lucy 8, 116, 117
Walking on Water (Paounov, 2018) 218
Wasson, Haidee 15
Waste Land (Walker, 2010) 8, 9, 116–17, 118, 123
Watermark (Burtynsky, 2013) 9
Ways of Seeing (Berger, 1972) 5–6, 8, 160
Welsch, Janice 132, 133
Wenchuan earthquake 83, 86
Westwood: Punk, Icon, Activist (Tucker, 2018) 175
White, Charles 12
Whitney Museum of American Art 129, 131, 139
Wilke, Hannah 132
Williams, Gareth 148, 154
Wintour, Anna 177, 178, 179, 183
Wiseman, Frederick 161, 163, 164, 165, 166, 167
Witkin & Witkin (Ziff, 2017) 191, 201–2, 217; picture format in 202; painting in 201; twins in 202; women in 201
Witkin, Jerome 191, 201, 202, 203, 217, 218
Witkin, Joel-Peter 191, 203, 217, 218
Woman's Building, The 137
Womanhouse 137
women; feminist art movement 15, 128–40; representation of 27, 28, 29; women artists 8, 128–40
Women, The (Cukor, 1939) 174
!Women Art Revolution (Hershman Leeson, 2010) 15, 128–40; as autobiographical work 132–4; Consciousness-raising and 15, 131, 137; feminist art activism and 15, 129, 135; feminist history in 129, 130–1, 132, 133, 138, 140; feminist methodology and 131; intersectionality in 136; paratexts of 129–30; radical techniques in 133
Women Artists in Revolution 132
Women's Action Coalition 138

Women's Art Program (Cal State) 136
Wong Kar-wai 162, 177, 178
Wood, Michael 148, 154
World, The (Jia, 2004) 71
World of Paul Delvaux, The, see Le Monde de Paul Delvaux
Wright, Frank Lloyd 4, 105

Xiao Wu (Jia, 1997) 69

YouTube 9, 107, 108, 209

Young, Cynthia 197

Zhao Tao 68, 72
Zhang Huan 75
Zhang Yimou 75
Ziff, Trisha 16–17, 191–203; biography of 191–3; challenging artistic hierarchies 197–8; curatorial work of 192–3; relationship between curation and filmmaking 193–5

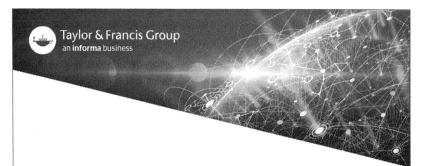